PRAISE FOR

Do You Want to Be Wealthier, Healthier, and Happier?
How to Unlock the Great WHH Continuum

"*Do You Want to Be Wealthier, Healthier, and Happier? How to Unlock the Great WHH Continuum* is a powerful exploration of the intricate balance between financial success, personal well-being, and the pursuit of true happiness. I spent over 30 years practicing Radiation Oncology while struggling to find a balance between wealth generation, health and happiness. I was privleged to help build the Arnold Palmer Cancer Center from its inception. This experience highlighted how Wealth altruism could be used to improve health outcomes for thousands of people.

Pete Roman brings invaluable insights into the intersection of wealth management, health challenges, and achieving fulfillment in the face of adversity. Drawing on years of experience, this book is not just a guide to financial and physical wellness, but a testament to resilience, growth, and finding joy through life's inevitable struggles. Having struggled with my diagnosis of Parkinson's disease during the last decade of my clinical practice, I found the Pete Roman's insight invaluable, as if he was talking directly to me.

For anyone seeking a holistic approach to living a balanced life, *Do You Want to Be Wealthier, Healthier, and Happier? How to Unlock the Great WHH Continuum* offers wisdom, practical advice, and inspiration from someone who has walked the path of both success and personal trials." —SANJEEV BAHRI, MD, FACRO

"FORE Systems was founded in 1990 in a tiny office above a pizza joint and hair salon by four professors from Carnegie Mellon University. I was very fortunate to join as the first "business" guy. We commercialized a complex technology–Asynchronous Transfer Mode (ATM), the backbone of the emerging Internet and nine years later sold the company for "billions". We had our Wealth box checked.

Many of us put our Health and Happiness on hold in pursuit of a wealth goal. As life went on, I realized the importance, no…. the necessity of having the proper balance of Wealth, Health and Happiness.

In his book, *Do You Want to Be Wealthier, Healthier, and Happier? How to Unlock the Great WHH Continuum,* Pete Roman has managed to distill and summarize the ideal timelines for optimizing all three. Pete's extensive research and interviews combined with his own experiences will save you precious time. Follow his success patterns to maximize your Wealth, Health and Happiness."   —MIKE GREEN-ENTREPRENEUR, PHILANTHROPIST, MENTOR

"As a team, John and I conceived, started, built and eventually sold an energy services business over a twenty five year span for millions.

Our journey had the inevitable highs and lows you can only experience when taking this life path. We say life path, as our Health and Happiness attainment became a challenge and at times was out of balance even though we significantly exceeded our financial goals.

After you read Pete Roman's *Do You Want to Be Wealthier, Healthier, and Happier? How to Unlock the Great WHH Continuum* you will have the knowledge and data to optimize your own life path."   —TERESA AND JOHN Z

"As an investment advisor for 40 years, and ranked in Baron's top 30 for many years, I can speak to Wealth creation and management.

Over these many years, the most successful clients were those who found a way to balance their wealth, health and happiness. They had dreams and aspirations they turned into goals. My job was to help them exceed and excel. If I can offer you the reader some advice.

Go gain knowledge.

One way is by reading and putting in to practice advice found in Pete Roman's book *Do You Want to Be Wealthier, Healthier, and Happier? How to Unlock the Great WHH Continuum.* He did all the research for you.

Last bit of advice, is timing…start earlier than later and you will succeed."   —STEPHEN HASBROUCK,
MANAGING DIRECTOR, LEGACY STRATEGIC ASSET MANAGEMENT GROUP.

Do You Want To Be Wealthier Healthier and Happier?

How to Unlock the Great WHH Continuum

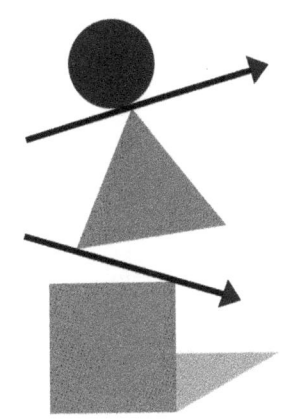

PETER JOSEPH ROMAN

Author's Disclaimer

The book provides information the author believes to be accurate on the subject matter. It is sold with the understanding that the author or the editor or the publisher are not offering advice tailored to any specific portfolio or any individual's particular needs. The author is not providing medical, health, psychological, accounting, legal or investment advice. Talk with your doctor, dentist, dietitian, mental health professionals before any actions. The author opinion is his own and as such should be verified by the reader. Past results do not guarantee any future performance. Data shared, laws and regulations change over time which can change the status of information and conclusions in this book. No warranty is made with respect to the accuracy or completeness of the information contained herein, and the author, editor, published and interviewee's specifically disclaim any responsibility for any liability, loss or risk, personal or otherwise, which is incurred as a consequence directly or indirectly, of the use and application of any of the contents of this book.

The information provided is for entertainment, educational and informational purposes only and does not constitute investment advice and it should not be relied on as such. It should not be considered a solicitation to buy or an offer to sell a security. It does not take into account any investor's particular investment objectives, strategies, tax status or investment horizon. You should consult your money manager, attorney or tax advisor.

The views expressed in this commentary are subject to change based on market and other conditions. These documents may contain certain statements that may be deemed forward-looking statements. Please note that any such statements are not guarantees of any future performance and actual results or developments may differ materially from those projected. Any projections, market outlooks, or estimates are based upon certain assumptions and should not be construed as indicative of actual events that will occur.

All information has been obtained from sources believed to be reliable, but its accuracy is not guaranteed. There is no representation or warranty as to the current accuracy, reliability or completeness of, nor liability for, decisions based on such information and it should not be relied on as such.

DEDICATION

To my parents, Joseph and Mary Roman, who allowed twelve-year-old me to ride my one-speed F1 Eliminator Banana seat bicycle eighty-nine miles from Connecticut to Massachusetts and back, thus beginning my quest for further adventure.

To Big Wonderful Wyoming, where I advanced from a College Boy Worm to a Roughneck and where I met my wife, Karen.

To Karen, for putting up with all my idiosyncratic behavior and "uniqueness."

And to my brother Vinny and my two sisters, Susan and Sally, who inspire me to be a better big brother to this day.

Contents

Preface. I

Introduction. III

What Is True Financial Wealth? 3

What Is True Health?. 47

What Is True Happiness? 101

How Your Personality Can Be Integral to Your Success or Failure . .171

Ego Drive and Empathy Application. 199

Time Factors 203

S.M.A.R.T. Goal Setting. 209

Wealth Health Happiness
Effort by Age Group© 213

Summary of
Wealth Health Happiness
Best Practices, Success Patterns,
and Actions© 217

Customized Client Lifecycle
Solutions© to Support Wealth Health Happiness Continuum 225

Notes and Sources 229

Acknowledgments 235

About the Author. 237

Preface

As the oldest sibling I felt responsible in some way for the happiness of my little brother, two sisters, and neighborhood friends.

I remember when I was about eight years old, Jonathan, my neighbor on Arbor Drive in Torrington, Connecticut, had just received a probably well-deserved spanking from his dad. He was crying, and I suddenly found myself doing a jig in front of him to cheer him up, get him to laugh through his tears. When I saw someone sad or upset in the neighborhood, I felt a need to find out why and then to try to help them be happy. To this day, when I see someone sitting alone I wonder why.

As time went on, I entered high school. I did not belong to any one clique, but a few of us, Alan Kittle in particular, moved with me from clique to clique, enjoying as many acquaintances as possible. We never broke through the shell of any of them. Maybe we were too shy to really put ourselves out there. Neither one of us went to the prom, as we were scared to death of having to dance.

I remember our class salutatorian, Mike C, telling me, "You are one goofy number." I was not sure what he meant then and still don't know what it means now. Maybe I was searching for happiness from clique to clique or maybe I was not able to commit to the "Jocks," the "Greasers," the "Heads," or any of the dozen or so distinguishable groups that made up what was then the high school experience. I do know that I was looking to fit in somewhere and be happy. Back then, being happy and accepted seemed to be paramount.

A few years ago, I was reflecting on my sixty-five years of existence and how fast time went by. I have experienced deaths of loved ones, a diagnosis of mild dyslexia (no wonder I can't spell), moves across the country nine times for the sake of my career, a happy marriage, world travel, business startups with failures and success, and appointed by the Dean, an adjunct professor position teaching entrepreneurship and marketing to Executive MBA students at Carnegie Mellon University (CMU). One thing I reflected on is how many friends I've made all over the world. Who would have thought that even possible for a kid without a clique? But then my thoughts drifted back to Jonathan, crying because his dad had spanked him.

So, now I asked: What if everyone could be happy? And then I added health and wealth to my question. Is this even possible?

The question wouldn't go away. In fact, I began to research it over the next two years. This book is distillation of that research, including interviews and experiences with thousands of people, who helped me come up with many practical solutions to help you maximize the Wealth, Health, Happiness Continuum.

No person I interviewed or studied for this book ever said, "I have more than enough time on my hands. Please, drone on." So, with the object of enabling you to be as productive as possible with your time, I organized this book in three parts, which correspond to three how-to lessons:

- How to Maximize your monetary wealth
- How to maximize your physical, spiritual, emotional health
- How to maximize happiness

I go on to provide actions, criteria, and examples to support the balance and blend needed to interlink all three "how-to" so as to maximize your life experience.

There are many what we may call "lead stories" in this book. I have boiled them down and purposefully condensed them. They may strike you as rapid-fire as they move from topic to topic. I want to save you time by getting you to the points quickly, effectively, and efficiently.

Whether you are starting out on the journey to maximize a WHH continuum or you feel that you have accomplished all your goals, I try to engage a perspective from your point of view. If you have questions on how to share these solutions with others, I provide you with some methods I learned in eighteen years of teaching at CMU. You can use or adapt the methods to train yourself, your family, and your friends.

This is your book. You can read it however it suits you to read it: from the first to the last page, or starting with Chapter 9, "Summary of Wealth Health and Happiness Best Practice Success Patterns and Actions."© By reading Chapter 9 first, you can get the gist of the best practices to maximize wealth, health, and happiness and drill down to other chapters that interest you the most. Either way you approach the book, I trust you will learn or validate at least one or two new and valuable ideas.

Introduction

Now that we have lived through the covid pandemic and its psychological and monetary ramifications, have perspectives on wealth, health, and happiness (WHH) changed?

How do we look at our wealth, health, and happiness, not as individual attainments, but as a continuum? How can we live life to the fullest?

Almost everyone interviewed and researched said they would like more Wealth, Health and Happiness. Counterintuitively (perhaps), wealthy people also yearned for more wealth, health, and happiness. So, why is it so few deliberately focus on maximizing their wealth, health, and happiness continuum? My research indicates that most people prioritize maximizing their wealth, doing it backwards, with no defined action plan. I will prove this bold conclusion and offer corrections to the approach.

I discovered that wealth transition and transformation enters the minds of many who are in their sixties and beyond. How do adults near retirement protect or transition their wealth? How does a business owner transition the business? How do we help people save for retirement late in life and without formal processes or plans?

The fact is that most young people avoid the topic of investing for retirement. Many delay, prioritizing current needs ahead of future needs. This is understandable, but it is human nature at its most pernicious. I will provide you with best practices that, if followed, guarantee a pathway for younger people to become millionaires. And this pathway to wealth comes with the right balance of health and happiness..

We need to ask some basic, clarifying questions.

What is true financial wealth? What is true health? What is true happiness? How much does work define us during our lives and after we retire?

I define wealth as monetary or financial in nature. The premise throughout this book is that wealth acquisition provides better health and happiness outcomes. Wealth acquisition earlier in life is better than later. Health is defined as physical, mental, and spiritual well-being. Happiness is a state of mind that draws from the wealth and health focus. As the philosopher Will Herberg wrote:

The moral principles of Western civilization are, in fact, all derived from the tradition rooted in Scripture and have vital meaning only in the context of that tradition....Cut flowers retain their original beauty and fragrance, but only so long as they retain the vitality that they have drawn from their now severed roots; after that is exhausted, they wither and die. So with freedom, brotherhood, justice and personal dignity—the values that form the moral foundation of our civilization. Without the life-giving power of the faith out of which they have sprung, they possess neither meaning nor vitality.

To maximize our wealth, health and happiness, we must invest time to grow the roots and avoid decisions that would cut us off from the roots. Most of us are neither philosophers nor botanists, but we certainly know that if you cut the roots of any plant, it will be short-lived.

Additionally, our personality traits play essential roles in maximizing wealth, health, and happiness. Different personality profiles produce different results. We will explore the patterns of success and failure associated with various personality traits. I will share what to avoid and what to enhance in your traits, including how to ethically modify your personality, ego drive, and empathy to produce better outcomes.

I will provide you with an adaptable personal wealth, health, and happiness assessment process to enable you to assess where you stand and to keep you on track toward your goals. Additionally, I will outline the optimum age-related ratio of effort required to achieve maximum WHH. Goals and goal setting methods are provided shared to help you to stay the course.

A Customized Client Lifecycle support methodology© will be provided and can also be applied for your family and friends.

Whether you own your business, work for a public or private company, or for the government, you deserve the right and opportunity to pursue maximum WHH. As you transition from necessary work, to optional work, to retirement, cashflow, health outcomes, and happiness must be balanced appropriately throughout your life. My experience, research, and interviews with thousands of people and hundreds of studies depict patterns of success and failure. My research will save you precious time.

Each stage of life requires different levels of focus or effort. This book will guide you in the timing required to achieve balanced results. Just be aware that in the work phase of life, "work" is not limited to earning a paycheck or volunteering or raising children or caring for loved ones. It encompasses all of these.

When you are in your early stage, especially in your twenties thirties, you must save as much money as possible. Unfortunately, this requires a level of guidance and maturity most of us do not have at this age.

When I asked my Carnegie Mellon University Tepper MBA students, Do you want to be a multi-millionaire? some said no. They told me they wanted to be altruistic and give their money away, an act that would create happiness for themselves and for others. No question that charitable acts soothe and nourish the soul. But I answered this response by inviting my students to apply the rule of 72 (which we will discuss) as well as WHH principles. Together, these will enable you to take life-changing actions on behalf of others and yourself, but only after you yourself attain millions.

Having attained wealth, become a major contributor to causes that matter to you. If you give away your money too early in your lifecycle, you cannot give the Rule of 72 the time it needs to work. It is like severing the roots of plants or pulling them out by their roots and expecting them to grow. If you use time to your advantage, you can be charitable in a truly life-changing way. Give a little now. Give much more later. It's all about the timing.

In your twenties, do what very few do: sacrifice. Work and save as much money as you possibly can. Do not spend money on fancy clothes, cars, or vacations. Practice austerity. I've interviewed numerous financially successful people in their twenties. Of these, many worked a full-time and a part-time job, logging over sixty hours a week. Many share rent or other housing costs with others. Some live with their family rent-free. Your main goal should be to save as much money as quickly as you can tolerate. Be an over-saver.

In your thirties, you need to tweak your effort slightly. Letting up just a bit on the wealth- acquisition throttle while you focus more time on your personal health actions. You can now look to invest in real estate and home ownership and other less liquid assets. Diversify. You have successfully incorporated a saving discipline. You now have the credibility to mentor people in their twenties, sharing with them what you have learned.

As you reach middle age, you approach the "Make work Optional" stage of life. The demanding success patterns of the early years become less rigid. You can toggle in and out of wealth acquisition efforts and devote more to health and happiness outcomes—always on variable, flexible basis. Think about how a light dimmer switch operates. There are going to be times when you will need to turn up the brightness so you can see your pathway forward.

Now, what if you find yourself in your forties, fifties, or sixties feeling that you have not yet acquired sufficient wealth? If we wait to acquire wealth, we must also delay a focus on "maximizing" health and happiness. The greater the delay, the more difficult it is to achieve the best possible WHH outcomes. Timing and consistency are key. If you believe you are not on pace to maximize WHH, don't despair. You will find later in this book strategies to help you catch up. I assure you, you are not alone in feeling behind.

If you are like most people, you want to find ways to be more productive and to find more time in your day to support your goals. I will share success practices for more effectively segmenting your efforts. These will help you to stay the course toward maximizing the wealth, health, and happiness continuum.

It is important to be in touch with your feelings about where you are in your WHH journey, but it is also vital to get a measurable reality check by measuring your WHH status compared to your peers. Using available data from U.S. banks, brokerages, and money managers, I was able to track 401K savings by age. Here is one example of many I found:

As of September 2024, according to The Vanguard Group, people under 25 have an average of $7,351 dollars saved. People 25-34 have $37,557 average savings. People 35-44 have $91,281 saved. People 45-54 have saved $168,600 on average. People 55-64 have $244,750 and people 65 plus have $272,588 saved. The median amounts are much less, as it takes only a few over-savers to skew the averages higher. Median amounts saved paint a more accurate picture of the population being measured. Now these amounts do not include other savings vehicles like bank accounts, non-401k/403b entities. I will share more benchmarks in future chapters.

We have not—yet—figured out how to go back in time to change behaviors. We know human time is perishable. We know through knowledge acquired and retained that we can pre-determine outcomes.

If you have ever been involved in manufacturing a new product, you know that most manufacturers "life test." Accelerated life testing helps to determine quickly, in a laboratory environment and before it is mass produced for sale to consumers, how long a product will last in a real-life environment. The product is put through a series of tests until it fails. What if we could life-test into the future or extrapolate ahead of time wealth, health, and happiness outcomes for ourselves and others?

We can look at past behavioral history of individuals who have failed or succeeded and the resultant outcomes to extrapolate how to maximize success today and into the future. That is what I have done through my research and experience.

Most people are behind in the amount of money required to have the same standard of living for their retirement years. Catchup saving for the future typically causes stress, unhappiness, and, over the long term, health issues. If you find yourself behind on your goals, what can you do? Let me share some approaches to minimize stress through behavior and diet as you seek to maximize your WHH continuum.

Some people do not need or want to achieve great monetary wealth. Think of the Tibetan monks, Hindu priests, and Roman Catholic clerics who commit to a life of austerity and poverty. We all can learn from them as we balance our efforts to achieve true WHH.

Many books have been written on the individual topics of Wealth acquisition, healthy lifestyle, and the attainment of happiness, but very few have focused on all three, what I call the Wealth, Health, and Happiness (WHH) continuum. I am not aware of any college curriculum that teaches this material. There are studies that speak to why wealth, health, and happiness are enhanced through the pursuit of knowledge. As we pursue knowledge of investments, health enhancements, and ultimate happiness, we form habits and success patterns we can use. By our example, these can help others as well.

Most of the research does a good job of extrapolating data from polling and surveys. Gallop is mentioned worldwide as a major source. The issue, however, is the data output is only "a moment in time in a lifetime of moments." Research is limited to one frame of an entire movie. That is a paucity of data. How many of us can decipher a movie by see just one still frame?

If you do not understand how to maximize wealth enhance your health outcomes, or maximize your happiness, acquire the knowledge. By reading this book you are well on your way. I have done the research, had the interviews, and have condensed it all for you. This book is a "one stop shop."

Henley & Partners, the leading international residence and citizenship advisory firm, has collaborated with global wealth intelligence firm New World Wealth to produce the second edition of the USA Wealth Report.

New World Wealth is currently the only known independent wealth research firm systematically tracking global wealth migration trends between countries and among cities. The firm tracks the movements of over 150,000 high-net-worth individuals in its in-house database, with a special focus on those with over USD 30 million in listed company holdings. The database's primary focus is on company founders (50%+ of the database) and individuals from high-value companies who hold the following positions: chairperson, CEO, president, director, and managing partner. If you want to become wealthy, study how wealth is accumulated by the wealthy. You should note that the studies reveal that even the super wealthy or extra-high net worth people do a poor job of wealth transition. In particular, wealthy small business owners fail to plan far enough ahead. Major economic, personal, or governmental calamities often bring the need to sell small businesses faster than what the owners envisioned.

**What follows is our first BEST Success Practice
to maximize the WHH continuum.**

Constantly acquire and apply knowledge.

We can obtain knowledge from sources outside of our usual interactions. I have researched extra high net worth sources for you. Many are not publicized. Among these, Tiger21, American Association of Individual Investors, and R360 come to mind. R360 deserves special mention as a by-invitation peer community of extraordinary leaders and wealth creators stewarding family enterprises that thrive through life's transitions. Their website is revealing:

> At R360, we believe wealth is about more than money. It's about cultivating capital in all its forms: financial, intellectual, social, human, emotional, and spiritual. Bound by shared values, R360 members wish to inspire future generations and use their abilities, wealth, and knowledge to become a legendary force for change. The pursuit of wellness and longevity technologies is of significant interest among R360 members, driven by both personal wellness goals and investment prospects. Members are actively seeking ways to optimize their health and are engaging in solutions for addressing health concerns, whether personal or within their families. Initiatives within the R360 community include pioneering blood tests for various cancers, and ventures into regenerative medicine, gene editing, and stem cell therapies. R360 members involved in our Health, Wellness & Longevity interest circle, including the managers of multiple billion-dollar biotech funds, tour biotech labs and learn about stem cell therapies, and though the group's main focus is longevity, members have also learned more about psychedelic drugs as treatments for addiction and mental health.

Knowledge does not reside in Western culture alone. I have included ideas from the Far East, India, South America, the Middle East and Asia among the sources that most influence me in creating the Wealth, Health, and Happiness continuum. I will share all my sources of influence with you to enhance your WHH perspective. With the knowledge we acquire, we have a responsibility in turn to create awareness, educate, and coach family and friends in the benefits of saving as early as possible for retirement. How we train is as important as the facts we are trying to convey.

Here is a macro example as it relates generally to adults. Every wonder why it's so easy to consume or purchase something? You go into a grocery store, pick out your items, go to the self-checkout counter, scan the bar or QR codes, tap the screen with your credit card, and off you go—minus a quantity of dollars but with basket of food. Industries have formed to simplify the shopping experience without the need to go to a store. The process goes from your laptop or smartphone to your front door. On the one hand, the streamlined process may prompt you to spend less time deciding. On the other hand, you do have access to a range of vendors and the ability to compare prices and features. It is a fast and simple education.

Now, how does a person save or invest money? Well, it's not like going to a grocery store or ordering food online. You go into a bank or brokerage firm, such as Fidelity, to open an account. You are required by law, to fill out applications, Security Exchange Commission (SEC) documents and other paperwork written by lawyers and politicians. Disclosures must be signed. Investing takes more effort and demands more knowledge than the buying experience requires. Our society is conditioned to consume more than to save. It is not just the technology and government regulations that discourage saving. Most countries in the world impose a Capital Gain Tax (CGT). What is a CGT? When, as an example, you buy the stock Nvidia at $100 and sell it for $125, the $25 dollar profit is taxed at a CGT rate. There are short term, long term and income level implications with varying degrees of complexity across the globe. The CGT rates go from 0 to a high of 42% (Denmark) and average 25% in the USA, on the sale of your investment gains.

"These taxes create a bias against saving, leading to a lower level of national income by encouraging present consumption over investment. Higher taxes also cause investors to sell their assets less frequently, which leads to fewer taxes being assessed. This is known as the realization or lock-in effect." Tax Foundation- Europe March 11, 2025 Alex Mengden.

If we delve into some neuroscience and physiology, we find that a pea-sized structure called the habenula, located in the brain above the pineal gland and the floor of the brain's third ventricle, plays a big role in the brain's anti-reward process. The habenula plays a role in connecting the forebrain—essentially the seat of intellect and consciousness—with the midbrain, which is associated with more autonomous functions, such as appetite, emotional response, and the like. Our brains are wired for craving pleasure and, therefore, reward. Rewards come in many forms, getting a good grade, receiving a financial bonus, winning at bocci, poker, golf, spelling bee … you name it. The lateral habenula is a kind of guardian that tries its hardest to keep our pleasure-seeking drives in check. The structure secretes dopamine and endorphin antagonists. Dopamine is a hormonal messenger active in the brain, which plays roles in movement, motivation, and reward-seeking. It is released when pleasure is experienced and drives the individual to repeat the pleasurable action. Endorphins are neurotransmitter hormones that relieve pain, heighten mood, and generally increase feelings of well-being. These are all good things—in moderation. And it is the dopamine and endorphin antagonists produced by the habenula that moderate the effect of these substances.

While we are wired to seek pleasure and reward, we are also counter-wired to avoid being overwhelmed by self-indulgent emotion. The less effort required to reward oneself with a purchase, the more likely it is that the dopamine and endorphin drives toward pleasure will prevail over the antagonistic efforts of the habenula. But if the action in question presents more challenges than simply tapping your credit card on point-of-sale reader, it becomes increasingly likely that the habenula's antagonist hormones will prevail over the substances associated with pleasure and reward.

When you are disappointed, you feel a sense of loss. When you are in a situation that presents the prospect of disappointment—effort unlikely to produce a gratifying result—the secretions of habenula counter the stimulation provided by endorphins and dopamine, increasing the likelihood that you will abort a contemplated course of action because you feel that you will be disappointed by failure.

Engaging in "retail therapy" is a common means of self-treatment. A recent study found that 62% of shoppers report that they make some purchases to lift their spirits. Buying is therefore easy. Saving? Not so much. The effort required may seem daunting, the doubts over your competence to make the "right" savings/investment decisions are discouraging, as you imagine how bad you will feel if you make a mistake—a bad investment. Indeed, investing is fraught with confirmation bias, which drives us to seek out information that confirms your pre-existing beliefs while ignoring even irrefutable contradictory proofs. Cognitive dissonance is discomfort experienced when you hold two opposing beliefs. As an investor, you experience cognitive dissonance by holding on to a losing stock to avoid the painful admission that you made a bad investment and should sell the position.

In short, the action required is to save, invest, and thus acquire wealth is far less fun than the action required for "retail therapy." The same study that found 62% of shoppers indulging in retain therapy also concluded buying things you enjoy or think you need can be up to 40 times more effective at giving you a sense of control in your life compared to not shopping and buying.

Throughout this book, I will share self-training methods to avoid biases against saving that are reinforced by the habenula. We will work on reversing the retail therapy effect by learning how saving money can be made "fun" and give you both control and a comforting sense of control. I will also share how adaptive adjustments to your personal WHH continuum are required—that's normal—but you need to know how to confront and manage the negative or even destructive feelings working on your WHH continuum can engender. There will be success as well as failure. We don't want to fall into the trap of equating a missed goal with failure. We want to fail fast and move on.

Case studies, surveys, interview details, personal experiences, and research that encompass a variety of demographics—geographic location, level of wealth, age, education—will be offered in support of maximizing WHH, and, most important, I will share methods of creating the WHH transition and achieving stability in the process.

So, this is a preview vision of what you are about to read. I have asked many questions that will get answered. I have made many promises and commitments to you. We will be undertaking a journey, which will cause you to question your current approaches and may disrupt your current way of life. I know it had that effect on me. And I am grateful for it.

Let's get started with the details of what is true wealth.

1

What Is True Financial Wealth?

We should feel better than we do about pursuing goals to be wealthy. It is what we do with our wealth for the good of others not just ourselves that provides the most satisfaction and happiness. In this book, I define true wealth as monetary in nature.

Some say "Knowledge is true power." True enough, but the right application of knowledge can be not merely powerful, but life changing! We must be willing to transition and transform as conditions around us change. Who could have predicted the Covid pandemic and how governments would close down most of society?

Conditions will change in the future. That much you can count on. Maybe the next catalyst will be AI or cyber warfare or digital currency disruption. Maybe blockchain and digital world currencies will become more mainstream. Maybe current global currencies will be aligned with more tangible assets. Global debt increases may cause hyperinflation, stagflation, and shortages. Point is we don't know what the future holds. Nevertheless, wealth will still be acquirable and available despite inevitable change.

You want to live in a world of change? Just spend ten minutes with a stock day trader. (I don't recommend day trading, as the volatility is extreme and not for everyone.) Every second of that trade can be the difference between profit and loss. Timing is one crucial element as we pursue true wealth.

As an example of life changing knowledge, I did not learn about the Rule of 72 application to wealth building in school or from my parents. Neither provided the knowledge, and I did not know what I did not know! I finally learned about the Rule from a Paine Weber (Now UBS) branch manager in Casper, Wyoming, when I was twenty-three years old. Pete Natoli and his assistant Donnie Claunch mapped out how I could become a millionaire if I followed the Rule. I'll share the details a bit later.

Right now, let's explore how and why it is quite possible for people ages 1-18 to achieve financial independence and become millionaires—eventually. Parents, grandparents, relatives, and friends all have a responsibility to educate young people on the benefits of building monetary wealth. For many, the opportunity to save a million dollars seems like mission impossible, barring a lottery win (very close to mission impossible) or we inherit someone else's wealth. Let me share a story from the point of view of adults in support of young people.

I went to a drycleaner and was greeted by a smiling young cashier. She was just sixteen. After the typical chitchat, her much older coworker started bragging about this young woman. He went on to say she had saved almost enough money to buy a used car. As it turned out, she had been infused with a wonderful work ethic by her mother. As I often do when I see a young person working and doing a good job, I ask: Do you want to be a millionaire?

She thought for a second or two, and then said no. She explained that it was not possible and, besides, she wanted to buy a car. She said the car represented freedom and how she would not have to rely on anyone for a ride and she could go anywhere. Ah, youth! The immediate freedom of a car vs a lifetime of freedom of choices.

Her response is typical. Most want to spend now and save later in life—a "later," unfortunately, that often comes *too* late. We are inclined by aspects of our neural makeup and further conditioned by brilliant marketing and advertising to consume goods and services *now*. This urgency, however, means that, as a society, we are doing things backwards. Redwoods and money need time to grow. We should save while we are young and let the money we save build wealth over time. Wait to save and invest? Time is the most perishable commodity there is. We'll have more to say about this in a chapter to come.

For many years now, I have been asking young people the same question: *Do you want to be a millionaire?*

I usually get one of two answers. The first is what the dry cleaner cashier told me: *No. I want to buy a car now.* The second answer is *Yes. But how is that even possible?* In fact, both answers are based on disbelief that the million-dollar goal can be achieved, but the second response is usually followed up with *Tell me more.*

And so I introduce the Rule of 72.

I begin by explaining the concept of compound interest—that is, interest calculated on the principal *plus* the interest accumulated over the prior period of time. It is interest on capital that is continuously growing ("compounding"). The opposite of compound interest is simple interest, in which the interest due is calculated not on a continuously growing principal plus interest but on the principal alone.

At an interest rate of 10%, $1 will double in 7.2 years. With this fact put out there, I define what the S&P 500 is and what company stocks and bonds are. Next, show how, since 1970, the S&P 500 index has returned 10.47% compound annual growth rate (CAGR).

"Let's do some math together," I suggest. The calculations are written on a piece of paper or a napkin, doesn't matter which.

By age 16, the drycleaner cashier, through hard work, discipline, and her mother's guidance managed to save $10,000. This $10,000 in savings, invested in an S&P index low-cost fund instead of a car, will double to $20,000 in 7.2 years, assuming the same CAGR as the previous years. As it doubles in value, the car would inevitably depreciate—lose value.

I continue to apply the Rule of 72 as follows: $20,000 becomes $40,000, becomes $80,000, becomes $160,000, becomes $320,000, becomes $640,000 becomes $1.2 million dollars. When? At 65 years old, the current 16-year-old, will be worth $1.2 million dollars—without having added to her initial investment of $10,000. This is the rule of 72 at work.

The linear representation of the S&P index results is not a straight line up but an average of all recessions/ depressions and market advances. Going back further in time, through the past 96 years, the S&P has returned approximately 9.9% compounded annually.

Let's take another example, this time focusing on a 21-year-old. His family, saving $1,000 per year for him from his birth to age 21, having invested in the low-cost S&P index fund with the same historic CAGR, will retire at age 65 with $5,000,000. Yes, a total of just $21,000 invested will produce $5,000,000. No other investment or savings needed! It is the rule of 72 at work, using time and early-investing discipline.

If you are a parent, uncle, aunt, or grandparent, making an initial contribution for a newborn child will give him or her a considerable financial advantage. The Wealth/Health/Happiness (WHH) continuum blended with the Rule of 72 supports balance in life. We will speak to exactly how this advantage is used positively in other chapters.

Pensions, Social Security, and other social programs tend to create dependency, causing many to wait before saving. Some adults wait for an inheritance instead of funding their retirement starting right now. We know what has happened to public and private company pensions over the years. The shift to defined contribution plans works as long as the employee contributes. If we rely on social programs or inheritance, we run the risk of not maximizing WHH.

BEST Success Practice #2 to maximize the WHH continuum:
Learn and apply the rule of 72 as early as possible.

Let me share another story.

A married couple spent lavishly throughout their lives. Very generously, they provided material gifts to their three children, but saving money was not in their lexicon. One could say they were "professional" consumers. Their children saw the example set by their parents. The more money the parents lavished upon them, the more the children were educated on consumerism. The children, as they grew older, were consuming instead of saving, the bad habit having been ingrained from a young age.

Flash forward. Now the married couple find themselves nearing retirement age waiting for the windfall of their parents' inheritance, estimated to be in the millions. You guessed it! Due to many factors, the amount of the inheritance was not as robust as anticipated. The parents lived well into their 90s, and a great deal of money was spent on health issues and eldercare. The investment portfolio mix was not diversified and took a downturn. What was left to the well-indulged children when their elderly parents finally passed was not enough for any of them to retire comfortably.

Instead of purchasing cars for their children when they turned sixteen, had they invested in the children's retirement and provided continuous financial education and discipline, financial stability would be ongoing. To make matters worse, they did not fund their own retirements, thinking that the wealth transfer of *their* parents would suffice. Call this an example of generational ignorance. They did not know the difference between a stock and a bond. They did not think it necessary to acquire financial literacy. In consequence, the stress of their past actions negatively impacts their personal WHH continuum today.

The consumerisms with which we are blitzed on an hourly basis keep most people from ever achieving true financial wealth. We manage our money backwards by purchasing cars, homes, toys, jewelry, and non-essentials first. By incurring debt, *paying* (not earning) interest, and not saving, we become indentured servants. We are dependent on institutions, programs, and others. We rob ourselves of maximum WHH. Vaccinate yourself against this outcome by saving money first and buying stuff second.

True, saving and investing is not as easy as buying and spending.

So, where do we find the money to save? Part of the save-money-first formula requires looking at where we are spending money in the first place. Here is a simple example. How many of us buy a coffee or latte every day? It may not seem like much—until you do the math. An average of $120 a month spent on coffeehouse coffee instead of making your own at home can cost significantly more than $120 a month. Let me explain what we call "lost opportunity cost." That $120 monthly *outlay* could have been invested to provide an income return *input*. Using the example of an 8% return, the future value of the $120 a month is not $10,080 ($120 x 12 months x 7 years). If invested at an 8% return in compound interest, it would be worth $12,848 dollars in seven years. See the habeshafinance.com monthly expense chart below for other examples of save first and spend later returns.

Monthly Expenses Compounded Annually at 8% Over 40 Years

Years	Future Value $10/mo (Entertainment Subscribption)	Future Value $120/mo (Latte, Coffee)	Future Value $200/mo (Cable/Internet)	Future Value $523/mo (Car Payment)	Future Value $2000/mo (Mortgage/Rent)
Year 0	$0.00	$0.00	$0.00	$0.00	$0.00
Year 1	$120.00	$1,440.00	$2,400.00	$6,276.00	$24,000.00
Year 2	$249.60	$2,995.20	$4,992.00	$13,054.08	$49,920.00
Year 3	$389.57	$4,674.82	$7,791.36	$20,374.41	$77,913.60
Year 4	$540.73	$6,488.80	$10,814.67	$28,280.36	$108,146.69
Year 5	$703.99	$8,447.91	$14,079.84	$36,818.79	$140,798.42
Year 6	$880.31	$10,563.74	$17,606.23	$46,040.29	$176,062.30
Year 7	$1,070.74	$12,848.84	$21,414.73	$55,999.51	$214,147.28
Year 8	$1,276.40	$15,316.74	$25,527.91	$66,755.47	$255,279.06
Year 9	$1,498.51	$17,982.08	$29,970.14	$78,371.91	$299,701.39
Year 10	$1,738.39	$20,860.65	$34,767.75	$90,917.67	$347,677.50
Year 11	$1,997.46	$23,969.50	$39,949.17	$104,467.08	$399,491.70
Year 12	$2,277.26	$27,327.06	$45,545.10	$119,100.45	$455,451.04
Year 13	$2,579.44	$30,953.23	$51,588.71	$134,904.48	$515,887.12
Year 14	$2,905.79	$34,869.49	$58,115.81	$151,972.84	$581,158.09
Year 15	$3,258.25	$39,099.04	$65,165.07	$170,406.67	$651,650.73
Year 16	$3,638.91	$43,666.97	$72,778.28	$190,315.20	$727,782.79
Year 17	$4,050.03	$48,600.32	$81,000.54	$211,816.42	$810,005.42
Year 18	$4,494.03	$53,928.35	$89,880.58	$235,037.73	$898,805.85
Year 19	$4,973.55	$59,682.62	$99,471.03	$260,116.75	$994,710.32
Year 20	$5,491.44	$65,897.23	$109,828.71	$287,202.09	$1,098,287.14
Year 21	$6,050.75	$72,609.01	$121,015.01	$316,454.25	$1,210,150.11
Year 22	$6,654.81	$79,857.73	$133,096.21	$348,046.60	$1,330,962.12
Year 23	$7,307.20	$87,686.35	$146,143.91	$382,166.32	$1,461,439.09
Year 24	$8,011.77	$96,141.25	$160,235.42	$419,015.63	$1,602,354.22
Year 25	$8,772.71	$105,272.55	$175,454.26	$458,812.88	$1,754,542.56
Year 26	$9,594.53	$115,134.36	$191,890.60	$501,793.91	$1,918,905.96
Year 27	$10,482.09	$125,785.11	$209,641.84	$548,213.42	$2,096,418.44
Year 28	$11,440.66	$137,287.91	$228,813.19	$598,346.50	$2,288,131.92
Year 29	$12,475.91	$149,710.95	$249,518.25	$652,490.22	$2,495,182.47
Year 30	$13,593.99	$163,127.82	$271,879.71	$710,965.43	$2,718,797.07
Year 31	$14,801.50	$177,618.05	$296,030.08	$774,118.67	$2,960,300.83
Year 32	$16,105.62	$193,267.49	$322,112.49	$842,324.16	$3,221,124.90
Year 33	$17,514.07	$210,168.89	$350,281.49	$915,986.09	$3,502,814.89
Year 34	$19,035.20	$228,422.40	$380,704.01	$995,540.98	$3,807,040.08
Year 35	$20,678.02	$248,136.20	$413,560.33	$1,081,460.26	$4,135,603.29
Year 36	$22,452.26	$269,427.09	$449,045.16	$1,174,253.08	$4,490,451.55
Year 37	$24,368.44	$292,421.26	$487,368.77	$1,274,469.33	$4,873,687.68
Year 38	$26,437.91	$317,254.96	$528,758.27	$1,382,702.87	$5,287,582.69
Year 39	$28,672.95	$344,075.36	$573,458.93	$1,499,595.10	$5,734,589.30
Year 40	$31,086.78	$373,041.39	$621,735.64	$1,625,838.71	$6,217,356.45

habeshafinance.com

Most of us work and, if we do a good job, get raises and bonuses. The other part of the save money first formula is to apply any raise or bonus to an investment or savings account. Not all of it, but at least half of it. Resist the temptation to spend. Instead, condition your mind to save.

Another example is what my in-laws do every year. Most of us pay taxes. My wife, Karen, is one of eight children. She tells the story of how, after receiving their tax refund, her mom and dad would splurge on Barberton Chicken dinners with all the sides for the whole family. The money spent was minimal compared to the money left over from the yearly tax refund. Her parents would save and invest the remainder. This is rare. How many of us have plans to spend the refund even before we receive it? Plan instead to save it and invest it in your retirement or your children's retirement. Found money should be automatically saved and invested.

As adults, even if we cannot fund our children's retirements, we can make a significant difference in their lives by instilling practices of saving early and often. Keep the Rule of 72 front and center. If you want financial stability for your young people, demonstrate to them a save-early-and-spend-wisely strategy over time. Make if fun. Make it exciting.

Invite family and friends to a one-hour money class—or call it what you want. If you want to focus on young people outside of your family, you will want to get parental approval and support, of course. The best way to proceed, however, is to invite the parents to sit in.

Provide snacks and a comfortable setting, a quiet place, with an easel and magic markers for visual aids. Get cash from the bank in the following denominations: $40 in five-dollar bills, $80 in tens, and $160 in twenties, for a total of $315. These are illustrative props. You aren't giving any of the cash away. But the educational impact of real money as opposed, say, to Monopoly money, is substantial.

Now, with a little showmanship to keep their attention, start by placing the $5 on a table and demonstrate how the five-dollar bill doubles to a ten-dollar bill, a ten-dollar to twenty etc. Keep going with doubling your real-money props across the table until you get to $160 dollars. This makes for a powerful demonstration, especially among children.

For an audience with children and their parents, make part of your presentation more meaningful to the adults by using an example of $10,000 in savings. Share with them the 90-plus years of 10% compounded annual returns for the S&P. Depending on the knowledge level of your audience, you may have to explain what the S&P is all about. You may have to share some examples of low-cost indexes or ETFs. And you must explain that past performance is never absolutely predictive of the future. Provide an easel with a large white easel pad paper and some magic markers. On the top of the paper write, "A one-time investment of $10K will double every 7.2 years. Next write $10,000 and below it $20,000, then $40,000, $80,000, $160,000, $320,000, $640,000," and, at the very bottom, in big bold letters, write "$1.2 MILLION." This is how an easel presentation illustrates a $10,000 one-time investment doubling every 7.2 years. It is a powerful visual.

I explain there are infinite ways to accumulate wealth included but not limited to, investing in Futures, Commodities, Real Estate, REITS, Bonds, Debt Instruments, International, Private Equity and what I call "Exotics" like Crypto and derivatives. I futher explain that I am not a registered or licenced financial advisor and you should seek out Wealth Advisory (WAS) and Registered Investment Advisor (RIA) experts.

If my audience consists of working-age people from sixteen to thirty 16-30, I use the a different approach. I was at a restaurant after a golf event and overheard a conversation between a woman sitting at the table next to me and a gentleman. I jumped into the conversation.

"Forgive me for eavesdropping, but did I hear that you are working three jobs?"

"Yes," she said. "I'm working a full-time job and two part-time jobs. Today is my first day off in weeks. I have worked seventy hours a week, give or take, for the last two years."

I did not ask her age but found out later she was in her late twenties. I asked her why she worked so hard. She volunteered that she was divorced and had a child she needed to provide for. The young lady was clearly driven and had a high level of energy. This made her a perfect candidate to hear about the Rule of 72. So, I took a chance and asked if she wanted to become a millionaire.

She looked at me and answered, well, yes, of course I would!" She had a big smile. "But how can you?" She went on to explain that no one taught this in school, and her parents certainly never mentioned becoming a millionaire.

I grabbed a napkin and a pen.

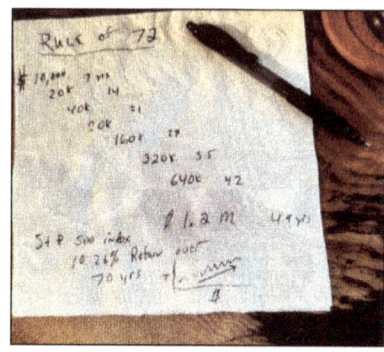

On the top of the napkin, starting in the upper left corner, I wrote $10,000, then $20,000, and going from top to bottom from left to right, I wrote $40,000, $80,000, $160,000, $320,000, $640,000, and, finally, on the bottom far right, $1.2 M, for "million." and then the progression of time, ending in with 49 years.

I explained the math, pointing out the doubling at seven-year intervals. Next, I asked if she had managed to save any of the money she earned. She said she had saved $12,000.

"You've done a super job of saving. You are obviously motivated."

We had built a rapport in the space of fifteen minutes. She volunteered that she had the money in a savings account at the bank earning 1%.

"My recommendation is that you talk with an advisor, open a brokerage account, and invest a *portion* of your savings in an S&P low-cost index or ETF."

"What is the S&P?" she asked—quite predictably.

I explained, using a few more napkins to scribble notes. She left the bar and headed home. Throughout the entire quarter-hour or so, he listened patiently. The gentleman sitting at the table with her was qualifying her. Turns out he is a realtor in the process of trying to sell her a house. Clearly, I had not helped his effort. He had earmarked her $12,000 as a downpayment.

"I've never heard of the Rule of 72," he said. Then he asked me if I could help him, so he could apply it for his three children. Could I repeat what I explained to her, and write it on another napkin? He offered to buy me an iced tea for my trouble.

So, I did a Ground Hog Day rerun. As I was doing this, a few curious folks came over. One happened to be the bar and restaurant manager, who had listened in on the conversation.

"What are you guys talking about?"

Ground Hog Day, Part II.

When he mentioned that he had heard of the Rule of 72, I asked if he had shared it with his employees.

"No, but I've used it on my family."

"Terrific," I said, and then suggested he share it at his next all employee meeting.

Why recommend and evangelize the Rule of 72?

Just imagine if we can help to double the number of millionaires in the United States. Less dependance, more freedom, and more choices in life? Absolutely! It starts with education. If we can get people into the habit of saving instead of spending, we are on our way!

> **BEST Success Practice #3 to maximize the WHH continuum:**
> **Save money for retirement first. Do not buy a car, house, or any large purchase. Open a Roth IRA and invest in a low-cost Standard and Poors 500 index/ETF first. Add to it each month. Diversify your portfolio to minimize inevitable corrections.**

Study after study I researched indicate that people with more wealth report being happier than those with less wealth. According to a psychological study of more than 4,000 millionaires worldwide, wealth can add to happiness. The study, which was published in *Personality and Social Psychology Bulletin 2018*, also found evidence that millionaires who earned their wealth were happier than those who inherited it.

Many people believe becoming a millionaire is out of reach, so why even try to study how to do it.

> *"Education is the ability to listen to almost anything without*
> *losing your temper or self-confidence"*
> —ROBERT FROST

Let's take a look at some statistics. For December 2023. (For the purposes of this report, "wealth" refers to an individual's liquid investable wealth, which includes only listed company holdings, cash holdings, and debt-free residential property holdings.) My source is New World Wealth.

Per the USA Henley and Partners 2024 report, there are 5.5 million millionaire citizens in the USA. As of January 2024, per a study by Abby McCain:

- There were about 22 million millionaires in the U.S. in 2023. (The difference between these numbers and those reported by Henley and Partners relates to how wealth is measured.)
- 33% of U.S. millionaires are women.
- There are about 62.5 million millionaires globally, a 11.4% increase from 2020.
- The world's 100 richest individuals earned their first $1 million at age 37, on average.
- The average millionaire is 57 years old.
- 42% of millionaires are baby boomers (between 57 and 75 years of age), the majority of any age group.
- 19% of millionaires are millennials (between 18 and 31 years of age).

Another study, by Ramsey Solutions, conducted in 2024 is the largest survey of millionaires ever, with 10,000 participants. This study finds:
- Eight out of 10 millionaires invested in their company's 401(k) plan.
- The top five careers for millionaires include engineer, accountant, teacher, management executive, and attorney. "Management executive" includes business owners.
- 79% of millionaires did not inherit any money from their parents or other family members.
- Three out of four millionaires said regular long-term consistent investing leads to monetary wealth.

BEST Success Practice #4 to maximize the WHH continuum:
Do not isolate yourself from others you love or trust.
Set S.M.A.R.T (Specific/Measurable/Achievable/Relevant/Time-bound)
goals to become a millionaire by a certain age. Share your commitment
to become wealthy with family and friends.

Also interesting, based on the research, is a connection between wealth and where people live. What cities are currently experiencing the most growth of millionaires?

The Henley and Partners Wealth Report 2024, puts the state capital of Texas, Austin, at number one in remarkable millionaire growth, which stood at 110% over the prior decade. With its booming tech sector, Austin has been dubbed "Silicon Hills," as several major tech companies have moved their headquarters to the city over the past few years, most notably Tesla and Oracle. Austin's top-end residential market has also been growing rapidly.

Number two city in millionaire growth is Scottsdale, the jewel in the crown of the Greater Phoenix, Arizona, metropolitan area. Scottsdale has seen a spectacular 102% millionaire growth in the past ten years. The town is home to a growing number of exclusive golf and lifestyle estates and is attracting large numbers of tech entrepreneurs from California as well as wealthy retirees.

Number three is South Florida's Palm Beach and West Palm Beach. These places are increasingly popular retirement hotspots for New York and California millionaires, with wealth growth of 93% over the past decade. A large number of affluent individuals are choosing to live and operate from this area in the post-Covid era, especially those in the fund management and entertainment sectors. There is a perception-turned-reality that these cities offer more financial freedoms. Certainly, regulatory regimes are less restrictive, and Florida, like Texas, has no state income tax.

Henley and Partners forecast that Austin, Scottsdale, and West Palm Beach will continue to lead in future millionaire growth over the next decade. Indeed, they will lead in general wealth growth. We also expect that Salt Lake City (Utah) and the Florida cities of Tampa and Naples will continue to attract rising numbers of high-net-worth residents.

Known for its beautiful mountain backdrop, Salt Lake City, which was recently named by WalletHub (https://wallethub.com/edu/most-stressful-states/32218) America's "Least Stressed City," is rising in popularity as a base for tech and financial start-ups. It is located relatively close to the resort town of Park City, a second-home hotspot for America's rich and famous.

Tampa and Naples are both located on Florida's booming west coast. A key business center, Tampa is also an emerging tech hub, while Naples is an increasingly popular retirement destination and is known for its top-end golf courses, beautiful beaches, and world-class shopping. Low taxes (no state income tax) and an excellent business environment are also attractive. We should note, however, that by 2024, there was growing evidence of an impending exodus from some Florida cities because of skyrocketing home insurance rates due to the incidence of increasingly numerous and severe hurricanes and tropical storms. Some insurance companies have ceased to write policies in the most vulnerable areas. Georgia and South Carolina are the recipients of some outflows from the state.

BEST Success Practice #5 to maximize the WHH continuum:
If you are in your twenties and thirties, work as many hours per week and save as much as possible. Work two jobs, if you can.

Now, where in the USA are the top states for earning the highest average paychecks?

According to Forbes advisor Belle Wong, JD, the average yearly earnings (or paycheck) in the USA is about $59,000 per year, as of the 4th quarter 2023. That is an average hourly rate of $28.34. She used the US Bureau of Labor Statistics and various payroll service companies as her sources. The states with the highest average salaries are Massachusetts at $76,000, New York at $74,800, and California at $73,200. The lowest is Mississippi at $45,180, Arkansas at $48,500, and West Virginia at $49,170 per year.

Average Salary by State in 2023

State	Annual Average Wage	Average Hourly Wage
Alabama	$50,620	$24.32
Alaska	$66,130	$31.79
Arizona	$58,620	$28.18
Arkansas	$48,570	$23.35
California	$73,220	$35.20
Colorado	$67,870	$32.63
Connecticut	$69,310	$33.32
Delaware	$62,260	$29.93
Florida	$55,980	$26.91
Georgia	$58,000	$27.88
Hawaii	$61,420	$23.35
Idaho	$51,350	$24.69

State	Annual Average Wage	Average Hourly Wage
Illinois	$63,930	$30.73
Indiana	$53,500	$20.24
Iowa	$53,520	$25.73
Kansas	$52,850	$25.41
Kentucky	$51,490	$24.76
Louisiana	$50,940	$24.49
Maine	$55,960	$26.90
Maryland	$69,750	$33.53
Massachusetts	$76,600	$36.83
Michigan	$58,000	$27.88
Minnesota	$63,640	$30.60
Mississippi	$45,180	$21.72
Missouri	$54,520	$26.21
Montana	$52,200	$25.11
Nebraska	$55,070	$26.48
Nevada	$55,490	$26.68
New Hampshire	$62,550	$30.07
New Jersey	$70,890	$34.08

State	Annual Average Wage	Average Hourly Wage
New Mexico	$54,400	$26.15
New York	$74,870	$36.00
North Carolina	$56,220	$27.03
North Dakota	$55,800	$26.83
Ohio	$56,530	$27.18
Oklahoma	$50,940	$24.49
Oregon	$62,680	$30.14
Pennsylvania	$58,470	$28.11
Rhode Island	$64,530	$31.03
South Carolina	$50,650	$24.35
South Dakota	$49,890	$23.99
Tennessee	$52,820	$25.39
Texas	$57,300	$27.55
Utah	$57,360	$27.58
Vermont	$59,190	$28.46
Virginia	$65,590	$31.54
Washington	$72,350	$34.79
West Virginia	$49,170	$23.64

State	Annual Average Wage	Average Hourly Wage
Wisconsin	$56,120	$26.98
Wyoming	$54,440	$26.17

Source: Forbes Advisor Embed

The statistics can be misleading, since some of the states with highest income earners have the highest taxes and cost of living. Remember, the whole idea is to save as much as possible for your retirement. Also, the statistics are based on averages, not median and individual pay, and not household total pay. As an example, in 2022, the household average income in the USA was $105,555, according to *Motley Fool.* Many households have multiple people earning incomes. The science of statistics can be misleading if the basis is not fully known.

> *"One of the great mistakes is to judge policies and programs by their intentions rather than their results."*
> *—Milton Friedman*

The data I just presented gives you a rough benchmark for where you stand compared to the average. Once you have your emergency savings and are on your way to accumulating at least the average amount of savings, you must consider diversification of your investment strategy. I know of many people who do not have a diversified investment strategy. They save a monthly amount on a disciplined basis at the bank, in a money market fund or certificates of deposits (CDs). At the time of this writing, the highest-yield savings account was 5.3%, with the average being closer to 4%. Not too long ago, the average was much lower. Some of us are very conservative with our saved money. Sometimes, personal circumstances make this conservatism necessary. As a rule of thumb—and common sense—the younger you are, the more forward-look horizon opportunity you have to be more aggressive with your investments.

With the data just reported and the knowledge we have gained, let's do some more math.

What if you are able to save 10% of the average household income of $105,000, $10,500, after taxes each year? You decide to go the ultra-conservative route and save through a CD instrument with a yield of 4%. How much can your savings and rate of return grow in thirty years? The answer? Approximately $562,100 dollars—not bad until you realize that when you retire, the cashflow 4% drawdown of the $562,000 equals $22,480 per year.

Here is another strategy to consider. The S&P index is an amalgamation of the top 500 publicly traded companies in the USA. You decide to invest the $10,000 in the S&P 500 index mutual fund or Exchange Traded Fund (ETF), and your return is 10%. The 10% is a historical average rate of return going back seventy years. Your total after thirty years will be $1,661,000 dollars. The cashflow generated by $1,661,000 times 4% equals $66,440 per year for your retirement.

The difference between cautious and moderate investment strategies proven by the numbers. Remember, portfolio balance and diversification must increase as we age.

Our behaviors define us. If you are under fifty and relatively healthy you want the stock and bond markets to go DOWN. Now this statement is counterintuitive to most thinking. Why? The younger you are, the more time you have to accumulate wealth. If the markets are down you can buy more with less money. You have the time constant within the rule of 72 on your side.

Dollar cost average your way into the market weekly especially when markets are trending lower. When markets are down I share with my nieces and nephews to buy the market especially large cap high dividend paying stocks. I also have family that have been waiting on the sidelines, for a major market downturn. It never happened. She waited for over five years and missed a 82% return in the S&P index. Her $100,000 dollars would have been worth $180,200 dollars. Instead her $100,000 dollars is worth $120,000 dollars. While you are young, invest every month whether the market is up or down…dollar cost average your way to wealth accumulation.

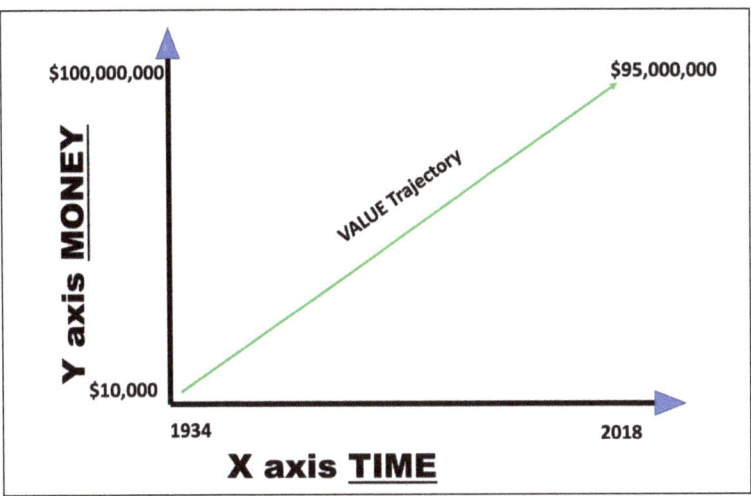

There are many charts from many investment platforms that show a graphical depiction of investment growth. On the "X" axis, (the line on a chart that runs horizontally from left to right) is where time is measured. On the "Y" axis, (the line on a chart that runs vertically from bottom to top of the page) is where the amount of an investment is measured. It is a graphical representation of how investing for the long term can maximize your wealth. One such chart representing the *American Fund* of the Capital Group investment platform, has returned over 11% compounded annually from 1934-2018. If you invested in this fund a one time amount of $10,000 in 1934 and left it to accumulate without any withdrawal, it would be worth over $95,000,000 today with dividends re-invested. The magic of the Rule of 72 and keeping your money invested is paramount. The Standard and Poor's 500 index has returned just at 10% compounded annually.

You can see the power of the Rule of 72.

Another example demonstrates the value of $100 dollars invested in 1928 into different opportunity vehicle's, and how they can vary substantially, in today's values. The low is 3-month treasury US government bills investment in 1928 was worth $100 and now today its worth $2,249 dollars. An investment in $100 of Gold in 1928 is worth $10,042 dollars today. The best return from 1928 to today is the S&P 500 US stock index plus dividends reinvested is now worth $787,018. Well what about Real Estate appreciation? The value of $100 dollars of real estate in 1928 is now worth $5,380. Clearly the best long term investment vehicle is the S&P 500 index with dividends reinvested. Source is A. Damodaran, New York University.

You can customize the amount and returns for your specific investments by going on-line to Saving.org. and follow the instructions. You will see government measured inflation calculators and inflation by year details to better understand your future cash flow. When you retire you must adjust from a wealth accumulation stage to a free cash flow management approach. You do not want to run out of cash. Plan to consider a measured transition of your portfolio at least ten years prior to retirement.

Risk management and diversification is enhanced through knowledge acquired and applied. As you get closer to retirement you must consider the volatility of the investments in your portfolio. Let's share an example. If you have a disproportionate percentage of stocks that have high price to earnings ratio (dividing the price of the company's stock by the earnings amount the company generates) or favor revenue growth over profitability, the trading price range will be more extreme. What do I mean by this? The higher the ratio the more expensive the company relative to its earnings. The stock price in good times will go up faster than the S&P index and in bad times will drop much lower than the S&P index results. Also, if you have a large percentage of your portfolio in individual stocks and bonds instead of an Index or ETF, you will have more volatility.

A Financial advisor and CPA can help you navigate the investment and tax options to optimize your pre-tax or after-tax strategy, whether you are the founder, owner of the company, or an employee. As an example, you may want to consider pre-tax saving through a SEP or 401K; or, after tax, you might choose a Roth IRA. A good advisor will educate you and help you evaluate your risk tolerances and your specific needs.

A millionaire is defined as a person whose financial wealth exceeds a million dollars in liquid assets and does not include a home unless it is owned free and clear. No mortgage. You must subtract any expenses/costs from your assets and the cumulative difference is what you total towards your goal of achieving a million dollars.

Defining true wealth in monetary form is the most straightforward dimension of the WHH continuum. Statistics and studies abound.

One study to ponder, especially recently, is how the value of a dollar has diminished. The need to save more as an offset against dollar deterioration has become obvious. Inflation affects all people, no matter their age, but it disproportionately impacts older people, especially those living on a fixed incomes.

According to *What Risks Do Near Retirees and Retirees Face From Inflation?* a study published in May 2024 by Jean-Pierre Aubry and Laura D. Quinby of the Center of Retirement Research, Boston College:

high inflation generally harms older households, but the magnitude of the impact depends on two offsetting factors: 1) the extent to which income and investments keep pace with rising prices; and 2) the amount of fixed-rate debt. These two factors lead to varying risk across the age and wealth distribution. Additionally, when recent inflation started to put pressure on household budgets, many responded by reducing new saving and increasing withdrawals from existing saving. Incorporating these behaviors into the scenario analysis shows that households largely offset the immediate loss of real income, but substantially reduce their wealth available to fund future consumption.

Aubry and Quinby continue:

For example, inflation harms retirees more than near retirees because– outside of Social Security – income is less indexed to prices, and retirees hold less debt. Similarly, top-wealth households see a smaller reduction in financial assets than their lower- wealth counterparts because they are more heavily invested in equities and businesses that grow with inflation; however, they ultimately end up with a bigger drop in consumption than lower-wealth households living off Social Security.

Older households react to rising prices by shifting consumption from the future into the present.

Aubry and Quinby's research goes on to prove inflation will reduce wealth, especially the wealth of those who are not diversified into equities. As measured by the US government's producer price index (PPI), inflation is up 19.4% and consumer price index (CPI) inflation is up 19.9% since January 2021. From January 2021 to June 2024, the average household has lost $24,000 of purchasing power due to inflation.

Earnings always lag Inflation. Economic uncertainty causes capital spending to pause, and this results in layoffs and less hiring. Inflation is a negative growth catalyst in the short term and the long term.

A report published in 2024 by LendingTree found that home insurance rates have risen 37% since 2020 due to many factors, including homes being built too close to bodies of water, repair cost inflation, an increase in extreme weather events, and rising home prices. The three states with the highest increases are Arizona, Nebraska, and Oklahoma. The US government does not measure homeowner's insurance costs, opting to measure only renter's insurance. They also do not measure energy costs or food prices when calculating personal consumption expenditures inflation index. Their logic behind these omissions? Food and energy costs are too volatile to measure! My point here is that by failing to measure key expenses, the government underreports the rate of inflation, which is generally much higher for the consumer than official talking heads would lead us to believe. In 2021, Warren Buffet said that the real US inflation rate for consumers was closer to 10%, even though the Fed was touting 5-6%. Many economists believe that the inflation we have seen since 2020 is due to government over-stimulation of the economy.

As we look to maximize our wealth, my logic is to over-save and over-invest, knowing that the actual inflation—and, sometimes, even worse, stagflation—will diminish our purchasing power for the future. Save early, and let the Rule of 72 work for you.

To get an idea of how destructive inflation can be, let's look at the past. In *What Could a Dollar Buy You in the 1940s?* (2024), Cameron Diiorio wrote, "Paying for what you need can be tough in today's economy. Inflation has blown up the prices of everyday goods, and 'shrinkflation' has you paying the same amount for less product. Additionally, homeownership, once part of the American dream, now seems an impossible feat for many."

According to the inflation calculator published by the United States Government, $1 in 1940 is equivalent to $22.31 in 2024. "This means that today's prices are 22.31 times as high as average prices since 1940, according to the Bureau of Labor Statistics consumer price index," the BLS explains. In fact, the value of the American dollar has decreased in the 84 years between 1940 and 2024. One US dollar in 1940 would provide a consumer with the ability to buy more products for their money. Today, that single dollar will not take you very far at all. Even "dollar stores," such as Dollar General or Dollar Tree, lack products that actually cost one dollar. Most of the time, a dollar will not even grant you an hour of street parking in a metropolitan area.

Of course, we cannot look at the value of the dollar in isolation. Prices for goods were generally much lower in the 1940s than they are now. The cost of living was much cheaper in the 1940s, including groceries. Salaries and hourly pay were, of course, also much lower. The National Archives reports that the average 1940 income in the US was $1,368 and the median income for a man $956, with women earning just 62 cents for every dollar a man was paid.

Today, Americans are spending hundreds of dollars to stock their pantries each week. In the last four years, 2020-2024, inflation has increased at a rate and level not seen since the President Jimmy Carter era. The average family spends more than $1,000 on groceries per month today, according to the most recent U.S. Census Bureau Household Pulse Survey.

Here are average grocery prices in 1940 and 2024, compared:
- According to *The People History*, a two-pack of Kellogg's Frosted Flakes cost approximately $0.35 in 1940. Today, a single 12-ounce box of Kellogg's Corn Flakes costs $5 or more.
- In the 1940s, large white eggs were $0.69 a dozen. Eggs have increased to over $6 a dozen in the current day.

- A tube of toothpaste cost around $0.47 cents in 1940; today, it costs over $4.

Home prices have also been greatly inflated with time. In 1940, the median price of a house was under $3,000. The median home price in August 2024 was $412,500, according to the National Association of Realtors, up from $384,000 in February of the same year, per Motley Fool.

The U.S. Census states that the average cost of rent in 1940 was $287. Now, the average monthly cost of rent for a two-bedroom apartment across the U.S. is $1,843, as of April 2024, according to a report from the digital rental marketplace Zumper.

Where we live, how much we spend and save all collectively effect our ability to maximize our wealth. As we go through different stages of life we can look at statistics to see if we are on track to meet our goals. In 2024 the average annual salary in the USA was $59,428. In 1940 it was $1,725 per year. Are we spending more than the average? Are we saving enough?

A GoBankingRates study, for example, found that you'd need over $1.1 million to fund a 25-year retirement in Miami, Florida, compared to nearly $570,000 in McAllen, Texas, or $2.8 million in San Jose, California – based on the annual cost of groceries, housing, utilities, transportation, and healthcare costs.

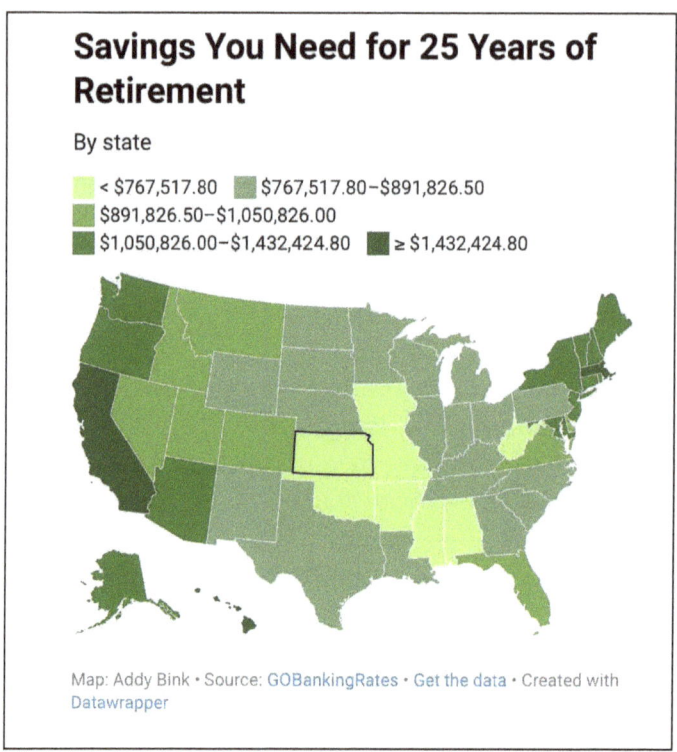

Savings You Need for 25 Years of Retirement

By state

- < $767,517.80
- $767,517.80–$891,826.50
- $891,826.50–$1,050,826.00
- $1,050,826.00–$1,432,424.80
- ≥ $1,432,424.80

Map: Addy Bink • Source: GOBankingRates • Get the data • Created with Datawrapper

When it comes time to retire, you want to make sure you're financially ready. Depending on where you live (and at what age you retire), how much in retirement savings you'd need to feel comfortable could be a just a few hundred thousand dollars—or a couple million.

In a recently released study, GoBankingRates reviewed data from the Bureau of Labor Statistics 2022 Consumer Expenditure Survey, the Social Security Administration, and the Missouri Economic Research and Information Center to determine how much you'd need to comfortably retire. To calculate that total, they analyzed the annual cost of groceries, housing, utilities, transportation, and healthcare for each state. GOBankingRates determined that, in 16 states, you would need at least $1 million to fund 25 years of retirement. In one state, Hawaii, the minimum retirement savings was even higher, at more than $2 million. Massachusetts had the second-highest minimum requirement at $1.6 million. Other states requiring at least $1 million were California, New York, Alaska, Washington, New Hampshire, Vermont, Maryland, Oregon, Connecticut, Rhode Island, Maine, New Jersey, Arizona, and Colorado.

On the other end of the scale was West Virginia, where you'd need just over $692,000 to support a 25-year retirement. It was the only state with an amount below $700,000. Mississippi came in at $701,000, Oklahoma at $702,000 and Kansas at $709,000.

That total would, of course, increase if you retired earlier. To fund a 30-year retirement, you'd need at least $1 million in 25 states. In addition to the states mentioned in the 25 year retirement discussion, Utah, Montana, Virginia, Nevada, Florida, Delaware, Idaho, North Carolina, and Wisconsin require $1 million for a 30-year retirement. Pennsylvania was close behind at roughly $998,000.

As you may have guessed, the city in which you live can also greatly impact how much you need to retire. GOBankingRates also reviewed what it costs to do so in the nation's 100 largest metro areas. Unsurprisingly, many of the costliest cities are in California. Retirees in San Jose are the worst off: GOBankingRates determined that, based on expenses, you would need almost $2.8 million to retire in the Bay Area city. In nearby San Francisco, you'd need $2.5 million. These are the only metro areas in which a retiree would require more than $2 million, but Honolulu isn't far behind at $1.9 million. Overall, you'd need more than $1 million to retire in 31 of the nation's largest cities.

The cheapest metro area in the report was McAllen, Texas. In the border city, a retiree needs slightly more than $569,000 to live comfortably.

Many of the states with the highest amount of savings are also the states that have the highest tax rates. Low tax States have a more affordable cost of living overall.

**BEST Success Practice #6 to maximize the WHH continuum:
Re-evaluate where you reside and determine if you can
move to a lower cost and lower tax area to keep and
invest more of your money.**

In May 2024, Ashleigh Jackson of Edward Jones compiled a report on how much the average American has in their retirement savings by age. She found that about 1 in 4 US adults 50 and older do not have retirement savings and plan to work well past the traditional retirement age of 65.

One way to benchmark your savings is to see how you compare with others in your age range, though, as Edward Jones's Jackson points out, it won't "tell you how close you are to your goal." The study is summarized here:

Retirement savings benchmarks notes on methodology and assumptions:

Below you'll find generalized age - and salary-benchmarks for investment levels that might let you retire comfortably, using broad assumptions about factors including taxes and spending preferences. For example, if you are 29, making $100,000, you would want a savings of $15,000 - $90,000 to maintain your current lifestyle. A 65 year old who has been earning $200,000 since their 20's should have saved between $2.7 million and $3.3 million. (The higher and lower ends of the range reflect differing assumptions about market volatility during your career.)

AGE	$50,000 salary	$100,000 salary	$150,000 salary	$200,000 salary
20	$0 - $0	$0 - $0	$0 - $40,000	$0 - $140,000
21	$0 - $0	$0 - $0	$0 - $65,000	$10,000 - $175,000
22	$0 - $0	$0 - $0	$0 - $90,000	$45,000 - $210,000
23	$0 - $0	$0 - $0	$0 - $115,000	$75,000 - $250,000
24	$0 - $5,000	$0 - $5,000	$20,000 - $140,000	$110,000 - $285,000
25	$0 - $10,000	$0 - $20,000	$45,000 - $170,000	$145,000 - $325,000
26	$0 - $20000	$0 - $35,000	$70,000 - $195,000	$180,000 - $365,000
27	$0 - $25,000	$0 - $55,000	$95,000 - $225,000	$215,000 - $405,000
28	$0 - $35,000	$0 - $70,000	$120,000 - $255,000	$250,000 - $450,000
29	$5,000 - $45,000	$15,000 - $90,000	$150,000 - $285,000	$290,000 - $495,000

Age	$50,000 salary	$100,000 salary	$150,000 salary	$200,000 salary
30	$15,000 - $55,000	$30,000 - $105,000	$175,000 - $320,000	$330,000 - $540,000
31	$25,000 - $60,000	$45,000 - $125,000	$205,000 - $35,0000	$370,000 - $585,000
32	$30,000 - $70,000	$60,000 - $145,000	$230,000 - $385,000	$410,000 - $635,000
33	$40,000 - $80,000	$80,000 - $165,000	$260,000 - $420,000	$455,000 - $685,000
34	$50,000 - $90,000	$95,000 - $185,000	$295,000 - $455,000	$495,000 - $735,000
35	$60,000 - $100,000	$115,000 - $205,000	$325,000 - $490,000	$545,000 - $785,000
36	$65,000 - $115,000	$135,000 - $225,000	$355,000 - $525,000	$590,000 - $840,000
37	$75,000 - $125,000	$155,000 - $245,000	$390,000 - $565,000	$640,000 - $895,000
38	$85,000 - $135,000	$175,000 - $270,000	$420,00 - $605,000	$685,000 - $950,000
39	$95,000 - $145,000	$195,000 - $29,5000	$460,000 - $645,000	$740,000 - $1,010,000

Age	$50,000 salary	$100,000 salary	$150,000 salary	$200,000 salary
40	$105,000 - $160,000	$215,000 - $315,000	$500,000 - $690,000	$790,000 - $1,070,000
41	$120,000 - $170,000	$235,000 - $340,000	$535,000 - $730,000	$845,000 - $1,135,000
42	$130,000 - $185,000	$260,000 - $365,000	$575,000 - $775,000	$900,000 - $1,195,000
43	$140,000 - $195,000	$280,000 - $395,000	$615,000 - $820,000	$955,000 - $1,260,000
44	$155,000 - $210,000	$305,000 - $420,000	$655,000 - $870,000	$1,01,5000 - $1,330,000
45	$165,000 - $225,000	$330,000 - $450,000	$695,000 - $915,000	$1,075,000 - $1,400,000
46	$175,000 - $240,000	$355,000 - $475,000	$740,000 - $965,000	$1,140,000 - $1,470,000
47	$190,000 - $255,000	$380,000 - $505,000	$785,000 - $1,020,000	$1,200,000 - $1,545,000
48	$205,000 - $270,000	$405,000 - $535,000	$830,000 - $1,070,000	$1,270,000 - $1,620,000
49	$215,000 - $285,000	$435,000 - $565,000	$880,000 - $1,125,000	$1,335,000 - $1,700,000

Age	$50,000 salary	$100,000 salary	$150,000 salary	$200,000 salary
50	$230,000 - $300,000	$465,000 - $600,000	$930,000 - $1,180,000	$1,405,00 - $1,780,000
51	$245,000 - $315,000	$490,000 - $630,000	$980,000 - $1,240,000	$1,475,000 - $1,860,000
52	$260,000 - $335,000	$520,000 - $665,000	$1,030,000 - $1,300,000	$1,550,000 - $1,945,000
53	$275,000 - $350,000	$550,000 - $700,000	$1,085,000 - $1,360,000	$1,625,000 - $2,035,000
54	$290,000 - $370,000	$585,000 - $735,000	$1,135,000 - $1,420,000	$1,705,000 - $2,125,000
55	$310,000 - $385,000	$615,000 - $775,000	$1,195,000 - $1,485,000	$1,785,000 - $2,215,000
56	$325,000 - $405,000	$650,000 - $810,000	$1,250,000 - $1,555,000	$1,870,000 - $2,315,000
57	$340,000 - $425,000	$685,000 - $850,000	$1,310,000 - $1,620,000	$1,955,000 - $2,410,000
58	$360,000 - $445,000	$720,000 - $890,000	$1,370,000 - $1,690,000	$2,040,000 - $2,510,000
59	$380,000 - $465,000	$755,000 - $930,000	$1,435,000 - $1,765,000	$2,135,000 - $2,615,000

Age	$50,000 salary	$100,000 salary	$150,000 salary	$200,000 salary
60	$395,000 - $485,000	$795,000 - $975,000	$1,500,000 - $1,840,000	$2,225,000 - $2,725,000
61	$415,000 - $510,000	$830,000 - $1,020,000	$1,565,000 - $1,915,000	$2,320,000 - $2,835,000
62	$435,000 - $530,000	$870,000 - $1,065,000	$1,635,000 - $1,995,000	$2,420,000 - $2,945,000
63	$455,000 - $555,000	$910,000 - $1,110,000	$1,705,000 - $2,075,000	$2,520,000 - $3,065,000
64	$475,000 - $580,000	$955,000 - $1,155,000	$1,780,000 - $2,160,000	$2,625,000 - $3,185,000
65	$500,000 - $605,000	$995,000 - $1,205,000	$1,855,000 - $2,245,000	$2,735,000 - $3,305,000

- In retirement, we assume you will maintain your current level of spending (adjusted for inflation). We calculate your current spending as current gross income minus savings and taxes.
- All savings are for retirement. Savings are pretax, equivalent to 15% of gross income, and adjusted assuming an inflation rate of 3% per year.
- Assume an effective tax rate of 25%, which is applied to gross income after deducting pretax savings.

- Assume your retirement portfolio earns an annual return of 6% pre-retirement and 5% post-retirement.
- Annual spending in retirement is adjusted assuming an inflation rate of 3% per year.
- Assume retirement at age 65 and life expectancy of 90. Benchmarks are only provided through the assumed retirement age.
- Assume in retirement, you have two sources of income to cover your spending needs: Social Security and withdrawals from your retirement portfolio.
- Assume the amount you receive from Social Security is the minimum between 35% of your gross income and $46,800 (which in 2024 is the maximum Social Security benefit if you retire at 67 having earned the maximum amount since age 22)
- Withdrawals from the portfolio are taxed at the effective tax rate of 25%.

EDWARD JONES

"Having a ballpark projection of how much money you need to retire comfortably can be helpful," Jackson writes. "However, relying on broad-based assumptions, they can't address individual circumstances such as your income, spending needs and risk tolerance.

That's where a qualified financial advisor comes in. After you evaluate your status with these tools, schedule a face-to-face meeting with a qualified WAS, RIA financial advisor to set a more precise goal." Jackson notes that the "relevant data point isn't what others your age have saved but how much money you need yourself. The answer depends almost entirely on you, your habits now and your plans for later."

Data from the Federal Reserve's most recent Survey of Consumer Finances (2022) indicates the median retirement savings account balance for all U.S. families stands at $87,000.

Below are the median amounts for individuals, categorized by age:

Age Range	Median Retirement Savings
Under 35	$18,880
35-44	$45,000
45-54	$115,000
55-64	$185,000
65-74	$200,000
75 or older	$130,000

Source: Federal Reserve

The average retirement savings account balance for all families is higher, at $333,940, since the wealthiest households tend to drive the average up. This also applies to individual account balances, as illustrated in the following table.

Age Range	Average Retirement Savings
Under 35	$49,130
35-44	$141,520
45-54	$313,220
55-64	$537,560
65-74	$609,230
75 or older	$462,410

Source: Federal Reserve

FEDERAL RESERVE				
YEAR	CATEGORY AGE	BEFORE TAX INCOME (THOUSANDS)	NET WORTH (THOUSANDS)	ASSETS (THOUSANDS)
2022	Less than 35	60,530	39,040	71,400
2022	35-44	86,472	135,300	310,399
2022	45-54	91,877	246,700	427,200
2022	55-64	82,149	364,269	473,500
2022	65-74	60,531	410,000	475,000
2022	75 OR OLDER	49,073	334,700	382,000

Continuing with the Federal Reserve statistics, they and basic accounting defines net worth as all assets minus all liabilities. This includes financial assets, such as investments, cash, and non-financial assets defined as non-investment real estate. Liabilities include both secured debt, such as home mortgages and vehicle loans, and unsecured debt, like student loans and credit cards.

A forty year old in the USA, the Federal Reserve said their household net worth is:

- Median: $135,300 (better reflects the situation of all households)
- Average: $548,070 (better reflects the total wealth in circulation)

If you're looking for another way to track your progress, Fidelity developed a guideline that factors in your age and salary. Fidelity says that by age 30, you should aim to have the equivalent of one year's salary saved. So, if your annual salary is $60,000, your 401(k) balance should ideally be $60,000.

Here's the full guideline from Fidelity:

- **By age 30:** Save 1x your income
- **By age 35:** Save 2x your income
- **By age 40:** Save 3x your income
- **By age 45:** Save 4x your income
- **By age 50:** Save 6x your income
- **By age 55:** Save 7x your income
- **By age 60:** Save 8x your income
- **By age 67:** Save 10x your income

However, it's important to remember that while this can be a useful tool, it's not a mandate. "These milestones are aspirational. You likely won't meet all of them," Fidelity explained on its website. "But they can serve as goalposts to help you make a plan to save enough to maintain your lifestyle in retirement."

Those who own their own business and are self-employed can "super" save. Contribution limits are significantly higher than traditional IRA's/401K. A simplified employee pension plan (SEP-IRA) allows employeers to contribute on behalf of their employees and themselves. The business can be any size including a one person (you) enterprise. A contribution of up to 25% of each employee's pay can be made with a cap. The cap for 2025 is 25% of an employee's total compensation, up to $70,000. For details, research irs.gov.

Another way to save more is to pay less in taxes. ...

So, what are the lowest income tax states per Fidelity?

At the top of the list are the 9 states with no state earned income tax: Alaska, Florida, Nevada, New Hampshire, South Dakota, Tennessee, Texas, Washington, and Wyoming. That's not to say these are no-tax states. Many make up revenues with higher property taxes, sales tax, and other taxes and fees. But if you are a high-income earner, the tax savings can add up. Imagine your earned income is $250,000. A move from Vermont, which has progressive tax rates with a base tax of $14,870 for taxable amounts up to $229,550 and tax rate of 8.75% on the remaining taxable amount, to New Hampshire, with a tax rate of 0% (for income not attributed to dividends or interest), could save you more than $15,400 in state income taxes. The same amount invested annually with a 7% return over 10 years would add up to more than $213,000.

Additionally, a single person earning $100,000 annually who moved from Oregon, which ranks in the top most expensive states for income for married and single filers, to no-income-tax states such as Florida or Texas could save approximately $7,200 annually by changing states. On the other hand, someone living in Nevada earning the same amount of money might owe approximately $4,000 more per year simply by moving to nearby Utah, where tax rates for individuals and married couples rank among the 30 most expensive.

10 highest and lowest marginal state tax rates

Among the 41 states with a state income tax, the top marginal state rate, which is the percentage at which your last dollar of income is taxed, ranges from a high of 9.3% in California to a low of 1.95% in North Dakota for a single filer with $100,000 of earned income. But no one pays that on all their income. So, if you want to know what taxes you might pay, it's better to consider your effective combined state and federal tax rate, which is the amount of your pay that goes to income taxes once you've factored in deductions and credits. Montana, Minnesota, Hawaii and Oregon have the highest overall total tax burden.

Fidelity researched the range of those effective income tax rates for both singles and married couples with $100,000 in income. You may be surprised about some of the best and worst states, depending on your marital status. As one example the combined FICA, effective state and federal income tax rates for a single filer earning $100,000 of income vary from a high of 29.16% in Oregon to a low of 22.72% in North Dakota. For a married couple filing jointly with the same income, the combined effective state and federal income tax rates range from a high of 21.64% in Oregon to a low of 15.89% in North Dakota.

Assuming $100,000 in annual earned income, the lowest-tax states offer a combined effective tax rate of 21.91% for single filers and 15.89% for married people filing jointly. That compares to a top rate of 29.16% for single people and 21.64% for joint filers in high tax states.

Here are some surprising details based on the same income parameters.

- ◆ While the Northeast has a reputation for having the highest-tax states in the nation, it turns out that Oregon has the highest effective tax rates for both single and married joint filers in the US. Hawaii comes in a close second with a top rate of 28.27% for single filers, and 20.44% for married filers.
- ◆ Minnesota, Maine, and Montana are also in the top 10 highest-tax states for income tax rates for both kinds of filers.
- ◆ While California ranked among the most expensive states for single filers, with an effective tax rate of 26.58%, it also ranked among the 20 best states for married people filing jointly, with an effective tax rate of 17.58%.
- ◆ New Jersey and Rhode Island are among the states with the lowest effective tax rates for married filers.
- ◆ West Virginia is nearly in the middle for all states for married couples filing jointly and single filers alike.

If you're looking to save money on taxes, you might consider Florida and Texas, despite their rising costs of living. But there's always North Dakota and Ohio, which also have favorable tax rates.

Another consideration if you own a home or plan to own a home, is the states property tax rate. Property values from 2020-2024, in the USA, have increased 26% faster than the high inflation experienced in the same time-frame. The average USA home sales price has increased from $370,000 to $525,100. Most property taxes are based on the assessed value of the home.

Which states charge the most in property taxes? New Jersey, Illinois, Connecticut, New Hampshire and Vermont. The states charging the least are: Hawaii, Alabama, Nevada, Colorado, and South Carolina. Research details for your own state through the *US Census Bureau, 2023 American Community Survey or the Tax Foundation.*

To continue to establish benchmarks and a basis for SMART goal setting, let's where you compare:

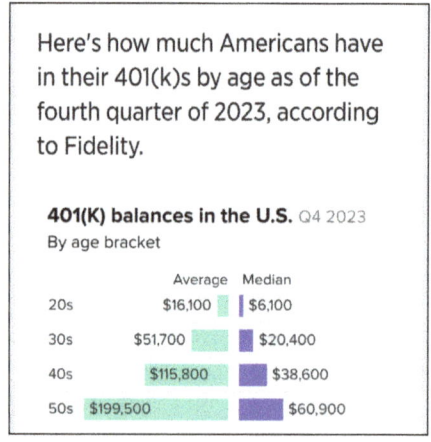

Here's how much Americans have in their 401(k)s by age as of the fourth quarter of 2023, according to Fidelity.

401(K) balances in the U.S. Q4 2023
By age bracket

	Average	Median
20s	$16,100	$6,100
30s	$51,700	$20,400
40s	$115,800	$38,600
50s	$199,500	$60,900

Your 401K or 403B should never be drawn down while you are working. There are severe dire circumstances that may exist of course. But as you can see in the chart below, the major "reasons for loans and withdrawals" are not severe and dire emergencies. Your secure retirement is best served by monthly savings year after year, decade after decade with no withdrawals until 59.5 at the earliest.

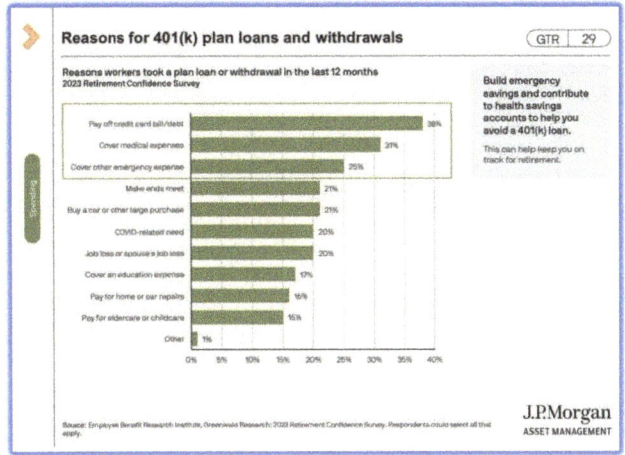

Assets – liabilities, costs, and expenses = net worth.

Monetary wealth is relative. A person can own a big company and give the appearance of wealth but is losing money. Their net worth could be zero or even negative. They must sell the company or transition the assets to achieve any gain and cash flow. Add in the timing issues along with resultant tax consequences, and you have the potential for no potential.

According to Schwab's 2024 *Modern Wealth Survey* (its eighth annual), 1000 Americans said it takes an average net worth of $2.5 million to qualify a person as being wealthy. But among the 48% of Americans who say they already feel wealthy today, the average net worth is $560,000—about a quarter of that loftier target. According to Schwab's survey, only about one-third (35%) of Americans have plotted their goals and documented a financial plan. Among those who do, seven in 10 say it makes them feel more in control of their finances and nine in 10 say they feel confident that they will reach their financial goals.

Then there are total assets vs liquid assets.

I lived in Wyoming for seven years. Ranchers in Wyoming require over an acre of grazing land per "cattle unit," which is defined as one 1000-pound cow and one calf. A 1600 pound cow with calf is 1.6 animal units. Raising sheep is a completely different dynamic and metric. How they gaze the land is now a mathematical effort. A rancher cannot use 100% of their grazing land. A utilization rate is calculated without irrigation and typically equals 50% usage for all grazing animals.

Rotation of the land is required to prevent over-foraging. The point is, ranchers must own, maintain, and protect thousands of acres of land to be successful. Many must invest in helicopters to traverse the property in search of predators and to respond to any cattle issues.

On paper, their land is worth millions. If they sell the land, they risk the business model. Cash flow, expense, and liquid asset management are their biggest challenges as they look to grow their monetary wealth and achieve optimum WHH.

A bigger problem for a generation of people lies twelve thousand miles away, in the Philippines, which exhibits yet a different type of wealth.

In Negros Occidental, site of the sugar plantations of the Philippines, sugar barons lived like royalty before the 1980s, selling sugarcane to the USA and worldwide. The sugar barons wore sharkskin white suits, drove high-end luxury cars, and lived in mansions. Families named Marino, Gaston, and Lacson still own heritage houses, preserving their rich sugar baron history. Don Marino built a mansion so spectacular, it was dubbed the "Taj Mahal" of Negros Island.

The eldest son of French born entrepreneur Yves Gaston, the first sugar cane producer in Negros, was Victor Gaston. He carried on the tradition. But the invention of artificial sugars and sweeteners in the 1980s changed everything. Exports to the USA and Canada all but dried up, and plantations became acres of non-producing fields. I met Victor's great grand-niece Melissa, who struggles to preserve and maintain the Gaston Heritage house. She told me they must sell their property hectare by hectare (a hectare = 2.47 acres) to pay their bills and fund their retirements, since much less sugarcane is produced on their land than formerly. It is a very different kind of wealth for her generation. Selling land is a long, difficult, illiquid task fraught with significant risks. On paper, their land is worth millions—until they *must* sell it.

I have shared some different perspectives on wealth accumulation and acquisition with you. I want you to be able to evaluate your status within the context of what others are doing or what you should have accumulated to meet retirement goals.

It is not all about measuring your status versus averages or what amount of wealth you should accumulate to have a financially secure retirement. Remember the cashflow strategy as you transition from work to retirement. Some examples below show how wealth accumulation was achieved. But at what cost?

The curious case of Uncle Stan's brother and the suit jacket speaks to another way to acquire true monetary wealth. It was one very cold snowy morning in New England. I was with my dad driving into town down Main Street in his orange VW Super Beetle. The sidewalks had not been shoveled, and there was a man, underdressed for the cold winter, wearing an old worn sports coat with the sleeves so short they fell just below the elbow--clearly two sizes too small for the man walking on the side of the road in the bitter cold and snow.

I said to my dad, "Is that a homeless man?"

"No," he said. "That's Uncle Stan's brother. His niece described her uncle as a walking scarecrow."

Uncle Stan's brother was an engineer for a local aircraft components manufacturer, Pratt and Whitney. He rarely owned a car and lived a very low key, humble existence. He kept to himself and married at age 72, only to divorce 6 months later, explaining only, "She was very weird."

Limos would stop in front of his meager home and drive him into New York City, where he attended major corporate shareholder meetings. As it turned out, Uncle Stan's brother was a multimillionaire and master investor.

Uncle Stan's brother had achieved monetary wealth through a very frugal, stingy life. His reclusive ways alienated family and the few friends he had. Was the WHH continuum maximized? No.

Another example is the story of a janitor in Vermont.

Warren Buffet has been credited with saying, "You don't have to have extraordinary effort to achieve extraordinary results. You just need to do the ordinary, everyday things exceptionally well." Well, this fits Ronald Read, gas station attendant and janitor, perfectly. How did he amass $8 million dollars on a way below average salary? He worked two jobs most of his life. He was frugal, buying secondhand clothes and appliances. He applied a simple formula, forgotten in today's buy-on-credit mentality. He spent less than he made, and what he saved he invested in the stock market month after month, year after year, into his nineties. He bought and held many value-based stocks, which paid consistent dividends. Was the WHH continuum maximized? Maybe. But those who knew him said he did not appear to enjoy life.

The librarian in New Hampshire who amassed $4 million is another example. He worked as a librarian for 50 years, lived a very simple life, and had disciplined saving and investing habits. He worked with money managers most of his life.

There are thousands of similar examples of achieving true monetary wealth—without maximizing WHH.

"It is impossible to live without failing at something unless you live so cautiously.... that you might as well not have lived at all,... in which case you have failed by default."
—J.K. Rowling

Most of us don't wake up in the morning and say "I am going to really screw up wealth accumulation and/or my health and/or happiness." Most of us never focus on these subjects at all, opting instead for minute tasks and activities to get us through the day.

We need to consciously shift into a different macro-think plan, with the goal of spending time on maximizing wealth accumulation, health, and happiness. The responsibility for all of us is to educate ourselves and inspire others. One great example of this approach is a seventeen-year- old who is reaching out to the youngest pre-earners and earners.

Her name is Rachael Kim, and she runs @financewrachael in Buena Vista Park, California. Her approach to creating awareness and wealth was featured on the *Nerd Wallet* website in a March 14, 2024, article by Alana Benson: "[Kim's] advice on her blog is to start early and educate yourself. Kim has also founded "Build UP," an organization that sends out free weekly newsletters to help increase financial literacy and to teach people all things personal finance."

Rachael Kim is a great "finfluencer" for our youngest family and friends. Who better to relate to than someone their own age?

Wealth can be accumulated but it can also be transitioned and inherited.

When I was on the Gold coast of Australia, walking on the beach after Sunday Mass at St. Vincent's, I heard and saw a helicopter hovering above. A voice from the helicopter boomed: "Move inland one mile!" The sky was blue, the sun was warm, and there were no clouds in sight. The voice continued to explain that a tsunami was approaching . Everyone moved off the beach quickly but only to the highest point in full view of the ocean. And so I saw my first and only tsunami. It was about two feet high and 30 or so feet wide. It rolled up the beach area and inland to the dunes. That was it. I was a little disappointed.

Well, there is a different tsunami coming. It is an inheritance tsunami from the baby boomers to their families and friends--who will not be disappointed with this tsunami. It is another kind of wealth accumulation: transition wealth.

According to *Forbes*, anywhere between $77 trillion and $90 trillion dollars will be inherited by the younger generations. This includes savings and business transitions from founders. The greatest wealth transition in the history of the USA is already in process. Some of this transition wealth will go to charities, trusts, and other causes, but, Jack Kelly of *Forbes* writes in "The Great Wealth Transfer From Baby Boomers To Millennials Will Impact The Job Market And Economy": "Baby Boomers were in the right place at the right time. Following World War II, this generation experienced immense economic growth and prosperity. The state of affairs afforded them the golden opportunity to accumulate much wealth in their lifetime. Boomers—born between 1946 and 1964—are currently the wealthiest generation on the planet."

Their mean total net worth falls between $970,000 to $1.2 million, according to *Fortune*. In the late 1950s through the 1980s, many families lived relatively well without the breadwinners having gone to college. There were plenty of good trade jobs, and you didn't need to take on six-figure debt to earn a college degree. Home prices were affordable. This cohort greatly benefited from an unprecedented 40-year rally in stock and housing prices.

The Silent Generation, or what many call, "the Greatest Generation"—the parents of the Boomers—and the Boomers themselves will pass down trillions in assets through 2045, with $72.6 trillion going directly to heirs, according to an analysis by financial market intelligence firm Cerulli and Associates. The transfer of wealth will create a wave of changes for Millennials in their ability to purchase homes, pay off student debt, travel, buy high-end products, and invest in the stock market. There is a very high potential for many to "blow" their new-found wealth. Do they have the knowledge and discipline to manage their inheritance?

I will detail in the upcoming chapters how to best transition this tsunami of monetary wealth while minimizing taxes, stress, and family issues. Maximize the WHH continuum is my goal for you.

Wealth Transition

Here's an example of a Wealth transition dichotomy: One of my students, who was getting his executive MBA at night, took one of my elective classes. He was the Carnegie Mellon Tepper School of Business Executive MBA class president. His day job was working for a Midwest venture capital private equity company. He was in his late twenties, newly married, and eager to plan his family's future.

The major emphasis of my class curriculum, "Business Development and Sales Management Leadership," involved either starting up a new (fictious or real) company and growing the top- end revenue profitably. Some students focused on their existing company, where they currently worked, and how to profitably grow sales and revenue. The class president, however, chose to do a startup. His value proposition involved identifying a gap where no one from Private Equity or Venture Capital would consider due diligence. Apply the filter and target small businesses with no succession plan. For most PE and VCs, the cost of targeting small companies is prohibitive, hence the market gap. He and another student created what they called the Stanford-Carnegie Mellon University Algorithm to identify best-in-class private business transition potential. The research they did produced a target market and demographic using a prior effort from the Stanford MBA program and their own "Carnegie Mellon University Method."

Many small private businesses (defined by the class president as revenue from

$1 million to 25 million) did not have heirs or family willing to carry on the business. Those founders wanted a succession plan to fund their retirements, provide for their loyal employees, and/or carry out the legacy of the business after they were gone.

These founders had nowhere to turn to and felt trapped in their own success. Many business brokers try to fill this gap through a real estate sales model and take a 10% fee. The algorithm, process developed, and subsequent interviews of hundreds of companies looking to transition identified a small business founder need. The need was legacy first and money second. They wanted the businesses they started to go on successfully through the new owners. This was in direct conflict with the priorities of most business brokers, who want nothing more than to sell the business quickly. The class president wanted to target the unserved business owners looking for a succession that would perpetuate their business successfully. He followed my class lectures and data examples over the next ten weeks or so and went to work on the new business model, applying what he learned and had already experienced.

Six months later, after raising working capital from eighteen individuals, including an owner of the Boston Celtics, to fund his and his partners' time effort, they applied the Stanford/CMU algorithm in search of company founders. The business plan was to provide the founder with a process to transition the business and eventually sell it by maximizing the founder's legacy needs. Part of the process was to install a co-CEO to be side by side with the founder and learn from the founder the customers, employees, and suppliers. The objective was also to learn the company's methods and markets and everything necessary to carry on the tradition through an equitable transition. It was partnership and a trust bonding between the Co-CEOs. It was knowledge acquisition and exchange.

The hundred or so company interactions over the next year produced a pattern.

Most founders could not let go. Their WHH equilibrium and continuum were out of balance. They thought no one was good enough to carry out the legacy they had started forty or more years ago. This spoke to why so many of these small businesses had no family members interested in taking the helm. The founder sought perfection, which pushed family members away. Happiness did not abound.

Had these founders sought professional advice from financial advisers, accountants, and other planning consultants throughout their business building career, an endgame plan would have been established early. Just as we should not wait until we are in our fifties to save money for retirement, founders seeking to transition their business should start planning early. Earlier planning is better planning.

For those who do not own a business to sell or transition upon retirement, cashflow management is paramount. You have spent thirty years or more of your life in the accumulation stage and now you have to manage investments and liquid assets and convert them into a cashflow plan. Complicating this, the government mandates that you withdraw from retirement accounts. The Required Minimum distribution (RMD) must initiate on your seventy-third year. You can withdraw earlier starting, at age 59.5, to minimize or manage the tax burden.

If wealth accumulation is your primary objective, wealth preservation is essential as you transition into your retirement years. No one gets a do-over.

What you withdraw and the sequence in which you withdraw can means success or failure. Failure is having to go back to work and earn a paycheck. No one wants to do that unless it is to keep the mind active or for the sheer joy of giving back. And some people just like to work. The point is to have control over your choices. Talk to a Wealth Advisory Service (WAS) or Registered Investment Advisor (RIA) for guidance and second opinions.

Julie, an insurance company attorney, retired after more than thirty-five years. She left her practice in good hands, including a trained replacement with a six-month orientation process under her belt. Julie and her husband bought a fifth wheel and a one-ton pickup truck and went off to see America, vowing never to return to the grind.

Less than a year later, she was called by the owner of the practice, who pleaded with her to come back. The practice had suffered loss of clients and a lot of employee turnover. Turns out that Julie had been doing the job of two lawyers, and her overburdened replacement quit.

The owner of the practice was near retirement age and had no transition plan. Julie, however, had choices! She did not have to go back to work, but her sense of loyalty motivated the action to help out.

Julie said yes to a part-time approach to revitalize the practice and help hire two replacements. This law firm owner is an example of poor business transition and succession. The owner has no action plan and much of his retirement portfolio is based on the sale of his business with the resultant cash. The timing of the sale could have major impacts on the amount he gains. Once he does sell, he now must determine where to invest the proceeds and how to draw them down. He has set himself up for both sequence and size of returns risk.

Writing in the June 2024 publication of the *American Association of Individual Investors*, Craig Israelsen counsels, "A few modest guidelines will naturally insulate a retirement portfolio from both sequence and size of returns risk during the early years of portfolio withdrawals." The owner of the law firm had no such options. He was a great lawyer but failed to achieve maximum WHH. Israelson writes:

Differences among retirement investing schools of thought tend to focus on two things:

longevity risk and sequence risk. They are both interrelated but different. How an investor should deal with these dual risks is an ongoing source of debate. Longevity risk is the risk of outliving your savings. In an economically perfect world, you will die with just one penny left in addition to what you intend to bequeath. We don't live in this world. More complicated and harder to predict is Sequence risk. Sequence of returns risk, is the risk of a bad period of returns—particularly early in retirement. The 30-year period of 1965–1994 is a good example. Large-cap stocks fell by 10.1% in 1966 (year 2 of retirement), 8.5% in 1969 (year 5), 14.7% in 1973 (year 9) and 26.5% in 1974 (year 10).

As you can see from the above example, almost 60% was lost. Just as we dollar-cost average our build-up of savings while we worked over time, we must plan our most effective sequence of withdrawals while we are in retirement mode. We must also consider the best tax minimization approach to withdrawals.

Israelsen goes on to say:

The general idea behind sequence of returns risk is that when we start pulling money out of a retirement portfolio, we are naturally more sensitive to the performance of the portfolio each year. In other words, making our withdrawal at the end of a bad year (or a bad sequence of years) will magnify the pain already inflicted on our portfolio by poor returns and the true personal, not government reported inflation.

Consider an example scenario. A person retires at the start of the year 2000 and has a 60% equity/40% bond retirement portfolio. The year 2000 was the start of the "tech wreck" and led a 60%/40% portfolio to incur a 0.68% loss. In 2001, things got worse with the portfolio losing 1.89%. The year 2002 was even worse with a loss of 10.20%.

This retiree must make annual withdrawals based on their need for income and/or their required minimum distribution (RMD). In the early 2000s, they were faced with the distasteful task of withdrawing money from a portfolio that has been beaten up by bad market returns. This is an example of a bad sequence of returns for a new retiree (or any retiree). Withdrawals from their retirement portfolio only exacerbate the negative returns experienced by their portfolio. Very simply, this is sequence of returns risk.

An understandable "reaction" to the possibility of being adversely affected by sequence of returns risk would be to build a more conservative retirement portfolio. Entirely logical, but likely the wrong choice for reasons that are only indirectly related to the sequence of returns experienced by a retirement portfolio....

Is there a lesson to be learned here? I suggest that the primary lesson is hunkering down in a very "low-risk" retirement portfolio (meaning 20% or less exposure to equities) exposes a retiree to size of returns risk while attempting to avoid sequence of returns risk. Size of returns risk often masquerades as sequence of returns risk.

A secondary lesson is that a withdrawal method that attempts to keep pace with inflation is a particularly demanding withdrawal strategy. The size of returns in a 20% stocks/80% bonds retirement portfolio (and to a lesser extent a 40%/60% portfolio) will likely not be high enough to sustain the demanding withdrawal schedule while counteracting the natural performance variability that sequence of returns risk is generally blamed for.

A new retiree could—in many cases—view themself as a long-term investor and, as such, consider the appropriateness of a portfolio with at least a 60% overall allocation to equities and equity-like asset classes (such as real estate investment trusts). Furthermore, retirees should consider using a percentage-based withdrawal method where possible. RMDs are, of course, percentage-based. Thus, percentage-based withdrawals will naturally happen with retirement accounts that are governed by RMD withdrawal rules. The RMD is easy to hate because it is forced upon us, but the percentage-based nature of the RMD is a feature that is genuinely advantageous.

These two modest guidelines—a 60% equity/40% fixed-income retirement portfolio (or an overall asset allocation in that ballpark) and a percentage-based withdrawal method—will naturally insulate a retirement portfolio from both sequence and size of returns risk during the early years of portfolio withdrawals.

Conversely, a withdrawal method that forces the withdrawal to increase each year—such as a mandated 3% or 4% annual COLA or a CPI-based COLA (which forces an increase in the next year's withdrawal a high percentage of the time)—exposes a retiree to the highest amount of sequence of returns risk—regardless of their retirement portfolio asset allocation.

Your portfolio rate of return and withdrawal rate must take into account your **personal and family** cost of living. Remember that the government's official rate of inflation does not include Homeowners insurance, energy, or food cost increases. Although tedious, you must keep track of every expenditure for a year prior to your retirement, including an accounting estimate of unexpected costs. Also, many publications observe a rule of thumb holding that when you retire, your yearly expenditures with be 80% of what you spent (plus inflation) when you were working. If your expenditures were $40,000 a year when working, some advisors say to take an 80% or 40,000 x.80=$36,000 expense estimation in retirement. In my experience, for your first five years of retirement, your expenses will **increase** 20%, not decrease: $40,000 x 1.2=$48,000 in expenses. Why? Now that you're retired, your free time will be used to travel more, eat out more, pursue hobbies, do special projects around the house, and the list goes on.

When I retired from Eaton Corporation, I was ready to take a break from all the national and global travel. My expense estimate for retirement, completed over the five years prior had very little budgeted for travel. After all, I have traveled everywhere. Travel, to me, was work. Well, I overlooked one very, very important fact—my wife, who said, "Just because you have been everywhere does not mean I have been there! Now that you have free time I want to travel and see…" She listed a dozen or so venues she wanted to visit.

During your budget estimation period before retirement, account for more inflation than the government publishes, and accrue for the inevitable and sometimes unpredictable costs. An example is your water heater fails, the roof has a leak, or your spouse wants to travel more. You get the point.

BEST Success Practice #7 to maximize the WHH continuum: Measure and record any and all of your expenses in the year prior to retirement. There are many free budget templates on-line you can customize to your specifics. Include an inflation rate 2% ABOVE the government reports. If the Government is stating 3%, use 5%. Increase your estimated budget by 20% each year for your first five years of retirement. Do not do your budget estimates in a vacuum. Include the input of advisors, family, and friends.

How do we better predict withdrawal rates and sequence of returns?

One way, although not perfect, is to ask your WAS/RIA to run Monte Carlo simulation scenarios. The results are one indicator or forecast to help manage your risk of withdrawal.

Your portfolio is uploaded into a algorithmic program called a Monte Carlo Simulation, which includes inflation rates, historical returns, and extrapolations brought forward in time. The outcome is your future potential investment value. The results help guide you on the risks of your withdrawal rates and the actual investments. The simulation takes into account market downturns.

BEST Success Practice #8 to maximize the WHH continuum:
Team with your WAS/RIA/trust attorney to run Monte Carlo simulations to mitigate your risk of suffering wealth longevity and withdrawal rate issues.

There are other wealth risk mitigation strategies. High net worth individuals (HNWI) and ultra-high net worth individuals should consider a Golden Visa (henleyglobal.com).

In its most basic form, golden visa acquisition, or residence by investment and citizenship by investment, denotes the process whereby qualified, vetted candidates are granted either full or dual residence or citizenship rights in exchange for a defined economic contribution to the host country. There are also other customized programs offered by some countries. When I was working on the Panama Canal Phase Three project in Panama, government official approached me with a program funded by the Panamanian government that would pay me $1,200 a month and provide me a rent-free office and secretary in exchange for 20 hours a week, three weeks a month, to advise and teach business to local Panamanians.

Golden visa programs give HNWIs the option of physically relocating to a favorable jurisdiction — either now or upon retirement — and becoming residents of that locale with full legal rights, including the right to live, work, study, and receive healthcare in that country.

A golden visa provides investors and their families with access to new markets and a host of business, career, educational, healthcare, tax, and lifestyle opportunities on a worldwide scale, for both present and future generations. Many golden visa programs allow the successful applicant to apply for full citizenship after a few years of residence. Providing increased optionality worldwide along with the ability to hedge against potential risk and volatility, golden visas allow HNWIs and their families to:

- Secure an alternative safe haven
- Enrich and expand their lifestyle and business opportunities
- Enjoy a high quality of life and access to excellent infrastructure
- Access world-class healthcare at leading facilities
- Attend first-rate educational institutions

If you are considering living abroad during retirement, contact local and national government authorities to see if there are any special opportunities available based on your skill sets.

Can we attain millionaire status early in life so we can maximize health and happiness throughout our lives? How important is timing and our personality as we journey forward?

Is there a deep connection between Wealth and Health?

Yes! Keep reading…

2

What Is True Health?

True Health consists of physical, spiritual, and mental health.

In *"The deep connection between your health and wealth,"* Nigel James Green reported:

> An academic study by researchers at the Urban Institute and Virginia Commonwealth University assessing the intricate connection between health and income backs up the approach. The main takeaway of the report is, in simple terms, that those who are healthier and who live longer tend to earn more. Health and income correlate across the socioeconomic spectrum. That is to say, the richest have fewer poor-health conditions than the upper-middle class, who in turn are fitter and healthier than the lower-middle class, for example, with the pattern continuing. The basics for creating a healthier lifestyle are widely accepted and known to many people. They include eating the right foods for your body, cutting out or limiting sugar, exercising regularly, not smoking or taking illegal drugs, limiting alcohol consumption, getting plenty of sleep and avoiding stressful situations.

We cannot avoid all stress. Indeed, studies show that some stress benefits our body and mind. The medical term for such beneficial stress is *eustress*, literally "good stress." Excitement without threat or fear is how positive stress is manifested. Good stress is a motivator that enhances concentration and performance. Remember your first date? Your first promotion?

Green goes on to say:

> The steps for devising, implementing and managing financial planning strategies are, arguably, not quite as simple due to the personal circumstances of each individual. That said, I believe there are some irrefutable cornerstones in this regard, too.
>
> Savings are a fundamental part of a robust personal financial plan. By building a savings safety net, you will be able to financially meet the costs of

unforeseeable emergencies without having to increase credit card debt, ask for loans from relatives or friends, or turn to other borrowing options that serve to increase unnecessary and avoidable hassle. The positive symbiotic relationship between Wealth and Health is manifested through savings and investing.

BEST Success Practice #9 to maximize the WHH continuum: Build a safety net emergency savings account to reduce negative stress and minimize the need for credit card usage.

Growing and protecting your retirement income is also a critical pillar for good mental health.

Preparing sooner rather than later for your retirement positions you to achieve your objectives more quickly and more effectively, so you can enjoy the retirement you desire and increase your health. Preparing early is more important than ever because life expectancy, for the most part, has been increasing globally, meaning that the money we put aside must last longer. Additionally, in the future, governmental agencies and company pensions may not be sufficient to support older people as they have for previous generations. There is also a burgeoning health and social care crisis.

In addition, investing some of your savings is recommended. A failure to do so can mean that inflation will erode your purchasing power in the long term, as outlined in the previous chapter. Tax efficiency should be prioritized, too, by making use of legitimate solutions, reliefs, initiatives, and approaches. And finally, insurance, including life and critical illness insurance, is another fundamental needed to help protect what is precious to you and your loved ones.

The connection between health and wealth is deep, and it is therefore important to create and roll out strategies to manage both, so that you can truly enjoy life-enhancing benefits and opportunities.

Bad stress is worrying about putting a financial plan in place. Good stress is completing and managing a robust financial plan successfully.

Here is a question for you to ponder: Let's say you have millions of dollars in liquid assets. For the most part you are happy.

But have you ever had a splitting headache or a bad toothache? The throbbing pain from these common maladies can be downright nauseating. Time seems to stand still for all the wrong reasons. The pain makes it drag on second after second, in step with your heartbeat and the ticking of the clock. At that moment, you are not happy, and your millions do not matter. All you want is relief from the pain.

Now, pain is relative.

I laugh when a physician asks, "On a scale from 1, being no pain, to 10, being intense pain, how do you score your pain right now?" It's relative. Some people can withstand pain and suffering better than others, but it is still pain. When you are in pain, your focus on being healthy trumps being wealthy.

"I will get healthy when I am not working so much and have time; meanwhile, I have a business to lead and customers, employees, shareholders and a board who depend on me." This is what a Fortune 500 Group President in his early fifties told me when I asked him about his health. His response is understandable but also dysfunctional. Health, after all, is foundational to everything else.

For the first time in my recent memory, the USA has recognized and implemented actions to address the increased overall unhealthy status of our citizens. In 2025, the "Make America Healthy Again" initiative has gathered momentum. The key premise is to help change unhealthy eating practices to lower the obesity crisis. This includes the root causes of childhood chronic diseases and shift toward prevention. Did you know a study published in the Journal of Food Composition and Analysis, investigated the sugar content in 73 USA infant formulas available in 2022? Researchers categorized these formulas into three types: standard, gentle, and lactose-free. Just 5 of the 73 infant formula's met healthy sugar standards sold in the USA. Ninety (90) percent of the carbohydrates in the formula came from the added sugars instead of the healthy lactose found in mothers breast milk.

Our newborn children are being conditioned to depend on sugar from birth!

The commission is chaired by U.S. Health and Human Services secretary Robert F. Kennedy Jr.

The Commission in 2025, identified the USA as having the highest age-standardized cancer incidence rate across 204 countries, nearly double the next-highest rate. From 1990-2021, the U.S. saw an 88% increase in cancer. The U.S. spends almost twice per capita what other wealthy nations spend on healthcare. The Commission is tasked with answering the question Why, and solutions to address the issues.

In this section of the book, I offer preventative or proactive practices to help you to achieve and maintain a maximum health state. I will also share habits, methods, and practices to slow down and even reverse adverse health outcomes. I focus on actions you can take to achieve more immediate positive results. By implementing these actions and recommendations over the long term, your longevity will likely be increased.

As you can imagine, there are thousands of practices you can choose from, and they run the gamut of what it means to be healthy. An important first step in embarking on a healthfulness journey is to define for yourself what health is. This will lead you to focus on the best practices that are truly best for you.

What is health?

There are physical, mental, environmental, consumption, medical, and spiritual health. Together, these make up the human condition. I can't possibly cover every conceivable aspect of health, so I have homed in on the key areas and practices that are likely to have the most positive impacts for you.

There is no nice way to say this, but many Americans are sedentary and overweight. While the general trend worldwide is toward greater longevity, here in the USA, the average life expectancy has declined in recent years. There is a correlation between obesity and longevity, and there is a correlation between bad stress and reduced longevity. At most risk in the business world are private company founders and public company executives. Stress reduction is not in their ethos. It should be, because bad stress is a killer. Fortunately, we can reverse this trend.

Many of us, due to our schedules or stubbornness or fear, put off seeing doctors and dentists. Maybe we had a bad experience or do not trust the medical insurance systems. Men tend to plow through aches and pains. Hypochondriacs we males—for the most part—are not! Yet uniformly points to a correlation between longevity and maintaining a regular routine of visits to doctors and dentists.

Mammograms, prostate exams, cardio stress tests are among the many essential tests we should have at regular intervals. This should begin at an early age, so that we establish benchmarks by which we can better gauge the dynamic state of our health as we grow older.

> **BEST Success Practice #10 to maximize the WHH continuum to help minimize illness: During your late thirties to early forties, schedule an "executive" physical every year, preferably with a physician who is not employed by an Insurance company or affiliate. See your Dentist twice a year, starting in your twenties. See your eye doctor every year, especially if you are past fifty.**

Many health studies are flawed or incomplete. For example, the spiritual dimension of health is typically either minimized or left out entirely. The self-assessment techniques and methods are framed. A simple question like, "Are you healthy?" can be answered yes or no, but "How healthy are you?" is relative. If your comparison data set is your family and friendship circle, your answer is already biased. The lateral habenula (the structure of the brain involved in motivation, decision-making, and the regulation of mood) tends to prompt us to make positive responses, even if these are inaccurate.

No survey is perfect. Life-long assessments—which are rare—are more representative of reality. Most health studies, however, capture only a point in time. For this reason, I focus on life-long studies. The most comprehensive life-long study I found was one that began in 1938 and continued to follow the same group of subjects for the next eighty years. As Liz Mineo reported in 2017 in The Havard Gazette, scientists tracked the health of 238 Harvard sophomores. The goal of the study was to look for links between happiness and health.

Of the original Harvard cohort recruited as part of the Grant Study, only 19 are still alive, as of 2017, all in their mid-90s. Among the original recruits were eventual President John F. Kennedy and longtime Washington Post editor Ben Bradlee. (Women weren't in the original study because the College was still all male.)

In addition, scientists eventually expanded their research to include the men's offspring, male and female, who now number 1,300 and are in their 50s and 60s, to find out how early-life experiences affect health and aging over time. Some participants went on to become successful businessmen, doctors, lawyers, and others ended up as schizophrenics or alcoholics.

During the intervening decades, the control groups have expanded. In the 1970s, 456 Boston inner-city residents were enlisted as part of the Glueck Study, and 40 of them are still alive. More than a decade ago, researchers began including wives in the Grant and Glueck studies.

Over the years, researchers have studied the participants' health trajectories and their broader lives, including their triumphs and failures in careers and marriage, and the finding have produced startling lessons, and not only for the researchers.

The surprising finding [from the long study] is that our relationships and how happy we are in our relationships has a powerful influence on our health," said Robert Waldinger, director of the study, a psychiatrist at Massachusetts General Hospital and a professor of psychiatry at Harvard Medical School "Taking care of your body is important, but tending to your relationships is a form of self-care too." That, I think, is the revelation.

Close relationships, more than money or fame, are what keep people happy throughout their lives, the study revealed. Those ties protect people from life's discontents, help to delay mental and physical decline, and are better predictors of long and happy lives than social class, IQ, or even genes. That finding proved true across the board among both the Harvard men and the inner-city participants.

The people who were most satisfied with their relationships at age 50 were the healthiest at age 80.

The researchers also found that marital satisfaction has a protective effect on people's mental health. Part of the study found that people who had happy marriages in their 80s reported that their moods didn't suffer even on the days when they had more physical pain. Those who had unhappy marriages felt both more emotional and physical pain.

Those who kept warm relationships got to live longer and happier, said Waldinger, and the loners often died earlier. "Loneliness kills," he said. "It's as powerful as smoking or alcoholism."

Our society is increasingly mobile. The transplantation of families due to job opportunities and the like has increased dramatically over the last few generations. I myself moved nine times since graduating from college. I remember how frustrated my wife was after one of those moves, upset that she would have to go meet, greet, and "find" a new set of friends. She said to a stranger at the horse stable, "Hi, I am going to be your friend. " Her logic was, "we both have and love horses so she must be a good potential friend!" Thirty-two years later Julie and Karen are still great friends.

**BEST Success Practice #11 to maximize the WHH continuum:
Develop and maintain an in-person social network throughout your life,
not just a set of online social interactions. There is no substitute
for in-person relationships. The alternative is loneliness.**

The Harvard researchers found that those with strong social support experienced less mental deterioration as they aged.

"Good relationships don't just protect our bodies; they protect our brains," Waldinger noted. "And those good relationships, they don't have to be smooth all the time. Some of our octogenarian couples could bicker with each other day in and day out, but as long as they felt that they could really count on the other when the going got tough, those arguments didn't take a toll on their memories."

Psychiatrist George Vaillant, who joined the team as a researcher in 1966, led the study from 1972 until 2004. Trained as a psychoanalyst, Vaillant emphasized the role of relationships, and came to recognize the crucial role they played in people living long and pleasant lives.

"Those who were clearly train wrecks when they were in their 20s or 25s turned out to be wonderful octogenarians," he said. "On the other hand, alcoholism and major depression could take people who started life as stars and leave them at the end of their lives as train wrecks." We all know people in our lives who peaked in High School and others who were late bloomers.

In a book called *Aging Well*, Vaillant wrote that factors predicted healthy aging for the Harvard men are:

> **BEST Success Practice #12 to maximize the WHH continuum:**
> 1. **Physical activity**
> 2. **Absence of alcohol abuse and smoking**
> 3. **Having mature mechanisms to cope with life's ups and downs, stress reduction**
> 4. **Enjoying a healthy weight**
> 5. **Having a stable marriage.**

"The study showed that the role of genetics and long-lived ancestors proved less important to longevity than the level of satisfaction with relationships in midlife, now recognized as a good predictor of healthy aging. The research also debunked the idea that people's personalities 'set like plaster' by age 30 and cannot be changed." I have devoted a whole upcoming chapter to personalities and their effect on the WHH maximization continuum.

Anyone who is interested in long-distance running has heard of Jim Fixx. His 1977 book, *The Complete Book of Running*, popularized jogging and other forms of running for health and fitness. My Torrington high school cross-country coach, Jon Hutchinson, spoke about him and used some of Fixx's training and running techniques. Fixx was the very picture of health and the literal poster boy for a healthy lifestyle. His book was a big bestseller, convincing many of the health benefits of running. His midlife was centered around exercise and cardio activity through running.

He died of a massive heart attack at age fifty-two.

His family had a history of heart disease, which motivated him to live a healthy lifestyle. But he could not alter genetics, although it is possible that Fixx might have died even earlier in life if he had not focused on his health, and it is likely that exercise enabled him to make the most of the years he did have.

I have found many studies indicating that cardio exercise 20-30 minutes a day combined with attention to diet can extend one's life by six to nine years. If we do minimal exercise each day and pay attention to diet, we can extend life by at least two years. But can we outmaneuver "bad" genes, as Fixx tried to do?

According to Franchell Richard-Hamilton, MD we can! Her 2021 academic study, "6 Ways to Outsmart bad genes for optimal health," published in *Psychology Today*, concluded:

Keep meals to 40% carbohydrates or less: Otherwise, multiple genes get triggered to work overtime.

Learn to relax: Studies show constant exposure to stress hormones forces a change in gene expression, putting one at risk for mood disorders.

According to experts, 80% of the way we age is influenced by the way we behave. Even if you do inherit bad genes, your overall health state will often be determined by your habits and your environment. What you do matters, and with proper techniques, you can give your body the "medical makeover" it so desperately needs and avoid activation of those unwanted genes.

I have used Dr. Franchell Richard-Hamilton's recommendations for the following six Best Success Practices for "outsmarting" your genes to achieve optimal mind and body health.

BEST Success Practice #13 to maximize the WHH continuum: Choose Healthier organic meals over "fast food" and keep meals to 40% carbohydrates.

Research shows that genes respond to the foods you consume. They impact gene expression. A diet packed with 65% carbohydrates triggers multiple genes to work overtime. The high-carb diet also leads to inflammation, which can get in the way of other gene-associated diseases such as type 2 diabetes, dementia and heart disease.

To outsmart your genes, consume more vitamins, nutrients, and minerals. For example, a healthy meal shouldn't have over 40% of carbohydrates. Otherwise, you can stimulate the genes to cause metabolic inflammation. Don't forget to add a lot of fruits and veggies to get the desired result.

BEST Success Practice #14 to maximize the WHH continuum: Break the Sedentary Lifestyle. Always be moving. Example: If you find yourself sitting down to hold a meeting ... stand up. You will burn more calories, and the meeting will be more productive, saving everyone precious time.

Many people are discouraged from exercising and often blame their laziness on their genes. The problem is, just thinking you have low-endurance genes can impact your body negatively. But, if you change that mindset, you can achieve an eye-opening and very positive experience.

Those who lack motivation and drive to be physically active, tend to give up easily. They see their efforts as fruitless and focus more on the negatives. By breaking the sedentary lifestyle, you can shift this negative mentality and help to boost endurance and muscle strength. This will energize you and help you to stay motivated.

Any kind of physical movement helps oxygen and nutrients get to the tissues, which means you are helping your heart and brain function better. In the long run, the lungs also improve, and you will have an easier time tackling the daily chores.

Physical activity not only helps with brain health but can mitigate stress responses that activate unwanted genetic mutations.

Photo by Chevanon Photography from Pexels

BEST Success Practice #15 to maximize the WHH continuum:
Minimize Your Emotional Stress to extend your life

Studies indicate that constant exposure to stress hormones triggers DNA modifications in the brain, forcing a change in gene expression. The longer you remain *stressed*, the greater the risk for mood disorders, anxiety and depression.

You want to try different coping mechanisms. For example, prayer, yoga, meditation, deep breathing, swimming, massage all help to relieve stress and reset the nervous system, allowing it to reconnect with its normal functions.

BEST Success Practice #16 to maximize the WHH continuum:
Change your surroundings or go outside

Sometimes, a change of scene can influence aspects of your life for the better. Spending time in a dirty or polluted environment or even a cluttered space can adversely affect your body, mind and mood. To feel more productive and motivated, try to work and live in clean, clutter-free spaces. If possible, spend time in a park or a forest, Give your mind and body a breath of fresh air.

BEST Success Practice #17 to maximize the WHH continuum:
Get Some Uninterrupted Sleep

Your brain is being fed information throughout the day and needs regular rest. Sleep is critical for health and well-being. Unfortunately, most people don't get enough shuteye, either because of their busy work schedule or because they want to cram in a few more amusements. The fact is your body needs sleep.

BEST Success Practice #18 to maximize the WHH continuum:
Enhance the quality of your sleep by ditching screens and other
electronic devices before bed

Using a smartphone, laptop, or tablet will make it harder for you to fall asleep. The blue light the screen emits interferes with melatonin production, which is crucial for regulating the circadian rhythm (the sleep and wake cycle). These devices also make you more alert and wakeful, preventing your brain from going into REM sleep because it is still processing what you have just read or watched. Set aside digital devices thirty minutes before going to bed. Just place them in a different room or somewhere that keeps you from habitually reaching out to them.

> **BEST Success Practice #19 to maximize the WHH continuum:**
> **Cardio exercise 30 minutes a day combined with attention**
> **to diet can extend your life six to nine years. Cardio is**
> **defined as exercise that increases the heart rate. The market**
> **is saturated with many cardio workouts and are freely**
> **available. Before doing any cardio to increase your heart**
> **rate check with your doctor.**

Here is an example of how to achieve a maximum health outcome by consulting an optimal health specialist outside of the traditional healthcare network. Vincent has over 85,000 hours of applied health and wellness coaching experience, some forty years. I asked him to tell me the top three things people over age sixty can do to stay healthy. In addition to 30 minutes of daily cardio, Vincent says, "Stay hydrated, get to sleep earlier, and walk more." He added a fourth action, stretch more regularly.

> **BEST Success Practice #20 to maximize the WHH continuum:**
> **Use the Black AXIS Foam roller to provide spine therapy**
> **and overall proactive spine health.**

Vincent believes that stretching is valuable to spine health but recommends professional evaluation before initiating a regimen. For some, initiating a vigorous stretching regime will cause more harm than good. He specifies one stretching exercise most people can do with little supervision. He explained that "our spine is a connection point for all our nerves, muscles, and organs. If your spine is out of alignment, many other physical issues develop over time. Of all the stretching we would do, if our spine is not in conformity, we are treating symptoms not the potential cause." He went on to say this particular stretch should first be done with a qualified trainer or physical therapist but added that if you can only do one stretch a day, this is the one.

Remember a parent or a teacher would say to you, "keep your shoulders back and chest out when you walk" or "stand up straight!" As it turns out, they were right. Everything is connected. If, over time, our spine leaves optimal alignment, our breathing is affected as our chest and lung function will not be maximized. A bent back compresses the lungs. If we are not oxygenating optimally, our blood flow is impacted. We tend to feel lethargic and want to sit down and "relax"—or, as my niece Jill says, "chillax."

You will need to purchase a product to use with the stretch technique, OPTP® Black AXIS® Firm Foam Roller - Round 36" x 6" Item No: AXR366. (I derive no monetary benefit from recommending this product and neither does the physical/mental health coach quoted above.) The Firm Foam Roller costs less than $25 dollars and consists of High-density, "6" round AXIS® Black rollers," which "offer the greatest stability challenge for balance and proprioception, as well as the ability to perform Active Release Therapy by rolling out tight tissues and trigger points."

Once you have the Firm Foam Roller, and working with a physical health specialist, set it on the floor. While holding onto a rail, chair, or helping hand, lower yourself so that you are now lying on the Roller. The Roller must be positioned in parallel with and not perpendicular to the spine angle. It should be positioned from your lower spine or coccyx (tailbone) lengthwise up to your neck and head. Make sure your spine is centered on the roller, with your feet in balance on either side of the roller device. For the first few times you do this, you may need a small pillow under your neck.

Now close your eyes and breathe through your nose. Slowly inhale and then slowly exhale through you nose with your mouth closed. You are now in an Active Release Therapy mode. Continue for one to two minutes once a day, preferably before you go to bed at night. You can build up to five minutes a day as your spine decompression health increases.

The roller product can be used for many other activities, including, physical therapy and high-use Pilates and yoga sessions. Used properly, the product will relieve tight or injured muscles, perform self-myofascial release on trigger points and knots, self-massage soft tissue, and roll away soreness. Professionals use high-density Black AXIS® Foam Rollers to roll out tough muscle adhesions in the heavier lower extremities including the iliotibial band (IT band), piriformis, hamstrings, or quads.

Vincent also told me that the four keys to better health—hydration, good sleep, walking more, and stretching—apply to people of all ages. "These are common sense solutions. It is my experience that most people know intuitively what to do but don't do it. A health coach or certified trainer will proactively support positive health outcomes and the discipline to continue the process."

MOTIVATION and coaching—we all need these at times. Vincent went on to point out that the people he coaches "say I bring whatever is necessary or missing to produce optimum health, body, mind, and spirit solutions." His client's stay with him for decades.

At the time of this writing, the world's oldest man is 111. He was interviewed by major news outlets and was asked for his secret to a long life. He said, "If you drink too much, or you eat too much, or you walk too much—if you do too much of anything, you're going to suffer eventually. No smoking, little alcohol, and a fair amount of good luck have contributed."

My research indicates that the more we delay implementation of good practices, the more difficult it is to get past an inflection point of no return. If we are not self-motivated, a coach or trainer is needed to help us initiate positive change.

BEST Success Practice #20 to maximize the WHH continuum: Drink less alcohol, smoke less, eat less meat, stay hydrated, get more sleep, walk more, and stretch appropriately. Find a disciplined approach or a coach to help you carry through what you know you need to do.

Mental Health is linked to physical and spiritual health.

I interviewed a clinical mental health therapist, Jessica Pretak, from Connecticut. She is a Licensed Clinical Social Worker (LCSW), currently working in private practice. She holds a master's degree in Social Work from Southern Connecticut State University and is working toward a doctorate. Her experience includes working in school, hospital, and community mental health environments. My objective was to interview someone who was highly qualified but had less than ten years of professional experience, as this cohort tends to be more keenly aware of the latest techniques and applications.

I asked her to list the top three things we can do to maximize our mental health. Jessica began by telling me, "I think the most common answer would be exercise, diet, and sleep" and then continued:

1. **Mindfulness:** prayer, meditation, tai chi, breathing, gratitude practices. Mindfulness: simply meaning "paying attention." I like to extend the definition by saying "paying attention to one thing at a time, without judgement." Full focus and attention to the activity you're engaged in (e.g. reading your book without the tv on in the background, going to yoga class and drawing awareness to your breath). Your mind will inevitably drift, and the act of mindfulness will be recognizing your mind is drifting, and slowly bringing your attention and awareness back to your activity. A "formal" practice of mindfulness can be meditation. Meditation can be listening to a guided meditation on your phone for 10 minutes or investing in a silent retreat. The benefits of mindfulness and/or meditation/prayer are mental clarity, an increase in distress tolerance, a sense of being in the present (being in the here and now both physically and mentally), decreased depression and anxiety,

increase in memory recall, an increased ability to regulate mood, which all create an opportunity for increased happiness.

2. **Connection to nature**: sunlight to balance circadian rhythm, be grounded by putting your feet in the grass. Our body and brain soak in sunlight which helps regulate mood and reset our circadian rhythm to boost consistent sleep. Humans are facing so much stimulation with staring at screens that being in nature is a stark difference in the vastness of what is real. Being in nature can quite literally be grounding as our feet touch the earth. Nature is a natural stress reliever.

3. **Therapy**- break the cycle and recover and heal from intergenerational trauma, increase awareness of behaviors, emotions, and thought processes that may not benefit well-being, boost connectivity to other people. Therapy can be a place to sit with a skilled trained professional to unpack days, years, or even generations of baggage and/or trauma. We hold our ancestors' pain and it can be played out in difficult dynamics with friends or family. If we acknowledge our feelings and try to make sense of them, we can not only grow as individuals, but we can halt passing on trauma to additional generations. In addition to trauma therapy, people go to therapy for many different reasons. A few common ones are difficulties with communicating needs in a relationship with a family member or partner, navigating challenging life events (e.g. death, divorce), understanding unconscious drives, boosting self-esteem, substance abuse treatment, changing destructive thoughts and behaviors, or overcoming fears.

BEST Success Practice #21 to maximize the WHH continuum:
Be more connected to nature to avoid nature deficit disorders, which lead to other maladaptive behaviors. Reflect on what is good. Be more positive knowing that today is a good day to have a good day.
If you are a person of faith, pray more.

There's an old song that tells us, "When you're smiling the whole world smiles with you." This lyric was not referencing the Joker in Batman movies and comic books or any snarky smirk. It was talking about a genuine smile. The late nineteenth-century American psychologist William James proposed the idea that *we do not run because we are afraid but are afraid because we run.* In other words, our emotions do not just influence our actions and beliefs but are also influenced *by* our actions and beliefs. Positive neural messaging is triggered by the act of smiling.

The wife of one of my friends sometimes really gives him the business—deservedly so, by the way. As she is scolding him, he smiles and smiles until his wife gets frustrated and walks away. His smiling made him feel better during the onslaught while also defusing his wife's anger. When I tried that with my own wife, she demanded to know how I could smile when she was upset. I learned there that there is an art to every communication strategy, especially where emotions are uppermost.

Science tells us that a physiological change occurs when we smile and, furthermore, there are such changes when others smile back. We produce endorphins when smiling and, even more, when exchanging smiles. Endorphins are neurotransmitter hormones associated with pain relief and happiness. A smile given and returned makes us feel good, reducing stress and thus benefitting our health. It's not magic or mysticism. It's body chemistry.

Buddhist author Thich Nhat Hanh said, "Sometimes your joy is the source of your smile, but sometimes your smile can be the source of your joy." William James would agree!

Being mentally, physically, and verbally positive has its psychological benefits. Studies of this behavioral area have been conducted for decades. The business world devours books and lectures endeavoring to teach the "power of positive thinking" and how to be positive and motivated for yourself and others. Many people really do change their attitudes with daily positive affirmations.

Dr. George S. Everly, Jr., of the Johns Hopkins School of Medicine write this about "positive psychology," a discipline that has been around for hundreds of years: "**Positive psychology is the study of our strengths, and how to maximize them. It's about flourishing. It's about wellness, stemming from the wellness movement that was founded in Greece over 2,000 years ago. Fast forward to the 20th century, and it was given a rebirth of sorts.**" Dr. Everly sees positive psychology as tying together physical and mental well-being. By focusing on strengths in both the domains of mind and body, we can better understand how to create happy and meaningful lives. "**Positive psychology is not a treatment, but it can help a person become the best person they can be, with a greater appreciation of what life has to offer.**"

**BEST Success Practice #22 to maximize the WHH continuum:
Find reasons for joy and thankfulness. Smile "out loud,"
and do so more each day. Be positive.**

Here is another action that will help to maximize your health. Breathing is both free and necessary. Since we have to breathe anyway, why not do it in an optimum manner to maximize our health?

"Breath is the bridge between the mind and body," says breathing expert Stuart Sandeman, author of Breathe In, Breathe Out: Restore Your Health, Reset Your Mind and Find Happiness Through Breathwork (2022) and the founder of Breathpod. An article in the Health and Wellness" section of The Epoch Times reports, "For centuries, cultures around the world have turned to breathing for its healing properties. From India's pranayama to China's qigong, breathing techniques have been pivotal to wellness practices. Through tummo meditation, Tibetan monks have demonstrated the power of breath by generating body heat to dry wet sheets wrapped around their bodies in freezing temperatures."

The effect of breathing on health is anchored in respiratory system physiology, which facilitates the essential exchange cycle of oxygen and carbon dioxide. Controlled breathing enhances respiratory efficiency, boosts blood oxygenation, and aids in eliminating waste gases. Furthermore, it stimulates the lymphatic system, which is crucial to body detoxification.

Shallow breathing patterns exacerbate discomfort and are less healthy for you.

Breathing directly affects the autonomic nervous system (ANS), which controls functions such as heart rate and digestion. Slow, deep breaths activate the parasympathetic nervous system, leading to relaxation, reduced stress, and lower blood pressure. Such breathing patterns can counteract stress—a key factor in chronic diseases.

These physiological changes caused by the activation of the Parasympathetic Nervous System emphasize breathing exercises' immediate and long-term benefits. Regular breath work can improve respiratory function, boost immunity, and foster mental and physical well-being. Breath is a powerful tool for aiding healing in many ways.

"There is a breath prescription for most chronic health problems. Through breathing, you can harness your body's natural ability to heal and recover," Sandeman says. He cites seven conditions that can be improved through breathing exercises:

1. Hypertension (High Blood Pressure)

Breathing exercises provide a simple and cost-effective strategy for managing high blood pressure, serving as a viable alternative to medication for many. Incorporating slow, deliberate breathing techniques into daily routines helps those with hypertension regulate and reduce their blood pressure.

A 2023 study, "Breathing Exercise for Hypertensive Patients: A Scoping Review," sheds light on this approach. Researchers discovered notable decreases in blood pressure among practitioners of controlled breathing, with systolic pressure dropping by 4, to 54.22 millimeters of mercury (mmHg), and diastolic pressure (the bottom number) by 3, to 17 mmHg. "Slow breathing can be used as an alternate, non-pharmacological therapy" to help people with hypertension reduce blood pressure, the study authors report. Millions struggling with high blood pressure might be able to alleviate their condition through breathing exercises.

2. Asthma

Breathing techniques are increasingly acknowledged as helpful in managing asthma, complementing conventional treatments. A review in the Cochrane Database of Systematic Reviews shows these exercises can improve quality of life, reduce hyperventilation symptoms, and enhance lung function for those with mild to moderate asthma.

The review highlights that controlled breathing strengthens the diaphragm and respiratory muscles, improving breathing efficiency and lung capacity. For those with asthma, these exercises can boost lung function, ease symptoms, and enhance lung health. The Asthma and Allergy Network points to such techniques as diaphragmatic and pursed lip breathing, which help improve respiratory muscle strength and flexibility of the rib cage and also control breathing patterns. Furthermore, the calming effect of deep breathing exercises can mitigate asthma triggers linked to stress and anxiety, potentially reducing the frequency of asthma attacks.

"Breathing exercises should be offered to all asthma patients with symptoms or impaired quality of life despite standard treatment," Mike Thomas, a primary care research professor at the University of Southampton, wrote in the journal Breathe. Regularly practicing these exercises can help asthma patients control their condition more effectively and enhance their quality of life.

3. Irritable Bowel Syndrome

Irritable bowel syndrome is often seen as just a digestive issue. Yet there's strong evidence that it's also connected to the broader relationship among the brain, gut, and autonomic nervous system (ANS). Problems with the body's stress response and digestive relaxation pathways are critical factors in IBS, making breathing exercises a promising complementary treatment. Cindy Huey experienced intense IBS symptoms, such as ongoing abdominal pain and significant weight loss, but found relief through diaphragmatic breathing. Although she initially struggled to breathe into her stomach, persistence paid off. "Within a few hours, my pain was reduced," she said. Two years later, she reported a full recovery. A 2022 study reinforces the efficacy of diaphragmatic breathing practices, showing that IBS patients practicing slow, deep breathing over six weeks saw substantial improvements. They reported less IBS discomfort, more regular bowel movements, and better stool consistency. Moreover, these patients showed enhanced vagal activity, indicating a healthier balance in their ANS.

4. Insomnia

Millions suffer from insomnia worldwide, experiencing a wide array of symptoms from trouble focusing to severe long-term health conditions. The go-to solution is often medication, but research suggests that deep breathing exercises may be equally as effective.

Slow, deep breathing boosts melatonin production, an essential hormone for initiating sleep. Slow breathing techniques promote relaxation and strengthen the body's rest-and-digest response. An increase in melatonin helps signal to the body that it's time to sleep, aiding in falling asleep faster and more deeply.

Deep breathing can improve vagal tone, which is essential for relaxation. Spend 20 minutes on slow-paced breathing before bed significantly helps with relaxation. Researchers have said that slow-paced breathing could be a practical, non-medication-based treatment for insomnia.

5. Chronic and Acute Pain

Many in the United States battle chronic pain and look for solutions outside of medication. Diaphragmatic breathing is a promising option that uses the body's own processes to ease pain. Johns Hopkins Medicine points out that this technique activates the diaphragm and vagus nerve, triggering a relaxation response vital for managing stress and pain.

As shown in a comprehensive review of clinical trials, studies highlight the effectiveness of breathing interventions in lessening acute pain. Findings suggest that slow, deep breathing is an alternative to usual pain management methods and promotes an active role in dealing with pain, contributing significantly to overall health and well-being.

6. Menstrual Discomfort

Say goodbye to heating pads, medication, and discomfort. Breathing is now recognized as a powerful, natural option for managing menstrual pain. By relaxing the body, enhancing blood flow, and soothing dysmenorrhea-related pain, this method helps overcome the body's natural tendency to tense up in pain. It stabilizes the ANS to lessen stress and the sensation of pain.

A study in a university holistic health class underscored the effectiveness of diaphragmatic breathing. The participants, who learned stress awareness and relaxation methods, experienced notable relief from menstrual pain. One 28-year-old participant said: "True benefit came when I started breathing at the first sign of discomfort. I have not had to use any pain medication since incorporating diaphragmatic breath work."

7. Type 2 Diabetes

Common strategies to manage Type 2 diabetes typically involve medications, dietary changes, and engaging in more physical activity. Yet breathing exercises have demonstrated significant promise.

As stated above, slow, deep breathing activates the parasympathetic nervous system, which calms the body and also lowers increased stress-related cortisol inducing a state of relaxation that helps stabilize blood sugar levels. Diaphragmatic breathing decreases oxidative stress, further aiding blood sugar regulation.

A 2023 study examined the effect of combining aerobic exercise with slow, deep breathing and mindfulness meditation for women with Type 2 diabetes. Six weeks later, those who had added breathing and meditation to their exercise regimens had notably lower fasting blood sugar and cortisol levels than those who did only aerobic exercise.

Adding breathing exercises to your daily activities can bring many benefits, such as lowering stress, improving lung function, and boosting your overall health. By sitting upright and allowing the abdomen to expand and contract with each breath, you can significantly alleviate discomfort and support healing. Advocate for a slower abdominal breathing method, in which the exhale is twice as long as the inhale, mimicking the serene breathing patterns of a baby or toddler.

Here are two simple methods you can start with:

1. Diaphragmatic Breathing
  -Focus on using your diaphragm for deep breaths to relax
   and ease stress.
  -Lie down or sit with one hand on your chest and the other
   on your belly.
  -Inhale slowly through your nose, letting your diaphragm expand,
   and your lungs fill with air. Keep your chest still
  -Exhale through pursed lips, gently pressing your belly to push all
   the air out. Continue for a few minutes, paying attention to
   your belly's movement.

2. Slow Deep Breathing (4-7-8 Technique)
   This calming method reduces stress and aids healing.
  -Find a quiet spot to sit or lie down. Close your eyes, and deeply
   inhale through your nose for a count of four.
  -Hold your breath in for seven counts.
  -Exhale fully from your mouth for eight counts.
  -Start with four or five cycles, gradually practicing for longer periods
   as you feel more at ease.

Diaphragmatic breathing has many health benefits, but it may not be suitable for everyone. If you've had recent heart surgery, injuries to the spine or rib cage, are pregnant, or have a history of severe respiratory problems, it's important to approach this practice with caution and under medical guidance. People who feel suffocated by deep, slow breathing should go slow. Beginners might find it easier to start lying down, gradually moving to a seated position. Listening to the body is extremely important. Always check with your Doctor.

Incorporating these breathing exercises into your daily life can unlock your breath's power to better your health and quality of life. Whether you're seeking stress relief, pain management, or tranquility in a hectic day, these simple methods are an effective way to achieve health.

Vincent, the *"Wellness Works"* expert referenced earlier, with 85,000 hours and 40 years of experience, says that "most people will try these techniques, but very few continue them. A routine and habit is formed by engaging health and wellness professionals and coaches.

We all have to breath, why not do it in such a way to enhance our health?"

BEST Success Practice #23 to maximize the WHH continuum:
Find a wellness coach to practice diaphragmatic breathing
and/or slow deep 478 breathing techniques.
Check with your Doctor beforehand.

Environmental Factors

I have focused on health practices involving our personal physiology and mental aspects, but what about the environment in which we live or work? What about what we apply to our bodies or what we consume?

If you resided in the Love Canal neighborhood outside of Niagara Falls New York before 2004, you grew up on a chemical dumpsite. It was named after William T. Love, who began digging the canal in the 1890s intended to link lakes Erie and Ontario. Work on the canal began in 1894, but was abandoned after only a mile had been completed. The resulting ditch remained unfilled, and during the 1920s became a dump site for the City of Niagara Falls. Hooker Chemical Company purchased the canal during the 1940s and dumped 19,800 tons of toxic chemical waste into it. The local school district acquired it in 1953. Although the dumping had stopped, toxic runoff seeped into the ground and groundwater.

Gradually evidence mounted of an unusually high incidence of diseases involving high white blood cell counts, including, most ominously, leukemia. The Love Canal "incident" became a public scandal and served to launch the federal Superfund, dedicated to cleaning up the Love Canal site and other pollution hotspots. The entire surrounding neighborhood was razed, people displaced, and, of course, many sickened, some fatally.

Harmful environmental pollution is not always an outdoor issue. Inside our own homes, we use toxic cleaning products, chemicals, parabens (preservative chemicals), and other chemicals. We use deodorants, anti-perspirants, body sprays, toothpastes, sun screens, some of which contain chemicals known to cause adverse reactions. Many products brought to market are from off-shore companies and escape domestic regulatory supervision. Long-term use may cause disease in some people. Even some foreign vitamin manufacturers have come under scrutiny.

Computers, smart phones, and tablets emanate light in the blue spectrum that causes sleep disorders in some people. Certain furniture we lounge on or rugs we walk on are manufactured with questionable materials from China and other sources where safety laws are lax or non-existent. We consume processed foods and apply lotions that have toxins. We drink water processed by treatment plants that contain fluoride, chlorine, chlorides, and additives, which may adversely impact our health.

Let's focus on water consumption first, since we all require water to live.

Initial decisions can be made and actions taken for what appear to be the best of reasons at the time. Fluoride was first added to drinking water in Grand Rapids, Michigan, in 1945, making it the first community in the world to implement water fluoridation to prevent tooth decay. This practice spread to other towns and cities after studies showed a significant reduction in cavities among school-children. How or why this happened is another story. It happened, and just about every municipal water system in the USA followed suit. In September 2024, two towns in New York, Yorktown and Somers, appear to be the first towns in the United States to have ended adding fluoride to water following a judge's ruling that "the evidence of risk to one's health was sufficiently high to trigger regulatory response by the EPA. Scientific literature in the record provides a high level of certainty that a hazard is present and fluoride is associated with REDUCED IQ."

In 2024, a published study from the National Toxicology program part of the Department of Health and Human Services, summarized fluoride use globally. The 324-page report from USA, Canada, China, India, Iran, Pakistan and Mexico concluded people, especially children are getting too much fluoride in their drinking water. In a 2025 study published by JAMA Pediatrics called "Fluoride Expose and Children's IQ Scores-A Systemic Review and Meta-Analysis" Principle Dr. Kyla W. Taylor after review of 74 global studies, identified issues. Fluoride in water at a level of 1.5mg/L or greater for children was a risk to their IQ.

Also, if that is not enough, chlorides are present in many water systems. A chloride is tasteless and odorless. It's an anion or negative ion. Without getting into all the chemistry and science of long-term consumption, the research concludes high chloride concentration in combination with other chemicals consumed, is bad for positive health outcomes. Increased risk of kidney cancer and heart risks are just a few of the health risks. Boiling the water will only evaporate some of the water leaving a higher concentration of chlorides. Boiling water only increases the risk, and chlorides promote corrosion in copper water pipes and plumbing.

Many public water treatment systems have chlorides. You can ask your water authority for a copy of their yearly test results. They are required to provide an annual Water Quality Report or Consumer Confidence Report. Or, since the test they provide is a moment-in-time result, you may want to purchase a home water test package from a state certified laboratory. If you are on a well for your water, test it regularly.

There are services and companies that will help you identify products used long-term, that may cause adverse health effects. They will come into your home or business and take an inventory of what you consume, use and store in inventory. The deliverable is a list of products with a 1-10 toxicity rating. With some services, they will recommend a less toxic replacement product.

Sarah Storie, one CEO of such a service company, has identified the top three issues found in almost every home and business assessed. She observed:

- Water/Air purity issues
- Too much salt and sugar in the food we consume and stored in our food pantries
- Toxic parabens and aluminum in topical lotions/sprays we apply to our bodies

Given almost everyone consumes water, I focused on a case study and research outcome by Sarah, the service company CEO. Here is an example of a client who has their water piped in by a water utility in Connecticut. Her service company researched the water utility and provided her customer the analysis on the next page:

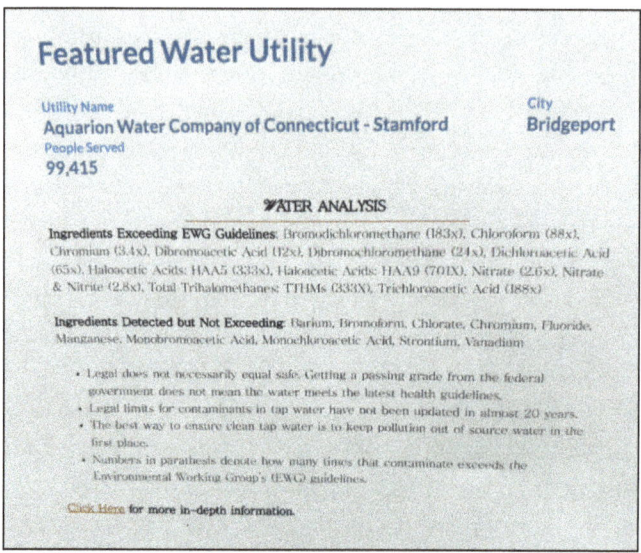

In her report to her client, numerous types of water filters were analyzed. Activated Carbon, reverse osmosis, and ion exchange types were ranked by contaminant removal, price and household filter location.

**BEST Success Practice #24 to maximize the WHH continuum:
Test your water. Purchase and install the best water
filtration system you can afford and change out the
filter regularly as required.**

Many products we use have not been life-tested. Time and space do not permit us to do a deep dive into all of them. Let's focus on one product as an example.

Everyone uses or has used anti-perspirants. Doctors now tell patients who have kidney issues, bone disease, memory disorders, and certain cancers not to use anti-perspirant products any longer. There is evidence that suggests the use of aluminum in products like these, which we consume or to which we are exposed may cause or exacerbate illness. Playing catch-up, the FDA now requires manufactures of anti-perspirants to list any aluminum used and how much. This labeling requirement did not exist when these types of products were introduced.

Anything we apply to our bodies or we inhale or we come in contact with must be checked for toxins, exotoxins, endotoxins and adverse effects. Think…pillows, hairspray, candles burning, air fresheners, cleaning products, baby crib mattresses, and so on. Talcum powder was long considered an totally benign substance—safe for the behinds of little babies—but it is now apparent that talc, the clay mineral from which talcum powder is made, is often found in combination with asbestos, a once widely used insulating material now associated with some types of cancers.

Read the labels.

There are hundreds of sources to help you. Among the most authoritative are *Journal of Toxicology and Environmental Health, Part B*; *Mayo Clinic*; *MD Anderson Cancer Center*; *Environmental Working Group*; and *Mindbodygreen.com*, to name a few. (I derive no economic benefit from these entities or any others mentioned in this book)

We are what we eat and drink

Before any change in diet, check with your medical provider or a registered dietitian.

I have researched what is best to consume and what to avoid. Earlier I commented how my research might challenge and even disturb you with facts we may not want to hear. This next section about the foods we consume produced for me, the highest level of guilt and discouragement. How did I not already know what I am about to share?

Let's address fruits and vegetables first.

Some fruits and vegetables harbor pesticide contamination, according to The Environmental Working Group (EWG). In its 2024 annual report, EWG analyzes data from tests conducted by the U.S. Department of Agriculture (USDA) and the U.S. Food and Drug Administration (FDA) on more than 46,000 samples of 46 popular crops to find which fruits and vegetables have the highest and lowest levels of pesticide contamination.

The dirty dozen, from worst to least-worse, are:
Strawberries
Spinach
Kale/Collard greens
Grapes
Peaches
Pears
Nectarines
Apples
Bell and Hot peppers
Cherries
Blue Berries
Green Beans

How to avoid pesticides? Organic is better than non-organic. Scientists at the Connecticut Agricultural Experiment Station found that washing produce with running water for two minutes reduced the amount of pesticide residue for 9 of the 12 tested pesticides.

In a study published in *Food Control*, researchers washed vegetables for 20 minutes in either a vinegar solution, a saltwater solution, or plain water to eliminate the residue of four common pesticides: chlorpyrifos, DDT, cypermethrin, and chlorothalonil. They discovered that a 10% salt water solution was effective in removing a large percentage of pesticides from produce, far more so than washing with plain water. A 10% vinegar solution was found to be equally effective, but using vinegar regularly might get expensive and can leave foods with an unwelcome vinegary flavor, making this less than ideal for a daily vegetable wash.

What may be the best and most affordable way to clean fruits and veggies comes from a recent study published in the *Journal of Agricultural and Food Chemistry*, which compared the effectiveness of plain water, a Clorox bleach solution, and a baking soda and water solution. Perhaps surprisingly, the baking soda solution was found to be most effective at removing pesticide residues from the surface of apples. The baking soda solution used in the study was very weak, a mixture of one ounce of baking soda with 100 ounces of water. It required 12 to 15 minutes of soaking to completely remove the pesticides.

So, what does all this mean for you? How should you use this information to wash your produce?

In the studies just mentioned, researchers cleaned produce much longer than most of us would do on an ordinary day, but this should not prevent us from putting their methods to use. Most people would never wash vegetables for longer than a couple of minutes, so I adapted the results of these studies to more practical everyday use. Admittedly, it won't be quite as effective as the time-consuming methods used in the studies, but it should be more effective than plain water.

Here's a quick and easy way to wash veggies using baking soda:

For leafy greens
-Fill a salad spinner with greens, then fill it with water.
-Add a teaspoon of baking soda and mix well.
-Soak your greens for ten minutes, swish, dump,
  then rinse and spin dry.
-If you don't have a salad spinner, you can add the greens, water, and
  baking soda to a bowl, let them soak, drain in a strainer, rinse, then
  pat the leaves dry with a clean lint-free kitchen towel or
  paper towels.

For mushrooms

There is some debate in the culinary world about how to clean mushrooms. Some chefs prefer to gently wipe mushrooms with a damp towel. However, to clean mushrooms thoroughly, you can gently scrub them using a mushroom brush and then rinse them quickly under running water. After that, blot the mushrooms dry with a clean kitchen towel or paper towel.

For other veggies

-Fill a large bowl with cold water.
-Mix in baking soda (about a teaspoon for every 16 ounces of water).
-Add the veggies
-Soak for ten minutes
-Drain
-Scrub with a brush
-And finally rinse of the veggies

Smooth-skinned fruits, such as apples, nectarines, and cherries, can be washed in a baking soda bath the same way as veggies.

Berries can be rinsed under cold water in a mesh strainer, then gently patted dry with a clean kitchen towel or paper towels just before you intend to eat them.

Although your instinct may be to rinse off berries when you bring them home, doing so actually increases moisture and accelerates spoilage, microflora, and mold. This is why it's best to rinse them shortly before you eat them.

If you want to know the cleanest fifteen fruits and vegetables, here they are:

Avocados
Sweet Corn
Pineapple
Onions
Papaya
Frozen sweet peas
Asparagus
Honey dew melon
Kiwi
Cabbage
Mushrooms
Mangos
Sweet potatoes
Watermelons
Carrots

Membership in the "Clean 15" is based on having the least amount of pesticides applied. That's a good thing, but there is one negative. Some of these have high levels of sugar, especially the watermelon. This group scores two out of three positives: low pesticides and high electrolytes, high sugar content.

Pesticides are a clear and present danger. An extensive study published in *Consumer Reports* was published on April 18, 2024, and updated on May 17 of that year.

"To get a sense of the current situation," Catherine Roberts writes:
CR recently conducted our most comprehensive review ever of pesticides in food. To do it, we analyzed seven years of data from the Department of Agriculture, which each year tests a selection of conventional and organic produce grown in or imported to the U.S. for pesticide residues. We looked at 59 common fruits and vegetables, over 29,000 documents, including, in some cases, not just fresh versions but also canned, dried, or frozen ones. Pesticides posed significant risks in 20 percent of the foods we examined, including popular choices such as bell peppers, blueberries, green beans, potatoes, and strawberries. One food, green beans, had residues of a pesticide that hasn't been allowed to be used on the vegetable in the U.S. for over a decade. And imported produce, especially some from Mexico, was particularly likely to carry risky levels of pesticide residues.

But there was good news, too. Pesticides presented little to worry about in nearly two-thirds of the foods, including nearly all of the organic ones. Also encouraging: The largest risks are caused by just a few pesticides, concentrated in a handful of foods, grown on a small fraction of U.S. farmland.

To come up with that advice, we analyzed the USDA's test results for 29,643 individual food samples. We rated the risk of each fruit or vegetable by factoring in how many pesticides showed up in the food, how often they were found, the amount of each pesticide detected, and each chemical's toxicity. (For details, go to CR.org/pesticidemethodology)

BEST Success Practice #25 to maximize the WHH continuum: Consume organic food from the USA. Clean fruits and veggies using the baking soda process—one teaspoon of baking soda per 16 ounces of water—before consumption.

In identifying best success practices, my research is somewhat biased toward entities that published results from a sample of thousands of subjects over long periods of time. One such study is from the Harvard T. H. Chan School of Public Health and other universities. As Melissa Rudy writes in the May 2024, researchers "analyzed population health data for more than 92,000 adults over a 28-year period. The participants' average age was 56 and none of them had heart disease or cancer." The study found that people who consumed over 7 grams a day of olive oil had a 28% lower risk of dementia-related death compared to those who rarely or never consumed it. As the researchers wrote, "Substituting olive oil intake for margarine and mayonnaise was associated with lower risk of dementia mortality and may be a potential strategy to improve longevity free of dementia." It has also been shown that olive oil consumption promotes heart health as well.

To continue with the we-are-what-we-eat theme, we have all heard of natural remedies, including Native American "plant-based" cures for illness. Here are a few to incorporate into our diet:

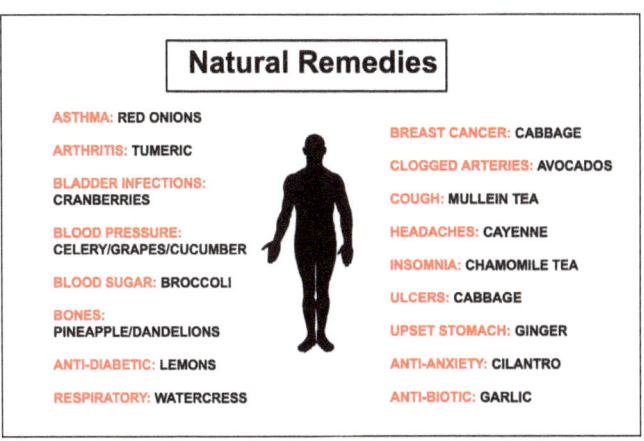

We are seeing increased amounts of diseases related to what we eat and drink. One example is colorectal cancer as well as other cancers of the digestive system. According to Dr. Jeremy Kortmansky's March 2023 interview on News 8 WTNH TV, as the associate professor of medical oncology at the Yale School of Medicine and clinical director of the Division of GI Medical Oncology at the Yale Cancer Center, there is a correlation between increased risk of colorectal cancer and—

- Widespread use of antibiotics
- Modern dietary habits
- High consumption of added sugars, including sweetened beverages and high-fructose corn syrup
- Widespread use of food additives, such as MSG, titanium dioxide, and synthetic food dyes
- Exposure to bright lights at night and changes in sleep

Other experiences and exposures early in life may also be associated with early-onset colorectal cancer, such as:

- Birth by Caesarean section
- Infant formula often replacing breast milk
- Increased maternal age at first and last childbirth
- Abdominal radiation therapy (especially early techniques that, due to precision issues, were more likely to damage normal tissues)

Another extensive study suggests that sugary foods, such as high-fructose corn syrup, may be a primary culprit, said Lewis Cantley, a professor at the Harvard Medical School Department of Cell Biology, published through Weill Cornell Medicine with New York-Presbyterian. He explained that the consumption of high-fructose corn syrup sharply increased in the 1970s, and over the next 20 years, the incidence of colorectal cancer rose in relatively young adults. These adults typically have KRAS mutations. The KRAS gene is an oncogene that can turn cells cancerous when mutated.

How do we maximize our health?

The foods and the amount of food we consume have a direct bearing on maximizing our health outcomes and longevity. The old adage "we are what we eat" still holds true. Lately, the U.S. government has been getting more serious about the nation's health, with the appointment of a "health czar" to shake up the Food and Drug Administration (FDA). More than 60% of what Americans consume is processed foods leading to less than positive health outcomes. Retooling the FDA is needed. Educate yourself using healthy food apps that scan the barcode and rank the product as healthy or unhealthy. I did the research for you. As an example watercress is the most nutrient-dense vegetable, receiving a perfect score of 100 in the Centers for Disease Control's long-standing ranking of "powerhouse" fruits and vegetables (PFVs). Chinese cabbage came in a close second, with a score of 91.99, followed by chard (89.27), beet greens (87.08), and spinach (86.43). These foods, among a total of 41 that qualified as (PFV's), were found to contain 17 nutrients, including potassium, fiber, protein, calcium, iron, thiamin, riboflavin, niacin, folate, zinc, and vitamins A, B6, B12, C, D, E and K. Others high on the list include Chinese cabbage, collard greens, kale, and arugula along with leafy greens such as chard, beet greens, spinach, chicory, and leaf lettuce. Yellow and orange foods, including carrots, tomatoes, winter squash, and sweet potatoes—along with allium, citrus and berry groups—landed in the bottom.

Let's return to watercress. When it comes to the top veggie, nutritionists agree that watercress offers a multitude of health benefits:

1. Rich in nutrients and low in calories

Watercress has "remarkable levels" of vitamins K, A, C and B, as well as magnesium, calcium and potassium, according to Serena Poon, certified nutritionist and celebrity longevity advisor in Los Angeles. Vitamin K, calcium, and magnesium are great for bone health, Poon told Fox News Digital, while vitamin C supports immune health, collagen production, and skin radiance.

"Watercress may be tiny, but it's one of the most nutrient-dense foods you can find," Poon remarked. "Plus, since it's low in calories, you get all these benefits without adding much to your daily caloric intake." Los Angeles-based registered dietitian nutritionist Ilana Muhlstein agreed, telling Fox News Digital that consumers can get more than 50% of their daily value of vitamins C, A, and K in three cups of watercress.

2. Supports heart health

Watercress is rich in antioxidants, which can help reduce inflammation and oxidative stress–two "key contributors" to heart disease, Poon noted. The vegetable also contains compounds such as beta-carotene, lutein, and zeaxanthin, which support heart health and improve blood vessel function. "Additionally, the nitrates in watercress are known to lower blood pressure, further protecting your cardiovascular system," Poon added. "Adding watercress to your meals could be a simple yet powerful way to give your heart some extra support."

All dark greens and cruciferous veggies contain "powerful levels of antioxidants, but typically get overshadowed by other things like berries," according to Muhlstein. "Greens are numero uno when it comes to healthy food," she said.

3. Could reduce cancer risk

As powerhouse vegetables are strongly associated with reduced chronic disease risk, watercress could also reduce cancer risk, according to Poon. "Watercress contains powerful phytochemicals, including glucosinolates, which have been shown to inhibit cancer cell growth. When you chew watercress, these glucosinolates are converted into isothiocyanates, compounds that have been studied for their anti-cancer properties." Previous research has suggested that watercress may help prevent DNA damage and reduce the risk of certain cancers, particularly those affecting the lungs and digestive tract, Poon points out.

4. Encourages hormone balance

Nutrient-rich watercress can also support hormone health through its high levels of B vitamins, calcium, and magnesium, nutrients that "play roles in neurotransmitter balance, stress response and metabolic function, which are all vital for maintaining hormonal equilibrium," Poon explained.

5. Aids in detoxification and liver health

The natural constituents of watercress, including sulfur, can enhance the body's natural detoxification process and support liver function, "This leafy green can help support the liver's ability to filter toxins and promote the elimination of waste products, making it a great addition to any detox-supportive diet," Poon told Fox News Digital.

6. Supports skin health

Watercress can also give the skin a natural glow, Poon noted, as antioxidants like vitamin C, beta-carotene, and lutein support skin elasticity and radiance. "Vitamin C, in particular, is essential for collagen production, which helps maintain skin firmness and can reduce the appearance of fine lines," Poon added.

Lessons from India

Now, let's look overseas to India. Vegetarians represent over 35 percent of the population in India, or almost half a billion people. Vegetarian Indians have significantly fewer types of cancer, lower risk of heart attack, circulatory diseases, and Type 2 diabetes than non-vegetarian Indians. Those who do not supplement with Vitamin B12, have a higher rate of depression.

Depression is one of the most common mental health issues in both India and the United States. Some 21 million U.S. adults—more than 8%—reported at least one major depressive episode in 2020. Studies, including one from University of Pittsburgh Medical Center (UPMC) suggest that what you eat can either contribute to depression or help you to avoid it. What follows is a discussion of foods that minimize depression, according to *UPMC Health Beat April 2024.*

Omega-3 fats are essential fats, which means you must include them in your diet because your body cannot make them. Your brain needs omega-3 fats to work well. People who get more omega-3 fats in their diet appear to have fewer depressive symptoms—although studies are ongoing to determine whether omega-3s affect or are affected by depression.

The best sources of omega-3s are oily, cold-water fish, including:

- Salmon
- Sardines
- Mackerel
- Anchovies

If you don't eat fish, add more walnuts, flaxseeds, and leafy green veggies to your diet. These also provide omega-3 fats.

The vitamin Folate, also known as folic acid or vitamin B9, helps your body make neurotransmitters. These chemical messengers send signals from your brain to the rest of your body. Some neurotransmitters (like serotonin and dopamine) help regulate your mood and emotions. Studies show that people with depression often have low levels of folate in their blood, which may make them more prone to depression. Further research is needed to fully understand how the relationship between folate and depression operates.

Leafy green vegetables and beans are among the best dietary sources of folate. Some small studies show that taking a methylated form of folic acid may help people when an antidepressant alone isn't effective. Broad use of this practice is not currently supported, however.

The recommended adult dietary allowance (RDA) of folate is 400 mcg a day. Pregnant women need 600 mcg, and those who are breastfeeding should get 500 mcg.

You also need healthy levels of vitamin B12 to make neurotransmitters, which may have the added benefit of keeping inflammation in check. Low levels of this vitamin appear to be linked to depression, dementia, and overall poor brain function. The specific connection is still being investigated.

Vitamin B12 is plentiful in such animal foods as:

- Meat
- Fish
- Poultry
- Eggs
- Dairy foods

Because plants don't have this vitamin, a vegan diet probably does not provide enough B12. Older adults and those with digestive conditions such as celiac or Crohn's disease may not absorb sufficient vitamin B12 from food. If you are in either of these groups, ask your doctor if you need a supplement.

Adults should get 2.4 mcg of vitamin B12 each day. Pregnant women need 2.6 mcg, and those who are breastfeeding should get 2.8 mcg.

Vitamin D is popularly known as the "sunshine vitamin" because our bodies make vitamin D when we expose our skin to sunlight. Many people experience mild depression in the winter months, and lower vitamin D levels may play a part. Some studies have shown that depressive symptoms may improve with vitamin D supplementation.

Vitamin D is not widespread in most diets. It is found mainly in:
- Fatty fish like salmon, rainbow trout, and sardines
- Fortified milk
- Eggs
- Mushrooms exposed to ultraviolet light

You might not get enough vitamin D if you don't eat these foods regularly, or if you live where there is relatively limited sunlight. If that's you, consider asking your doctor about taking a vitamin D supplement.

Children and adults under the age of 70 need 600 IU (15 mcg) of vitamin D each day. If you're over age 70, you need 800 IU (20 mcg) daily. Vitamin D is stored in your body, so don't take a higher dose unless your doctor recommends it.

A protein deficiency is uncommon, but you might not eat the right kinds of protein. Protein foods supply amino acids, which our bodies use to make neurotransmitters, some of which play a role in feelings of happiness and well-being.

You need the amino acids tyrosine and tryptophan to make the neurotransmitters serotonin and dopamine. Without sufficient levels of these neurotransmitters, you may experience a low mood and feelings of aggression. You can get plenty of these amino acids from animal proteins, quinoa, and soy. If you don't eat these, you can rely on other plant proteins, which contain these amino acids, albeit in lower amounts. It is crucial to eat a good amount and variety of plant proteins every day, including:
- Nuts
- Seeds
- Beans
- Whole grains

Hypothyroidism or underactive thyroid is an often-overlooked reason for mild to moderate depression. Your thyroid regulates the metabolic functions in your body. When it's not working well, you can experience subtle symptoms, including feeling more tired and depressed.

Your thyroid needs enough selenium and iodine to make thyroid hormones. But getting too much of these trace minerals from supplements may be harmful. Instead, try to eat fish and seafood—most types have both minerals along with healthy omega-3 fats.

The RDA for selenium is 55 mcg a day for adults and 60 mcg for pregnant women. If you're breastfeeding, you need 70 mcg. The RDA for iodine is 150 mcg a day for adults and 220 mcg for pregnant women. Breastfeeding moms need 290 mcg daily.

No one nutrient is more important than rest for depression. And there's no magic bullet that can cure depression. However, nourishing your brain with a healthy and well-rounded diet is an essential step in your journey to feeling better.

What about fish and seafood? For a long time, we were all told that both are necessary for a balanced diet. But not so fast … All fish and seafood contain a level of mercury, some more than others. The Food and Drug Administration (FDA) has listed the best (least contaminated) to consume:

- Anchovy
- Atlantic croaker
- Black Sea bass
- Butterfish
- Cod
- Flounder
- Haddock
- Herring
- American Lobster
- Pollock
- Salmon
- Sardines
- Smelt
- Sole
- Squid
- Canned light tuna
- Whitefish
- Whiting

Stay away from farm-raised fish. especially from the warm waters of China and Southeast Asia. Stay away from catfish, carp, freshwater bass, and other fish harvested in small lakes, canals, and Intercoastal waterways. Always check with your doctor, but my suggestion is that you limit fish and seafood consumption. Adults should limit themselves to 8 ounces per serving twice a week.

Researching all this data can be overwhelming. Initially, it was for me. How can all my habits, my food consumption practices be so wrong? I must admit, I took the attitude that it was too late in my life to make a positive change. For a time, I stopped researching because I did not like the results. After all, who wants to be proven wrong?

But then I read how making even small changes in food habits and topicals can make a positive difference. The best analogy I can come up with is smokers who quit smoking experience measurable improvement in the condition of their lungs within weeks, provided they are not in the end stages of disease. The objective is to achieve progress, not perfection. Don't be discouraged. In upcoming chapters, I will share action plans and a SMART (Specific, Measurable, Achievable, Relevant, and Time-Bound) goal methodology you can use to start your journey to maximize WHH.

BEST Success Practice #26 to maximize the WHH continuum:
Follow a more restricted caloric intake, take a probiotic each day, and adopt a more vegetarian diet. Avoid red meats.
Depression can be treated, at least in part, through diet.

We need proteins to create balance in our diet for good health. Proteins contain some or all of these nine essential amino acids:

- histidine
- isoleucine
- leucine
- lysine
- methionine
- phenylalanine
- threonine
- tryptophan
- valine.

A "complete protein" contains all nine. Complete proteins can be found in animal-based sources, as well as some plant-based sources. Incomplete proteins lack one or more essential amino acids but certainly can be combined with specific foods to create a complete protein source, which provides all the essential amino acids needed by the body. The following are what nutrition expert Vanessa Rissetto, MS, RD, CDN, calls the Ten Perfect Proteins, which can fuel and energize your journey toward optimal wellness:

1. Eggs

Eggs are widely recognized as a nutritious source of protein. They contain all nine essential amino acids are thus a complete protein. Eggs have many health benefits. According to a 2020 scientific review found in Nutrients Magazine, the protein in eggs supports skeletal muscle health and protects against sarcopenia (muscle loss), as well as decreases appetite, which results in a reduction in caloric intake from the next meal. This promotes healthy weight loss.

One large egg provides about six grams of protein, as well as vitamins B12 and vitamin D, as well as minerals such as iron, selenium, and zinc. These nutrients are important for supporting immune function, brain health, and red blood cell production.

2. Lean chicken

Chicken is a rich source of high-quality protein, providing approximately 31 grams of protein per 3.5 ounces. Chicken contains all the essential amino acids the body needs for muscle repair, growth, and maintenance. To maintain its lean protein profile, you'll want to choose lean cuts of chicken, remove the skin, and use cooking methods that minimize added fats.

3. Greek yogurt

Greek yogurt typically contains around twice the amount of protein found in regular yogurt—and often less sugar, too.

Greek yogurt is packed with protein, usually containing around 20 grams per six-ounce serving. Greek yogurt often contains live and active cultures, which are beneficial bacteria that can support good gut health and digestion. These probiotics aid in maintaining a healthy balance of bacteria in the gut.

4. Salmon

Salmon is a fish rich in protein—a 3.5-ounce serving of cooked salmon provides around 22 grams of protein—and nutrients like selenium, B vitamins and vitamin D. Salmon is also an excellent source of omega-3 fatty acids, particularly eicosapentaenoic acid (EPA) and docosahexaenoic acid (DHA), fatty acids that have been linked to numerous health benefits, including heart health, brain function, and reducing inflammation in the body.

Make salmon tacos! Just fill whole wheat or pure corn tortillas with grilled or baked salmon, along with fresh vegetables, salsa, and a dollop of yogurt or avocado for a tasty and nutritious meal.

5. Lean beef

Lean beef is considered a good source of protein. It is particularly valued for its high-quality protein content, which means it contains all the essential amino acids that your body needs. A 3.5-ounce serving of cooked lean beef boasts about 26 grams of protein. Beef is also a rich source of iron, zinc, and vitamin B12, which play vital roles in maintaining healthy muscles, supporting cognitive function, and contributing to overall well-being. Cuts from the loin or round typically have a lower fat content compared to fattier cuts.

6. Lentils

Lentils are a versatile legume, which provide an excellent plant-based protein source. (They're also an amazing comfort food in cooler months!) In one cooked cup of lentils, you'll get around 18 to 20 grams of protein.

Lentils happen to lack the amino acid methionine, so they are not quite a complete protein. The good news? Pairing them with rice—as many delicious South Asian dishes do—will help make them a complete protein.

Lentils are also high in fiber, folate, and iron. A 2023 systematic review and meta-analysis in the journal *Advances in Nutrition* examined the impact of legume consumption on cardiometabolic health and found that consuming legumes like lentils can help prevent cardiovascular disease.

7. Quinoa

Quinoa is a plant-based complete protein, containing all the essential amino acids your body needs. Quinoa is also rich in fiber, complex carbohydrates, and vitamins and minerals like iron and magnesium. Quinoa offers around eight grams of protein per cooked cup. One study explored the effects of quinoa consumption on blood sugar and found that individuals who incorporated quinoa into their diet experienced improved blood sugar management.

Quinoa makes a fantastic base for salads or can be transformed into a tasty pilaf by sautéing onions, garlic, and vegetables.

8. Chickpeas

With approximately 15 grams of protein per cooked cup, chickpeas are a staple in vegetarian and vegan diets. They are a plant-based protein option highly nutritious and rich not only in protein, but in fiber and antioxidants such as flavonoids and polyphenols, which help protect against oxidative stress and inflammation in the body.

Chickpeas lack the sulfur-containing amino acids methionine and cystine, but you can pair chickpeas with rice, oats, or wheat to make them complete. Incorporating chickpeas into your meals can help support muscle function and promote digestive health. They can be enjoyed in many dishes such as in salads, stews, curries, hummus, or roasted as a crunchy snack.

9. Tofu

Tofu is made from soybeans and is considered a complete protein, providing all the essential amino acids your body needs. It offers approximately 10 grams of protein per 3.5-ounce serving. It is also low in saturated fat.

In addition to protein, tofu is a good source of iron, calcium, and other minerals and is also rich in plant compounds called isoflavones, which have been associated with such potential health benefits as reducing the risk of certain chronic diseases when consumed in moderation.

Tofu is versatile. It can be prepared in various ways, such as grilling, stir-frying, baking, blending into smoothies, or adding to scrambled eggs. Its mild flavor allows it to take on the flavors of other ingredients.

10. Pistachios

Pistachios are a good source of plant-based protein, healthy fats, fiber, vitamins, and minerals. They also contain antioxidants and may aid in weight management. Pistachios offer approximately six grams of protein per ounce and are a nutritious snack option that can contribute to your overall protein intake, especially when combined with other plant-based protein sources.

Pistachios can be enjoyed in various ways: mixed with other nuts and dried fruits, added to salads for a crunchy texture, incorporated into baked goods, or sprinkled on top of yogurt or salad. You can also make delicious homemade pistachio butter.

By including a diverse range of protein sources, you can ensure that you are obtaining a wide spectrum of essential amino acids and other important nutrients that are vital for optimal health and wellbeing. Each of these protein sources offers unique health benefits and nutritional profiles, contributing to a well-rounded and balanced eating routine. Individual protein needs vary based on many such as age, gender, activity level, and overall health status. For personalized protein recommendations, it's important to consult with a registered dietitian nutritionist or other licensed or certified health professional.

What to avoid?

Lots, but one group in particular is artificial sweeteners, which, unfortunately, are extensively used in food and drink.

In "This Artificial Sweetener Can Permanently Damage Your DNA, New Study 2023," Dr. Patricia Varacallo, DO, writes: "If you're proud of the strides you've made to reduce the amount of sugar you consume, major kudos—healthier habits take intention and discipline. However, that sugar substitute may not be great for you and *may* not even help stave off weight gain. In fact, a new toxicology study found that one popular low-calorie sweetener may have a major impact on your biology."

A May 2023 North Carolina State University and University of North Carolina at Chapel Hill study published in the *Journal of Toxicology and Environmental Health, Part B* revealed that digesting sucralose can lead to a "genotoxic" effect. Genotoxic is a term signifying that it disrupts DNA structure. This compound isn't just a byproduct, it's also present in minute quantities of the sweetener.

Splenda is one brand name for sucralose. Some generic sucralose brands come in yellow-colored packaging that's meant to call Splenda to mind. Sucralose is sucralose-6-acetate, a fat-soluble compound that's produced in the gut after sucralose is ingested. Previous work by the same North Carolina research team established that several such compounds are made in the gut, but the discovery of sucralose-6-acetate stands out. Susan Schiffman, PhD, a study author and adjunct professor in the joint department of biomedical engineering at NC State University and UNC at Chapel Hill, reports: "Our new work establishes that sucralose-6-acetate is genotoxic. We also found that trace amounts of sucralose-6-acetate can be found in off-the-shelf sucralose, even before it is consumed and metabolized." The implications of this discovery are not to be taken lightly. The European Food Safety Authority has a threshold of toxicological concern for all genotoxic substances of 0.15 micrograms per person daily.

Dr. Schiffman warned, "Our work suggests that the trace amounts of sucralose-6-acetate in a single, daily sucralose-sweetened drink exceed that threshold. And that's not even accounting for the amount of sucralose-6-acetate produced as metabolites after people consume sucralose." This is supported by the *in vitro* experiments the researchers conducted, exposing human blood cells to sucralose-6-acetate and monitoring for markers of genotoxicity. Schiffman said, "In short, we found that sucralose-6-acetate is genotoxic and that it effectively broke up DNA in cells that were exposed to the chemical."

Apart from the genotoxicity, Schiffman's team explored how sucralose-6-acetate affects gut health. Notably, they found that both sucralose and sucralose-6-acetate can cause a leaky gut, a condition that can lead to harmful substances being absorbed into the bloodstream."

Positive gut microbes are reduced by 50% when consuming sucralose, which also stimulates the appetite, thereby offsetting any weight-loss benefits.

The mounting evidence against sucralose and its metabolites raises many concerns about the potential health effects associated with this and similar substances. Dr. Schiffman says, "It's time to revisit the safety and regulatory status of sucralose, because the evidence is mounting that it carries significant risks." It's not just about counting calories but also about understanding what you put into your body. Dr. Schiffman's advice? "If nothing else, I encourage people to avoid products containing sucralose. It's something you should not be eating."

Francesco Branca, MD, PhD, WHO Director for Nutrition and Food Safety, explained "Replacing free sugars with [non-sugar sweeteners] does not help with weight control in the long term. People need to consider other ways to reduce free sugars intake, such as consuming food with naturally occurring sugars, like fruit, or unsweetened food and beverages.

Turns out the USA should have continued its importation of pure sugarcane from the Philippines instead of embracing sugar-free substitutes. During my research, I wanted to focused on all age groups and specifically how certain foods or behaviors had long-term effects. I identified another food to avoid: certain types of baby food. Many foods marketed to parents of infants may lead to obesity and chronic illness. Processed baby food in pouches for 6 to 36 month-old infants and sold in grocery stores failed to meet protein and sugar requirements per the world health organization. There has been a 900% increase in food-pouch consumption by infants over the last thirteen years (September 2024 WHO and George Institute researchers).

What else should parents and caregivers avoid feeding to young children? Fruit and cereal bars, including puffed snacks. Read the labels and focus more on organic foods in preference to processed foods.

Researching food can be pretty frustrating, since one study often contradicts another. The New England Journal of Medicine is a top-ranked medical source, which has been publishing since 1812. It provides clinical medical data and advice, including on food, to 175 countries. In one 2023 study, the conclusion was that coffee consumption was harmful to the heart. The study found that coffee was implicated in "cardiac ectopy and arrhythmias." Another study concluded that coffee had beneficial effects, including reduction of the incidence of diabetes due to the stimulative effects of caffeine and a resultant increase in movement and exercise.

I have discovered many additional contradictions throughout my research. Studies proved non-organic strawberries had the highest concentration of pesticides. If you are a regular consumer, over time, the life health effects are detrimental. Here is the frustrating part: properly cleaned strawberries are one of the best foods for delaying the onset of dementia. Based on the most recent studies, dementia is on the increase.

The solution is to create your own a food and drink ranking system based on your unique and specific needs. If scientific studies have produced contradictory results—as in the coffee and strawberries example—you can rank the food in the middle quartiles. If we rank the health effects of sucralose/aspartame/neotame lifetime consumption, it will rank in the bottom lowest-value quartile and should be avoided. Bottom quartile food and drinks in your personalized sort system should be avoided.

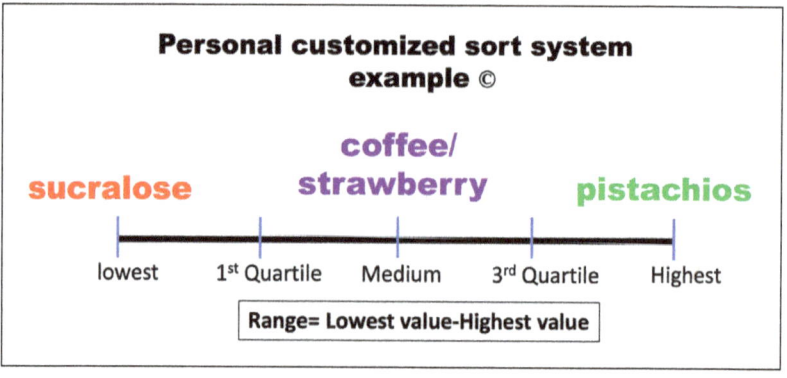

> **BEST Success Practice #27 to maximize the WHH continuum:**
> Formulate a list of the top 20 foods and drinks you consume in a week.
> Research them and sort them, using the template above. Those that fall
> into the lowest quartile on the left should be avoided. Study the DASH
> Dietary Approaches to Stop Hypertension, Mediterranean, and MIND
> (Mediterranean Intervention for Neurodegenerative Delay) diets.
> Stay away from sucralose-type artificial sweeteners.

If you find that most of your consumables fall into the lowest or left quartile, you most likely need to make some different consumption choices to maximize your WHH.

I promised you in the Introduction I would move "staccato like" from topic to topic to cover key areas to maximize your WHH continuum. Exercise is a crucial element for your success.

We all know we need to do more to get our heart rate up for at least thirty minutes a day. Since there is an inexhaustible supply of books and available data on exercise, my inclusion in this book are minimal basics already shared.

There are other ways to enhance our physical, mental and spiritual health. Some are traditional and some are less known, but scientifically proven. A great example was Ivermectin for covid. The US Food and Drug Administration, published in the National Library of Medicine details approving ivermectin as a anti-parasitic agent. Dr. Ravindra S. Godsi said "ivermectin has been used in India for years in support of curing and minimizing parasitic sickness, including covid."

Often Overlooked: The Health Benefits of Music

Okay, ready to tap your foot? I get pumped when I hear Queen's "We Are the Champions of the World." No wonder it is played in sports arena's nationwide. Same goes for "We Will We Will ROCK YOU." The emotions we experience when we hear certain songs or beats can be measurably therapeutic. I am not the only one who gets goosebumps hearing "The Star-Spangled Banner" at a hockey game or "Amazing Grace" in church. Why do those who participate in drum circles have such a strong reaction to drum beats?

Music and other sounds can calm, sooth, incite, as well as inspire and motivate. But can music and sounds heal or provide a better health outcome?

Yes.

The Cleveland Clinic referenced PubMed Health Psychology (M. DeWitte 2022), which reported that "Music therapy helps people of all ages (children, adolescents and adults) and from all walks of life. It may benefit many different aspects of your well-being, including: mental, emotional, physical, social, and cognitive.

I interviewed Jessica Lee, a jazz/blues advisor, writer, producer, composer, and vocalist. She is also an entrepreneur, who holds a law degree from Duke. I asked her if there is any basis for the healing powers of music or sound?

"As a professional singer with over twenty years of performance experience," she responded, "I am still amazed at the healing power of song and sound. A few of my favorite secrets of music's power are listed below, which I have learned from my invaluable music mentors":

The Power of Humming

Simply humming for 10-15 minutes each day stimulates the vagus nerve, which runs through the neck, and has been reported to decrease depression and anxiety, reduce blood pressure, lower heart rate, improve sleep and mood, increase immune system strength, and more! Each morning [Lee reports], I wake up, sip a coffee with brown sugar and cinnamon added, and I hum away! Deep breathing and the vagus nerve stimulation of humming are simple pathways to better mind-body health.

The Power of the Song "Play List"

Creating a play list with a) three songs with sad lyrics followed by b) three songs that have lyrics of faith and hope followed by c) three songs with joyful lyrics . . . has been shown to decrease depression and anxiety and improve mood. This play list is customized by each person to include songs that he or she likes to sing from any genre of music. The emphasis is on the lyrics and energy of the songs, which begin with sadness and the blues, move into flickers of faith and hope, and end in joy and concepts of unconditional love given and received.

The Power of Rhythm

Years ago, I participated in a two-day HealthRHYTHMS Basic Training presented by Remo Drums. This program helps trainers to understand the science of the mind-body connection in the context of rhythm making with hand drums. This program, which involves communicating concepts in a small group using phrases chanted in rhythm with the hand drumming, has been proven to:

- Lower levels of cortisol (stress hormone)
- Increase Natural Killer (NK) Cell Activity
- Decrease burnout
- Improve mood state
- Improve anger control
- Improve school performance
- Decrease levels of depression and improve self-concept
- Improve interpersonal problems
- And more . . !

This program consists of one hour of group hand drumming a week for six weeks (led by a trained facilitator), with the positive mind-body impact lasting months after the program's sixth and final session.

The Power of Gathering & Inspiration

Even more than the benefits of song and sound is the power of beautiful Jazz & Blues-based music (consisting of interesting and sometimes complex rhythms, harmonies, melodies, and lyrics, some of which are repetitive and form-based and some of which are improvised) to bring people of all ages, stages, and walks of life together and to uplift and inspire.

Jessica Lee went on to say, "One summer evening I was singing an outdoor concert, and two men who had been fighting bitterly on social media were seated at tables next to each other. I saw this from the stage, and I intentionally began singing songs with lyrics of friendship, love, and forgiveness. By the end of the show, these two men had become friends once again! They were laughing and talking at the show's end, and the polarization of their social media messaging seemed to now be forgotten and a thing of the past.

Equally moving to me was the time that a gentleman walked up to me after a Jazz & Blues show. He told me: "Your music saved my life." I was shocked and asked him how the music had saved him. He confided in me that shortly after both of his parents had passed he had become depressed. He decided to end his life one day. That evening he was having dinner with friends and heard some music. He found a small combo performing in a nearby room, and I was singing. He sat and listened for thirty minutes. He said: "Something in me changed." He then explained that the music was so beautiful to him that it touched his spirit and reminded him that – although his parents were no longer alive – there is still much beauty in this world, beauty to live for. He changed his mind that evening and decided to live.

So, I do believe that the power of song and sound is profound. The old phrase "whistle while you work" may have some wisdom hidden . . . and perhaps the phrase should include some humming too!".

A deeper look into sound and music therapy from a more scientific approach reported in 2024 by Flora Zhao in, *The Epoch Times*:

- A gray-haired older woman sat motionless with her gaze lowered. In the late stages of dementia, she no longer spoke to others or made eye contact.
- When Ayako Yonetani started playing the violin, the woman slowly lifted her head.
- "Her mouth moved, and her eyes brightened as if she heard my music and was trying to follow it," recounted Ms. Yonetani, a concert artist and professor of violin and viola at the University of Central Florida School of Performing Arts.
- Those who spent time with the older woman were astonished. "They had never seen her react like this before," she said. But this was only one of many times that Ms. Yonetani had seen such a thing.

One study published in the 1990s in The Journal of Nature drew attention. Three groups of participants were instructed to either sit in silence, listen to a relaxation tape, or listen to Mozart's Sonata for Two Pianos in D Major (K448). Ten minutes later, the group who listened to Mozart's music showed a significant improvement in spatial IQ score—nearly 10 points higher than the other two groups. Since then, scientists have used Mozart and other classical music in various experiments on animals and humans, obtaining similar results: Listening to classical music or learning to play an instrument leads to higher school grades and stronger spatial reasoning skills, reduces the risk of brain atrophy, and slows cognitive decline.

In an interview with *the Epoch Times,* Kiminobu Sugaya, who has a doctorate in pharmacology and is a professor of medicine at the University of Central

Florida College of Medicine and head of neuroscience at the Burnett School of Biomedical Sciences, remarked that the "Mozart effect" truly exists. In experiments with local community residents, he found that when this type of classical music was played, "we saw a 50 percent increase in brain function."

Certain types of classical music not only enhance cognitive abilities but are also used to treat brain disorders such as epilepsy or Parkinson's disease. "The Mozart effect is clear evidence that you can alter the brain function and abnormalities with music," Dr. Michael Trimble, professor emeritus of neurology and neuropsychiatry at the University College London Institute of Neurology and a Fellow of the Royal College of Physicians, told The Epoch Times. Sometimes, epilepsy difficult to control with medication can be managed with carefully selected and edited classical music to "train" the brains of epilepsy patients, normalizing their brain waves and diminishing electroencephalographic abnormalities.

A study published in Interdisciplinary Science Reviews in 2022 indicated that "to this date, [Mozart's] K448 and K545 have remained the only anti-epileptic music selections that have been verified by repeated experiments." The study also cited data from a 2020 meta-analysis, which found that "approximately 84 percent of participants in the reviewed studies exhibited significant reductions in epileptic brain activity while listening to Mozart's K448." As people age, their brains gradually shrink, resulting in a gradual loss of neurons. However, one study found that in orchestral musicians, certain parts of their brains do not shrink over time and can even increase in size.

MRI tests conducted under Mr. Sugaya's supervision also produced similar findings. The brain is composed of gray matter and white matter. Gray matter, consisting of neurons, has been observed to increase in volume following musical activities. A Ms. James, who was interviewed by Kiminobu Sugaya, explained that this increase is not due to an increase in neurons but rather "because the connections between the neurons get stronger." On the other hand, white matter refers to short or long axons of neurons, which act together as the brain's communication network, similar to how local roads and highways connect different cities. When listening to music, the network becomes better built and better oriented.

Additionally, the hippocampus, a deep brain structure associated with cognition, memory, and emotion, "lights up" when people listen to music attentively, said Ms. James. The hippocampus plays a critical role in cognition, memory, and emotion. Our memory of music seems to last longer than memories of everyday events or experiences from certain stages of life. This phenomenon explains why some older individuals can effortlessly recall and sing songs or melodies they enjoyed in their youth. The hippocampus also helps people understand music. If this part of the brain is not engaged, one will not comprehend what they hear, It's like listening to a foreign language.

There are more ominous tunes being sung in many households and businesses and on many social networks.

The lyrics to this "song" include the words; Cyber-attack and what is AI implementation going to do our world. I struggled on where to introduce this topic as it impacts each of the WHH continuum. Recently with disturbing regularity, we have experienced a breach of our most private and sacred data. Personal medical records have been stolen from our doctors, hospitals, Insurance companies, and health care administrators by nefarious cyber criminals. What happens when our doctor patient private relationship is violated and the data is sold on the black market? Happiness, health and potentially wealth are impacted by the breach. How do we minimize the massive negative stress and anxiety? First, we must understand the problem. No longer can we depend on our healthcare administration doctors and hospitals to keep safe and secure our medical records.

Strictly from a health perspective, we need to have a backup plan for the digital world we live in.

Given what has happened in 2024 at the Kaiser Permanente, Change Healthcare, and more recently at Ascension hospital networks, we must fend for ourselves.

Let me explain…Kaiser Permanente has forty hospitals and 618 medical offices. Ascension owns 140 hospitals. Both were cyber attacked and lost access to millions of patient's data and operational disruption occurred. This speaks to how vulnerable the US health care system has become.

Administrators were telling patients to provide their own detailed medical records before surgeries! This is a wakeup call to do just that. Keep a hardcopy of your and those you advocate through legal healthcare proxy estate plans. Ask your healthcare provider for the data before you leave from your appointment. Store the hard copies under lock and key preferably in a fire proof file.

BEST Success Practice #28 to maximize the WHH continuum: Whenever you visit a doctor, dentist, hospital, or clinic, make sure you leave with a copy of the tests, diagnostics, and all images. Keep a list all medications, allergies, past surgeries. Gone are the days of trusting medical administrators to keep our records. Keep a file for each family member and be prepared to advocate and articulate details.

In the Happiness section upcoming, we will share more on cyber fraud awareness and prevention as it relates to your medical records.

My research touched on some of the more salient points of what you can do to bring about optimum health outcomes. By no means have I explored all aspects of personal health, as there are many other sources available. My interest here is about the correlation of Health to Wealth and Happiness. With this purpose, I spent weeks researching many products. The last of these I want to comment on are parabens, a group of chemicals that are used as preservatives in many products, including pharmaceuticals, cosmetics, infant care products (such as baby wipes), and foods—as well as many other products.

For years, we have been applying sunscreen to help prevent skin cancer, which is a good and necessary thing to do. Yet applying these products comes with a potential danger caused by the parabens or p-hydroxybenzoates, used to preserve the products. Parabens are a class of preservatives that have been used since the 1920s to prevent bacteria and fungi from contaminating a wide range of products. Despite their long track record, parabens have not been adequately tested for health safety. The Cleveland Clinic November 20, 2024 as stated in their Health Essentials Newsletter, parabens have been shown to cause hormone issues especially in pre-puberty girls, fertility issues, premature births, and some cancers. The studies continue.

The alternatives to paraben-infused products are plentiful. Look up paraben-free products with your Duck Duck Go search engine. As you consume or acquire products, get into the habit of reading the labels. What additives does the product contain? What is the product's country of origin?

BEST Success Practice # 29 to maximize the WHH continuum: Use paraben-free skin care, shampoo, shaving cream, and sunscreen products. Throw out any products with paraben's including some cereals, beer, frozen dairy products and flavored syrups. Read the labels of the products you use or consume.

Faith and Health

At the intersection of Health and Happiness, as it turns out, are church services. If you have faith, going to church, temple, synagogue, mosque, or meeting house— even just for the sake of going—may well have significant health benefits.

A study by the world's foremost expert on longevity, Dan Buettner, interviewed and studied 263 people, 100 years old and older. Blue Zones founder, Dan Buettner is an explorer, National Geographic Fellow, award-winning journalist and producer, and *New York Times*-bestselling author. He identified the five original "blue zones," the places in the world with the healthiest, longest-living populations, including Okinawa, Japan; Sardinia, Italy; Nicoya, Costa Rica; Ikaria, Greece; and Loma Linda, California.

What follows are some of his findings and those from other sources, as reported by Ben Johnson in *The Daily Signal.*

Attending church services may open the door to eternal life—but it will also extend your life on earth even more than diet or exercise, according to the foremost expert on global longevity.

Dan Buettner, who won three Emmy Awards for his groundbreaking 2023 documentary *Live to 100: Secrets of the Blue Zones*—which I recommend to you—revealed the deep benefits that faith in God renders to those who want to live a long and prosperous life. Although America faces an epidemic of chronic diseases, "only about 20% of how long you live is dictated by your genes," Buettner told the Fox Business Channel's *Mornings with Maria* on August 30, 2024. A healthy lifestyle incorporating diet, exercise, and stress management means the average person can live "12 more years in good health."

But the statistics Buettner shared indicated that an active faith in God, in community with others, including weekly church attendance, had potentially the biggest impact on extending earthly life. Buettner's documentary investigated regions in the world known for having the longest average lifespan. Researchers interviewed 263 centenarians and found all but five "belonged to some faith-based community." The healthiest elderly had a common characteristic: "having a faith. We know people who go to church—or temple, or even mosque—and show up four times per month are living four to 14 years longer than people who aren't." The figure came from Buettner's study finding that regular church attendance lengthened the average American's life by seven years—and 14 years for African Americans.

These numbers clearly exceed those achieved by other, more intuitive life-hacks, including regular exercise and diet. "For a 20-year-old," Buettner told Fox's Maria Bartiromo, "if you move away from the standard American diet towards a Blue Zone diet—which is to say whole food, plant-based—it's worth about 10 years of extra life expectancy, and for a 60-year-old, it's still worth about six years."

One food stood out above others in Buettner's findings: beans. "If you're eating a cup of beans a day, it's worth about four extra years of life expectancy over getting your protein from less healthy sources." Buettner raved about minestrone soup: "Every time that you mix a grain with a bean, they come together, they make a whole protein. ... These are cheap foods, they're shelf stable, and every American can afford them."

Those in the healthiest lifestyle moved organically, about every 20 minutes, without sitting for long periods of time. But anyone can benefit from simple exercise, such as walking. "If you have zero physical activity in your life, you can raise your life expectancy three years if you just walk 20 minutes a day," Buettner told Bartiromo.

Strong family relationships also add years to your life. Centenarians agree on "putting family first, keeping your aging parents nearby, investing in your partner, investing in your children. ... People who are in a committed relationship are living anywhere from two to six years longer than people who are alone in life," Buettner said.

If you're keeping track, you can add three years to your life with exercise, four years by eating beans, six years by being in a committed relationship, six to 10 years by eating a whole foods and plant-based diet, and seven to 14 years by going to church every week. These are not all cumulative but will increase your well-being.

Another aspect of church attendance that may lengthen your life is stress management. A key factor in living to 100 is what Buettner calls "downshifting: either through prayer, meditation, or simply expressing gratitude before a meal." Regular prayer incorporates "making sure our day has certain times where we lower the stress of the human condition, lower inflammation."

Environmental factors—including the people and businesses around you— also play a role. "If you live in a neighborhood with more than five fast food restaurants within half a mile of your home, you're about 35% more likely to be obese than if there are fewer than three," Buettner adds. "If your three best friends are obese and unhealthy, you are 150% more likely to be overweight yourself."

The Buettner documentary project is but one of many studies that have found physical, mental, and psychological benefits in faith, Bible or other scripture study, and church attendance:

- Surgeon General Vivek Murthy issued a report in March 2023 stating that an epidemic of loneliness has produced health impacts "even greater than that associated with obesity and physical inactivity." Americans' health may be undermined "by their declining participation in "[r]eligious or faith-based groups."

- Regular "religious practice has significant effects" in reducing the odds of dying from suicides, drug poisonings, and alcoholic liver disease, according to the 2023 study.

* The Blue Zones commend cultures that promote a sense of purpose. "[R]eligious Americans tend to believe their life is meaningful more often than do those who are not religious," the 2023 study reported.
* Americans who believe in God and value marriage are more likely to be "very happy" than isolated secularists, according to a *Wall Street Journal-NORC* poll. While only a thin sliver of Americans (12%) consider themselves "very happy," 68% of the happiest people surveyed say they believe in God.
* Eighty-two percent of Christians describe their outlook as optimistic and take pride in their church, according to the 2023 study.
* Christians who regularly read the Bible report a higher score on the Human Flourishing Index—which measures "happiness & life satisfaction," "mental & physical health," "meaning & purpose," "character & virtue," "close societal relationships" and "financial & material stability"—than nonpracticing Christians or the non-religiously unaffiliated, per the 2023 Harvard Institute for Quantitative Social Science study.
* "Young-adult Gen-Xers in the *strongly religious* class across the three measurements generally reported better mental health when they reached established adulthood than those in the *nonreligious* class," reported a 2022 Syracuse University study.
* Women who attend church at least once a week had a 68% lower chance of dying a "death of despair" (death from suicide, drug and alcohol poisoning, or liver disease) than non-churchgoers; men who frequently go to church lower their risk of such a death by one-third, according to a 2020 *Harvard T.H. Chan School of Public Health* study.
* Americans who attended religious services regularly were 44% more likely to say they were "very happy" than the religiously inactive, concluded a 2019 Pew Research Center survey.
* Even if they leave behind religious practices, "people who attended weekly religious services or practiced daily prayer or meditation in their youth reported greater life satisfaction and positivity in their 20s—and were less likely to subsequently have depressive symptoms, smoke, use illicit drugs, or have a sexually transmitted infection—than people raised with less regular spiritual habits," a 2018 study from Harvard University's T.H. Chan School of Public Health found.
* Research by Vanderbilt University found people who attend regular s ervices at a church, synagogue or mosque are less stressed and live longer. The study, focused on middle-aged (40-65) men and women, reduce their risk for mortality by 55%. Professor Marino Bruce

authored the study, *"Church Attendance, Allostatic Load and Mortality in Middle Aged Adults with Keith Norris professor of Medicine at the David Geffen School of Medicine UCLA, 2017."* They surveyed 5000 people of all races and both sexes. SUMMARY: Compassionate thinking to improve our lives and the lives of others through a connection to a body larger than ourselves, reduces stress.

- Attending church more than once a week reduces a woman's likelihood of premature death by 33%, a 2016 Harvard study concluded.

I have in my church, St. Martin De Porres, in Jensen Beach, Florida, a wonderful lady who is 106 years old. Up until recently, she got around with a cane; now she uses a walker. She is the mother of one of our priests, who is semi-retired. She walks down the center aisle and sits in the front row every week. What an inspiration for a life well lived!

A whole ecosystem of change methods is available to extend heath outcomes. The Blue Zone lifestyle is one such approach. I am not endorsing it, but it is one of the most visible of many approaches.

All the research and experiences indicate that having true wealth and health will support an ecosystem in which happiness will flourish. And, counterintuitively, happiness can be achieved without monetary wealth or even good health. I think back to my silent retreat with the Benedictine Nuns at St Emma's. They exuded joy and happiness despite health issues and their vow of poverty. As a state of mind, and free will, happiness can reside within anyone.

Chapter 3

What Is True Happiness?

Let's explore the spiritual side of Happiness first....

Christopher Kaczor in his "How to Find Happiness" (*Columbia Magazine*, 2010) wrote, "We all want to be happy. Every day, in whatever we do, we seek this goal—one that we share with every other person on the planet. But what exactly is happiness? And how can we find it?"

Each of us has our own experience and examples of happiness. Society's definitions of happiness can be manipulative and are generally focused on secular humanism. This focus limits the characterization of true happiness. We have all seen commercials of "happy" smiling people on a beach dancing and drinking this or that brand of beer. The producer of the commercial wants us to believe drinking a beer provides happiness.

Specificity notwithstanding, our humanity produces a general level of what is typically defined as happiness. Regardless of where we live, who we are, whom we associate with, there are general definitions of happiness that traverse the human condition. Can happiness be singular and specific to each person?

To answer this question, Sonja Lyubomirsky, in *The How of Happiness: A Scientific Approach to Getting the Life You Want* (Penguin, 2007), examines hundreds of empirical studies. She writes, "Studies show that 50 percent of individual differences in happiness are determined by genes, 10 percent by life circumstances, and 40 percent by our intentional activities." She continues:

Some people, it turns out, are naturally more optimistic, joyful and upbeat. Therefore, we should not feel bad if we find ourselves with a less cheerful temperament than others. At the same time, circumstances of life — great wealth, good weather, a promotion at work — have a relatively minor effect on our long-term level of happiness. Changing our circumstances will only slightly affect our outlook, as we quickly adapt to our new circumstances. Yet, while we cannot alter our genetic back-ground, and altering our circumstances will not make much of a lasting difference to our happiness, we can dramatically change our intentional activities — that is, our goals in life. Engaging in work toward meaningful goals that strengthen our relationships with others can make us much happier. And regardless of our circumstances, we can become happier if we choose our priorities wisely.

The WHH continuum best success practices identified throughout and summarized in the last chapter will help shape our priorities and set our goals.

"Whoever is happy will make others happy too. "
"The best way to cheer yourself is to try to cheer someone else up."
—*Mark Twain*

In his *Columbia Magazine* article, Christoper Kaczor goes on to cite an interesting source:

Drawing on the work of St. Thomas Aquinas, Jesuit Father Robert J. Spitzer distinguishes four levels of happiness in his book Healing the Culture (Ignatius, 2000). Level one happiness is bodily pleasure obtained by drink, food, drugs or sex. Level two happiness has to do with competitive advantage in terms of money, fame, power, popularity or other material goods. Level three happiness involves loving and serving other people. And level four happiness is found in loving and serving God. Although we may desire each level of happiness, not every level provides equal and lasting contentment.

We are not guaranteed any level of happiness and must work at creating our own proper balance of WHH. As Kaczor writes, "Why don't additional amounts of money make us happier in a lasting way? Research indicates that we eventually get used to whatever level of financial success we achieve and then begin to seek higher levels of affluence." As the Rolling Stones sang, "I can't get no satisfaction." The lyric is an expression of our human nature with very little of our spiritual nature. Kazor continues:

We tend to compare ourselves with those who are richer than we are, rather than the vast numbers that live in poverty. The average middle-class person today enjoys luxury and comfort unknown even to medieval kings.
But maybe having not just more money, but lots more money, would lead to higher levels of happiness. Empirical research is not clear. Lottery winners— after the shock wears off—report being no happier than they were before win-

ning. Fortune 500 executives on the whole have average levels of happiness, and 37 percent of rich business leaders are less happy than the average person.

Research by financial advisors make it clear that happiness does increase when one crosses the $15 million liquid assets threshold, but Kaczor notes that "St. Thomas Aquinas pointed out more than seven centuries ago, we want many things that no amount of money can buy. And we cannot find true happiness in more fame, power or 'winning' of any kind." He continues:

There is nothing inherently wrong with worldly success or with bodily pleasures, such as eating. Rather, the trouble comes when we think that these are the ultimate goals of life. Even if we had all the money in the world, all the bodily pleasure we could handle and all the worldly success possible, we cannot be happy without true friendship and true love. Happiness, Aristotle taught, is activity in accordance with virtue. In order for us to be objectively happy, we need to engage in activities that accord with virtue, especially the virtue of charity. Without choosing higher levels of happiness, even if we subjectively feel good (for a while), we are missing out on objectively being happy. …Commenting on Aristotle, who argued that human happiness necessarily involves friendships, St. Thomas Aquinas added that we can be friends not only with other human beings but also with God. Psychological research confirms this ancient wisdom. The happiest people have meaningful work that serves others (activity in accordance with virtue), and they have strong, loving relationships with their family, friends and God. On average, people who practice their faith report greater happiness than those who do not.

Kaczor researched Wendell JeanPierre, noted Lecturer who said:

The Bible doesn't promote a morbid obsession with death. It reminds us to be honest about the inevitable (Memento Mori). The wise and the elderly remember the brevity of life. Exercise and eating right will probably increase our quality of life. Modern medicine may grant us a few more heartbeats. But the best way to live is to be honest about what's most important.

The constant worry of many today about illness, pandemics, loss of income, set-backs from unforeseen natural disaster, is an obsession which takes away from life even that little material happiness which good health and proper living can bring. As a result, modern man lives with the heavy yoke of fear around his neck.

This is the bitter fruit of living without God. If the spiritual, everlasting part of our makeup i.e. the soul, was wearing the crown of existence we would not tremble as we do. The body is perishable, temporary and always com-

*plains about discomfort. I feel bad says the body! I believe this too shall pass
says the soul.*

*Let us trust our faith and not our feelings. Living in the spirit is not easy
in a culture that is concerned and anxious only about giving joy and pleasure
to the body. But with help from the Lord the weak becomes strong, the fearful
become heroic and the self-serving, becomes charitable in service to others.
By putting God first, it becomes easier to remove the emotional and spiritual
burdens that weigh us down.*

Studies show that those who practice a religious faith live happier and healthier
lives than those who do not.

**BEST Success Practice #30 to maximize the WHH continuum are:
People of faith live happier lives and less worry by practicing
their faith in congregation with others.**

I remember a Power Ball lottery winner who lived about 100 miles away from
me. Prior to winning, he was a successful contractor. He won $300 million, or
$113 million after taxes. It ruined his life. He made one bad choice after another.
It is shocking that so many people who suddenly come into wealth are miserable.
Life changing? Yes, but not in a good way. This Mega Lottery winner ended up
losing everything. Clearly, he and his family's WHH continuum was out of balance. He was one of many whose sudden windfall derails his life's journey toward
maximum WHH.

I am not advocating against the acquisition of wealth. I am advocating for the
right balance of Wealth, Health, and Happiness. We need to acquire, retain, and
grow wealth to be able to give it away if we choose. In one of my religious education classes at Providence College, I well remember the professor speaking about
how the Bible was most likely interpreted over the millennia, from language to
language. Hebrew, Greek, Aramaic, Latin to English. The professor used an example from the Gospel of Matthew: "Truly I tell you, it is hard for someone who
is rich to enter the kingdom of heaven. Again I tell you, it is easier for a camel to
go through the eye of a needle than for someone who is rich to enter the kingdom
of God."

This biblical passage has always bothered me, as I wanted to be rich. The professor said that in ancient times, the "eye of the needle" referred to the entrance
to a walled city with a semi-dome higher than the surrounding wall, suitable for a

camel to walk through, on the next page. The person riding the camel must bow down to the level of the camel's head or risk a blow. It's ok to be rich as long as you are humble, bowing your head in thanks and with humility.

We should feel better about pursuing goals to be wealthy. It is what we do with our wealth for the good of others, not just ourselves, that provides satisfaction and happiness.

"Happiness wasn't about feeling good. It was about doing good."
—Jeffrey Rosen, President of the National Constitution Center

As individuals, families, and business owners we all have life priorities. In my research, I have discovered that very few of us include saving for retirement as a life priority. People think about it from time to time, yet a well-funded retirement can be the difference between maximizing WHH and failing to do so.

Why isn't it a priority for most people? Why is it that 28 percent of the US population has 0 retirement savings—ZERO—according to *Motley Fool* (2024). My research indicates that anywhere between 28 percent and 50 percent of Americans have no retirement savings. Life gets in the way, and saving for retirement falls further down the life-priority to do list. The realization hits some of us when we are in our late forties and early fifties. So, we begin playing catch up. Investment requires time, and time is far more precious than money. We must change our values, placing retirement saving ahead of a trip to Europe or buying a car for a sixteen-year-old, or buying a new car instead of a used car, or dining out, or making "retail therapy" purchases. This change can be achieved by cultivating a new mindset. If you don't save a little each month when you are young, you will need to save thousands a month when you are in your forties. With time short, it's the only way to save an amount sufficient to retire comfortably. Sadly, some people must work way past normal retirement age. Some can never retire. To be sure, some folks do not want to retire, and that is fine if it is a desire freely arrived at. But to be forced to work because there is no more time to save and invest—is this happiness? Of course not.

Being both happy and wealthy is possible.

A fifty-year life study published in Economics of Education Review (volume 17, Issue 3, June 1998) by Joop Hartog and Hessel Oosterbeek looked at a group of Dutch people born in the early 1940s and followed them until they were fifty years old. I've noticed in my research that the Dutch are quite focused on defining happiness, and this study is one of many examples of this interest. They Hartog and Oosterbeek studied family dynamics and IQ. "The most fortunate group is the group with a non-vocational intermediate level education. They score highest on health, wealth and happiness."

This study ended more than twenty-five years ago. More recent trends suggest a slight shift away from general college degrees with more emphasis on specific vocations after college or no college at all.

Is going to and graduating from college a necessary ingredient to maximizing happiness and becoming a millionaire? Increasingly, over the last ten years, with the amount of dept incurred and time spent in college experience, many graduates find themselves in a deep financial hole upon graduation. Let's do some math. According to the *US News and World Report magazine article on USNEWS. com 2025*, the average public college is $11,000 per year and the private college is $43,505. Housing, food, transportation, insurance, textbooks, social events, and "party money" is all extra cost averaging over $8,000 per year. Let's next take a simple average of public and private cost. $43,505+11,000=54,505/2=$27,252+ $8,000= $35,252. TOTAL estimate per year x 4 years of college equals **$141,000**. This does not include the interest cost to borrow the money, assumes no scholarships and does not account for the lost time value of money opportunity costs.

Contrast this scenario with an April 2024 report from Fox News Digital:

> Welding is a profitable career that can provide America's youth with a steady income free of debt in a trade that is in high demand in the market. A leader in the industry, Tyler Sasse, the owner and founder of Western Welding Academy (WWA) in Gillette, Wyoming, told Fox News Digital that social media has allowed the welding school to grow and spread the word about the "incredible" opportunity that welding provides. We started with ten welding booths and about ten students, and now the school runs 24 hours a day [in] three, eight-hour shifts and 98% of our students come from all across the country," he said. "You don't have to go to college to get a really, really good career, you spent six months of your life to make $100,000, which is, if you

got the work ethic, the accountability, the integrity to do it, it's incredible the money that you can make, and we tell those stories all day, every day." He reflected on the colleges that shut down their campuses during the COVID-19 outbreak, but still expected students to pay full price at the same time that artificial intelligence (AI) was really breaking into the mainstream market.

The April 2024 news report continues with Tyler Sasse, who says:
"For three generations, we've been telling our kids, if you want to be s omething in life, you need to go to college and now, a lot of them are out in the marketplace really struggling because AI is just taking over," Sasse said. "The accounting functions, the banking functions, a lot of these white-collar jobs or even engineering ... AI is decimating a lot of these white collar jobs, but it doesn't matter how rich or poor you are, you still need a toilet, you still want to live in a house, you still want all these things, you want to put gas in your car and those are made possible by welders and blue collar people."

Let's continue and compare the cost of the college degree math previously calculated with a welding trade diploma. Using the welder example above, the cost for the 6-month training for the 18 year old out of high school is $35,000 (includes housing costs). I will round up to $40,000 for incidentals. In a perfect scenario for illustrative purposes, the student graduates in 6 months at 18.5 years old with a job paying $100,000 per year. Lets assume the student can save $50,000/year through 22.5 years of age will total $200,000 saved minus $40,000 tuition=$160,000. Next the 22.5 year-old welder makes a one-time investment of the $160,000 in a S&P 500 low cost index fund. Let's assume an 8% compounded annual return with dividends reinvested for 40 years. The investment total at the welders age 62.5 will be worth $3,475,920 dollars. No other investment required.

Contrast the 22 year-old college graduate situation who has a $141,000 debt. The average starting salary for a college graduate is $77,000 per *Thomas Caldwell Louisiana State University December 2024 research article.* The college graduate saves 20% before taxes, expenses and student loan debt or $15,400 per year. Saving 15,400 per year for 40 years at the same 8% compound annual rate as the welder, the college graduate will have saved $4,348,000 at age 62. Almost one million dollars more than the welder! Not so fast....the big difference is the welder made a one-time investment where the college graduate made yearly investments for 40 years.

If the welder at age 22.5 continued to invest the same yearly amount as the college graduate of $15,400, the welder will have saved the same $4,348,000 PLUS the $3,475,920 totaling $7,823,920 at age 62. The power of the Rule of 72 and compound interest and the power of time value of money. The welder had a four-year head start.

Welder $7,824,920

College Graduate $4,348,000

These hypothetical examples assume no increases in pay or savings for the welder and college graduate.

Many so-called college degreed or white collar jobs may be supplanted by AI. Companies like Google (Alphabet), Microsoft, and global chip manufacturers are building the infrastructure necessary to launch AI solutions. This is not going to go away but will fundamentally change many professions and open up new career frontiers.

The fifty-year life study published In Economics of Education Review (volume 17, Issue 3, June 1998) by Joop Hartog and Hessel Oosterbeek goes on to say, "We find that IQ affects health, but not wealth or happiness. Family background level increases wealth, but neither health nor happiness. With a father who worked independently, health, wealth and happiness are higher. Women are a miracle: compared with men, they are less wealthy, equally healthy but they are definitely happier."

The conclusion of this 50 year study, 25 years ago, indicates the more we are open to learning and applying what we learn, like the rule of 72, the more likelihood we will enjoy maximum Wealth, Health and Happiness.

Iain Murray, OP-EDS Competitive Enterprise Institute CEI.org, wrote in *Health Wealth and Happiness (10/14/2004):*

The argument, laid out in a article from The Wall Street Journal, comes from a recent re-evaluation of international surveys of happiness, which generally use a seven-point scale where "1" equates to "not at all satisfied with my life" and "7" equates to completely satisfied. The analysis found that the consistent correlation between a nation's GDP (Gross domestic product-defined by a nations total monetary value of all finished goods and services produced) and its happiness level is seemingly illusory. The Journal summarized, "[T]he money-can-buy-happiness idea ... ignores one thing. Wealthy nations tend to be democracies that respect human rights and have a fair legal system, good health care, and effective, honest government. All of these contribute to well-being.

Yet this assumes that one person's happiness is interchangeable with another's. At one level, this is true, but would a happy millionaire be as happy if he switched places with a Masai tribesman? While some would be, it is probably safe to say that most would not. The question gets more interesting when asked the other way round. We have empirical evidence in the form of immigration statistics that people from the poorer countries want to enjoy the benefits of higher GDPs. Very few of them return home to a supposedly equal state of happiness.

It should be apparent, then, that a "happiness point" in Calcutta India might be worth somewhat less than a happiness point in Manhattan NYNY.

Murray concluded:

A survey of economic freedom by the Dallas-based National Center for Policy Analysis concludes that free economies not only grow GDP, but provide the following benefits: life expectancy at birth is 76 years in the free countries, 54 years in the least free ones; infant mortality is 9 times lower in the freest quintile than in the least free; the freer countries do better in health, education, living standards and other measures; the free ones have less corruption in business and government; and there is a correlation between economic freedom and political rights and civil liberties.

Health, wealth, and happiness go together. It is economic freedom, not social justice policies, that best guarantees all three.

BEST Success Practice #31 to maximize the WHH continuum are: Pursue and vote for more policies and laws that promote economic freedoms, not social justice policies.

In The International Journal of Indian Psychology, Dr. Kumud Kumari published "The Concept of Happiness in India" (December 31, 2022). He wrote that "happiness" is not commonly understood among people across different societies and cultures, even though several research studies reveal that it has a universal appeal across the world. Almost everywhere and everyone wants to be happy. People who are already happy search for more happiness in life, while those who are unhappy wonder how others can enjoy their lives despite so much hardship and problems all around. There are others who have attained the summit of their career and have more worldly possessions than they ever dreamed of but still feel hollow, incomplete, or not in control. Even in high-income group families, or in the case of successful businesspeople, or people in any society that is "very developed materially," the proportion of wealthy unhappy people remains higher than those who are less financially well off. Under the facade of external affluence, many such people tend to undergo mental strife within, which contributes to their frustration, pointless quarrels, addiction to drugs, alcoholism, that sometimes even leads to suicide.

Globally, several research studies have shown that when asked to rank in order of priority their life desires, people rank their "quest for happiness" at or near the top of the list, well above the worldly possessions such as wealth, fame, status, a good job, big house, and so on. This holds true for individuals across ages, regions, religions, cultures, races, and lifestyles (World Happiness Report, 2012).

Socrates and his student Plato tried to view happiness from an objective and absolute standpoint, by suggesting that happiness was the "secure enjoyment of what is good and beautiful" Happiness has been termed the "holy grail of human existence, the be-all and end-all of life." Aristotle called it the "goal of all goals."

Many of us who started with nothing, placed great emphasis and devoted much time to acquisition. Acquisition of money, possessions, and fame became a perceived pathway to happiness. Those who already had money or considered themselves "loaded" looked happy and may well have been. Once most of us attain a comfortable level of materialistic success, we do realize a level of happiness, and studies indicate that monetary wealth does provide happiness—at least to a certain level, after which comes a leveling-off effect. Pursuing monetary wealth as the sole or main strategy for attaining happiness has its downsides. For some, this life strategy causes fear and provokes illogical actions.

A happiness and economic survey was conducted online within the United States by Qualtrics on behalf of Intuit Credit Karma between November 3, 2023 and November 9, 2023 among 1,004 adults ages eighteen and older. The results, published on the Intuit Credit Karma website, November 16, 2023, reveal the top economic concerns among Americans: inflation (56%), cost-of-living increases (50%), and unaffordable housing (23%). Of those who are concerned about the economy, nearly half (48%) say that not having enough money to afford necessities like food, clothing and rent worries them the most about how a poor economy could impact them, followed by going into debt (34%) and not being able to spend money on things that bring them happiness (30%).

Younger generations are also concerned about how the challenging economy will impact their future job prospects, earning potential, and happiness. Nearly a quarter of Gen Z respondents (23%) say they're most worried about a lack of high-paying jobs, decreasing wages (21%), and generally poor job security (16%).

The conclusion is not hard to reach: Americans are worried about their money. According to the Qualtrics study, two thirds of Americans say the economy gives them anxiety about their finances, with Gen Z and millennials being most likely to report feelings of financial anxiety (71%).

To cope, many Americans are doom spending (27%). For the purposes of the Qualtric study, "doom spending" was defined as spending money despite concerns about the economy and foreign affairs to cope with stress. This phenomenon, most common among younger generations (35% of Gen Z and 43% of millennials), has risen at the same time as Americans' concerns about the economy have gone up (64%).

During late 2023 and early 2024, half of Americans in the Qualtrics study reported their financial situation had worsened, with 42% saying they struggled to afford enough food for themselves and/or their household and another 56% living paycheck to paycheck. Yet, more than a quarter (27%) of Americans said they were spending more money now than they had six months earlier. This was especially true among Gen Z and millennial, one-third of whom (33% of Gen Z and 34% of millennials) reported that their spending had gone up over the prior six months. This increase in spending correlated to a rise in debt among consumers.

According to the study, nearly one third (32%) of Americans' debt level had increased over the prior six months with millennials and Gen X-ers being the most likely to report increased debt levels, 38% and 35% respectively. Of those with debt (74%), a quarter estimated they currently held more than $10,000 in debt, a significant amount, especially amid record-high interest rates.

Doom spending may also impact the savings rate among Americans. Within the last six months prior to the November 2023 Qualtrics study, nearly half of Americans (47%) reported that they are saving less money that they had been saving. More than half (52%) estimated that they had less than $2,000 in savings or none at all.

Altogether, financial instability could be causing Americans to lose hope in the economy. According to the study, nearly a quarter (24%) were not optimistic about the economy in 2024. This was especially among older generations; 40% of respondents aged 57 or above said they were not optimistic about the economy in 2024, compared with 28% of Gen X respondents. Of those who are optimistic, 24% say they're hopeful inflation will level out, while others are hopeful that wages will increase (13%) and the job market will improve (12%).

With the new USA administration in place in early 2025, optimism in general has increased.

"In 2024, much like doom spending, (there is scrolling), where people mindlessly shop on line scrolling to soothe concerns about the economy and foreign affairs, which could take a toll on their financial well-being," said Courtney Alev, consumer financial advocate at Credit Karma. "If you're feeling stressed – you're not alone – there are things you can do to get back on track. Start by doing an assessment of your finances to understand how much money you have coming in and out each month, as well as how much debt you owe. This will help you make a plan for how you're going to spend your money moving forward. To get in the habit of better spending, consider using cash instead of cards until you get your spending in check. That way, you can limit your chances of overspending. Also, if your card information is stored online, you might consider deleting stored card information through your browser to make shopping online less frictionless." The easier it is to shop online, the more likely it is that you will click on buy impulsively.

Where is the Happiness?

A new Gallup poll in 2024 identified the primary source of happiness among the Gen Z cohort. A sense of purpose, whether at school or work, was the driver of happiness. The survey included 2,271 young adults in the U.S. between ages 12 and 26. Gallup senior education researcher Zach Hrynowski, the Washington, D.C.-based author of the study, observed that at least 60% of all Gen Zers who are happy feel that they do something interesting every day and are motivated to attend work or school. "The challenge that we see from the research is that about 40% to 50% of Gen Zers say they don't feel like what they do every day is interesting. … They don't feel like it's important. They're not motivated to do it, and they're not getting enough time to sleep and relax."

Hrynowski revealed that there's been a shift in the workplace away from more traditional measures of success. Factors that are more important to older generations, such as earning more money and getting promotions, have become less important to Gen Z and millennials, he noted. "The most important factor in the workplace for millennials and Gen Z is that feeling of purpose," said Hrynowski. What is important were: "Are you making a difference in the world? Do you feel like what you're doing is important? Do you have opportunities to learn and grow every day?" Other key drivers of happiness included the ability to fulfill basic needs, such as having enough time to sleep and relax during the week." Social pressures also have a direct correlation on happiness, as Gen Zers who spend a lot of time comparing themselves to others are less likely to report feeling happy and twice as likely to experience anxiety. That, to me, suggests we're not doing a great job of setting Gen Z up to step out into the world, into their adult lives — and to be in a place that makes them feel like what they're doing as adults is really purposeful," Hrynowski said. "Adult Gen Zers who have any level of post-secondary education, are married or have children are 'markedly happier'than their peers, according to Gallup."

What do the survey results mean about the maximization of WHH?

Each generation, as it matures to the next, has different values and motivations. When we were young, we didn't know what we didn't know. Experience is a great teacher. If you make a choice, can you unring the bell? No. Our decisions and choices can make or break the maximization of WHH.

As some younger employees see it, the purpose of a regular job—a day job—is to demand as little time and effort as possible so that they are free to pursue free-time activities, including freelance 1099-based gig jobs or sub-rosa occupations. All of this is done to achieve happiness.

The soft sciences often promote a do-less-work lifestyle to win more free time. Some politicians are advocating for a 32-hour work week instead of the current 40-hour standard.

It sounds good until the realization sinks in, we are competing with other countries. Countries who's citizenry are working more than 40 hours per week. We are a global economy. One of those competitive countries have publically stated in 2025, they are at economic war with the USA and the rest of the world. Think China Communist Party (CCP). The People's Republic of China is a misnomer as only 7% of the population of China belong to the ruling class. The remaining 93% must pull the communist yoke and policies.

I was invited along with 200 others to have an audience with then Alan Greenspan, Chairman of the Federal Reserve of the United States and the Ambassador of China. Decades ago, at the time of this meeting, Greenspan advocated for permanent normal trade relations which would allow Chinese goods to flow into the USA on a low or no tariff basis.

When one of my fellow colleagues asked the Ambassador of China, through an interpretor, a economic question of reciprosity with the USA and other countries, the answer was…and I quote, "Oh, we will do what is best for China".

Today, 25 years later, the China Ambassador was true to his word to the economic detriment of many industries in the USA.

In 2025, the new USA administration is seeking to balance and force tariff reciprosity with China.

Numerous websites teach and promote how to to fool the boss into thinking you are putting forth more effort than you are. These approaches were unheard of among Baby Boomers or, for that matter, Gen `Xers.. Erica Lamberg (Fox Business, April 2024) *"Why the viral trend 'Chronoworking' is making waves among employees and employers."* reported:

Viral work trends often have negative tones. Think of "resenteeism," " bare-minimum Mondays," and "quiet quitting," for example.

But the latest career trend, known as "chronoworking," might actually be beneficial for all involved, provided that it is implemented with care in the business environment. Chronoworking prioritizes flexibility for employees based on their work styles. In chronoworking, people work according to their "chronotype," their individual circadian rhythm. This means more flexibility. A person's circadian rhythm can impact how awake he or she feels at different points in the day, and the working arrangement would take that into account. For example, a perpetually exhausted night owl can shift their schedule, so they have the energy they need to socialize or run errands after work—or employees with families can also adjust their hours to better accommodate their home life, while still delivering quality work and meeting company goals.... The work-life balance benefits can be significant.

This sounds great for some businesses, except for a few key issues. What about the customer? Many have immediate needs. What about the public companies that have a fiduciary responsibility to the shareholders? What about the first responders behind the scenes, who we never need until there is a disaster? If you are sick, do you want your doctor to say, "Sorry. I can't see you until next week, as I have an imbalance in my circadian rhythms." We also have to consider if we really want to have surgery performed by a team that has not had the proper rest prior to our surgery.

The point is that many of the work/life balance opportunities and trends need to take into consideration the complete product or service lifecycles. The work-from-home productivity levels are never as high as those from the office or the field. The benefits of the on-site in-person watercooler anecdotal discussions with more experienced colleagues can't be discounted. In-person mentorship is better than remoted sessions conducted from afar.

The current trends and outside influences portend less productivity from off-site younger workers.

A CEO of a Fortune 50 company was asked by his staff employee, "How did you become a CEO?" He answered, that he was at the time, just a recently hired employee out of college. His boss was anguishing over a role for which she could not find a suitable candidate. The young man asked her what the problem was. She told him that it is a difficult role requiring someone who can overcome many obstacles. The young man replied, "I will give it a try, if it involves a promotion." This led to an insight that would guide him all the way into the role of CEO. When faced with a choice, take the path of *most* resistance, not the least. Throughout his career, he kept taking on and successfully doing work most people did not want to do. He developed a reputation for taking on the hardest assignments and most difficult projects. After thirty years of this, Frank became a CEO.

But did he attain maximum WHH? Sadly, no. His Wealth and Happiness continuum was high on the scale, but his Health was not. He did not take care of himself and suffered from many issues, including blindness and debilitating diseases, some of which could have been prevented.

> **BEST Success Practice #32 to maximize the WHH continuum are:**
> **If you are in the early stages of your work life (16 to 40 years of age), find ways to do more at work, not less. Ask someone who is successful to be your mentor. If you are past forty, offer to be a mentor to a promising person.**

One size does not fit all for each generation. Not all that long ago, there was no such thing as social media. Today, any circumstance or event, the momentous and trivial alike, is instantly blasted across various social media "news" platforms. The increased and immediacy of social media is a positive and negative influence. On the positive side, social media provides access information and data and may build a sense of belonging. The downside, especially in the case of younger minds less developed, includes depression, technology addiction, and an emphasis on instant gratification rather than long-term happiness.

There is a dark side to technology. For many, social media causes great stress and sadness. Most of us have been conditioned to believe that technological advances would invariably make life easier and people happier. Well, even the brightest among us are being duped. I want to share with you some details to create awareness of the hazards and to help you avoid the financial and emotional pitfalls social media presents.

The latest statistics, from Barclay's Bank, published in *The Financial Analyst* (January 6, 2025), reveal that one in five people over sixty fall victim to at least one financial scam in their lifetime. Barclays surveyed 2000 banking consumers. That's bad enough, but it is not just people over sixty who are targeted. Recently, families vacationing on spring break were targeted by cyber criminals and a rash of break-ins and burglaries resulted nationwide. Organized cyber criminals used online technologies to find vulnerable residence's and sell the information on the dark web, Christine Coulter reported on *Fox News* in 2024.

There are dozens of scams and thousands of criminals posing as administrators, officials, and customer service reps to compromise Medicare, IRS, and

Social Security accounts and to perpetrate fraud in the form of phony sweepstakes, reverse mortgages, and other criminal scams.

Of all the scams out there, the most insidious involve preying on people's trust in and love of family. This creates a vulnerability that high-tech swindlers exploit to extract money and then disappear into the digital ether.

Here is how it often works, as someone I know and trust revealed to me. A person—typically a senior citizen—receives a phone call. This is not a random call, but one that the criminals have prepared for using social media tools. They have identified who you are, who your children are, and even who your grandchildren are. They troll Facebook, Snapchat, Linked-in, and other web-based resources to compile a dossier on their target. How many people post pictures while on vacation, record voice messages, send seemingly innocuous information to hundreds of friends? Cyber crooks can hack through so-called privacy settings in seconds to build a profile on an their target, often the elderly.

"Hello, Grandma? This is Brittany," announces the caller.

Brittany is in fact the name of the target's granddaughter. She is crying and sniffling on a slightly static connection, so Grandma has a hard time hearing her and identifying her voice. "Brittany" tells her she has been in an accident, and a lawyer wants to talk to her Grandma. She finishes the conversation by pleading, "Grandma, please do not tell anyone!"

Next, fake Brittany's fake lawyer gets on the phone and , very authoritatively and lawyerlike, he tells Grandma, "To keep Brittany out of jail, I need you to overnight $5000 in cash by FedEx. It must be cash, so we can post bond. To keep this out of the press and off Brittany's record, I have convinced the judge to issue a gag order. So, you must keep this quiet for now. Let me be clear, Brittany is in significant trouble, but I can help her."

Brittany gets back on the phone and says in a tearful voice, "Thank you Grandma!"

The scam unfolded over six more days, with the fake lawyer providing reasons that Grandma needed to send even more money. In this way, he extracted some $30,000 dollars from her.

Sadly, family members initiate many of the financial scams to tap Grandma. This real-life example above was not an inside job, however. This case involved multiple countries, drop zones, mules, a scam call center, fake phone numbers, social media, and elderly target profiling. It is part of a multibillion-dollar criminal enterprise.

What can we do?

If you are a bank, train your tellers to ask questions. If an elderly customer is uncharacteristically withdrawing large amounts of cash over a short period of time, ask why and alert the supervisor.

If you are the police or law enforcement and suspect a scam is in process, recognize that fast follow-up is essential. Each police department should have a financial scam hotline, so departments can quickly respond and communicate between jurisdictions. Most police departments are not equipped to deal with interstate let alone international scammers. These scam artists operate in a small window of time and then move on to the next target. Police agencies should regularly educate the public with awareness seminars, using non-social media tools. Many seniors do not use Facebook or Snap Chat. Newspapers, community events, churches, and senior centers are a good start for reaching this cohort.

If you are Fedex, USPS, or UPS, develop policies to ensure your fraud divisions electronically tag overnight envelopes that contain cash. Realize that your best-in-class delivery system is being used as a pipeline to move cash illicitly. Provide the records to the police while balancing privacy rights.

If you have elderly parents, grandparents, or friends, keep in touch with them on a regular basis so they remember your voice. Proactively tell them you would never ask for cash over the phone. Have special code words that identify you, so that an AI-generated voice cannot succeed in deception.

Minimize your social media usage. Do not share that Grandma gave you $500 dollars for Christmas. Many videos are trolled, voices are extracted, digitally re-cordered, and then transformed to reach out to the unsuspecting elderly target. One piece of data is not significant, but the accumulated information can be a powerful tool enabling criminals to fool honest people.

If you are a senior citizen, *never* send cash, wire money, or leave cash on a doorstep. *Never* share your social security number, account numbers, or other financial information. If you suspect a scam, hang up the phone and call the police immediately. Share the details of the call. Next, call your loved ones and share the details.

To help maximize happiness and avoid financial loss or even ruin, we all need to work together to put these criminals out of commission and in jail. Communicate and create awareness with family and friends.

BEST Success Practice #33 to maximize the WHH continuum are: Create a special family code phrase to verify that you are speaking with family, loved ones and friends. Change the code periodically in person or by phone, not through text/email or social media.

I have listed some suggestions for you to enhance your fraud awareness. Always ask yourself, who or what is real, given the spread of AI tools and usage for criminal purposes.

Precautionary measures...
Do:

Proactively overcommunicate. Visit with family and friends. On the phone, have a family and friend code word as an identifier.

- Use dual-factor authentication or two-step verification.
- Create passwords with at least twelve distinct characters, and change passwords often.
- Limit social media usage.
- Turn off "Location Services" on cell phones.
- Engage in proactive charity giving rather than reactive charity giving.
- Minimize online banking and call your bank's headquarters phone number if suspect check fraud. Require the bank to initiate a special code that only you know before making any transaction in person.
- Limit online purchases, especially from individuals, brands you do not recognize, or informal platforms such as Craig's List.
- Trust your intuition. If something feels bad, it probably is. Be aware that no government or banking entity will proactively reach out to you.
- Establish a Virtual Private Network (VPN) for sophisticated communication. Supplement with Norton LifeLock or other identity protection
- If you live in or have family living in Florida, contact the police and the Florida Attorney General's Department of Elder Affairs at 1.866.966.7226 if you suspect any fraud.
- Research how to prevent cyber hacks and elder fraud.

Elder Fraud Awareness...Who or what is real?
Precautionary measures...
Do Not:

- Do not keep quiet or isolate yourself from family and friends.
- Minimize the use of TikTok or Zoom for communication. Consider a more secure platform, such as Microsoft Team Meetings.
- Do not Use Alexa, Amazon Echo, or Siri, as they record all your conversations and track movements. Apple Air Tags do not record, but they are used to track movements. Limit your usage of these devices and platforms.
- Do not use a debit card except at your bank for cash, and do not save credit card or debit card data on any website.
- Do not answer any phone call you do not recognize.
- Do not answer any text or email you do not recognize.
- Do not use online money-sending and receiving platforms. 13 percent of users get scammed.
- Do not Respond to any first contact email or phone call from Social Security/IRS/Medicare/Reverse Mortgage co. etc ...only USPS letter delivered or you proactively contact them.
- Do not Use Google. Instead use DuckDuckGo search and Proton email.
- Do not send cash by Fedex, UPS, USPS, or leave in a mailbox.
- Do not Use unencrypted Wi-Fi hotspots. Always encrypt.
- Do not share or have your DNA extracted.

Elder Fraud Awareness...Who or what is real?
Precautionary measures...

Have a special family code when communicating by phone, since bad actors use AI in conjunction with social media to imitate voices.

Where can I research to protect myself and my loved ones?
Here are a few reliable sources:

- Scam.org
- ScamAmerica.org
- FL St Attorney General dept of Elder Affairs 866.966.7226
- Better Business Bureau
- Cyberguy.com/Newsletter
- Kim Komando Today podcast
- Readers Digest Oct 19,2022 Jaime Stathis article
- FTC
- FBI Internet Crime Complaint Center
- Oig.ssa.gov/report
- ANY CPA or Law firm for Estate/Tax/POA or Trust issues
- AMAC fraud prevention
- Your Bank's Fraud division

These precautions may seem draconian. They can be burdensome to implement. And you may ask yourself how you can give up Alexa or online banking or cash apps. We have become so dependent on how technology accelerates our daily experience and makes our lives easier, we forget that we open ourselves to risk. The price we pay for convenience is an exponentially increased likelihood of being scammed and hacked.

Here are more steps to consider:

The law offices of Keane Thomas and Pinnacoli in Jensen Beach Florida advised people to manage and encrypt their digital assets. Digital assets are more susceptible to fraud. A digital asset includes airline accounts, websites, financial accounts, streaming services, credit cards, emails, X, etc. Their research indicates the average person has over 100 online accounts during a lifetime. They need to be addressed in your estate plan.

Start with a complete inventory. It may be daunting but imagine how much harder it would be for your spouse or adult child managing your estate. There are commercially available password protection systems. However, a pad of paper will do just as well. If you create a spreadsheet on your computer, be sure to encrypt it to prevent access by bad actors.

Your list should include the following:

- URL or website address
- Name of the company
- Account number and name

- Password and Username
- Any additional access information, i.e., third party verification (TPV) where a code is sent by email or text to verify the user.
- Whether the platform allows the user to give another person access after death, often referred to as a "Legacy Contact," or if you can provide directions to have the account deleted after death upon proper notification.

BEST Success Practice #34 to maximize the WHH continuum are: Minimize your online social media exposure and interactions.

So far much of what I have shared with you is mental or spiritual happiness. Can you achieve happiness physically?

I am not talking about pleasure derived from sex. That's a no brainer. What about working physically or mentally hard at something. In today's thinking, many of us try our best to avoid what is considered difficult. In his blog for *Epoch Times* (February 2024), Mike Donghia reviewed Angela Duckworth's research in *Journal of Personality and Social Psychology* (2007) and found that "isolated grit, which can be thought of as the ability to work long and hard toward a goal, [is] a powerful predictor of success across multiple domains. Hard work is a variable most directly under our influence." In simpler terms, hard work equals long-term success. We have been conditioned to accept a path of least resistance or a low bar to be considered successful. But Donghia believes: "There are few things sweeter in life than a well-earned reward. When your leisure time is preceded by hard work, the pleasures of rest and novelty are heightened to the utmost degree. In fact, you may find the harder you work, the less time and effort you'll need to put into entertaining yourself."

What comes to my mind when I read this is retired Pittsburgh Steeler linebacker James Harrison. I was having lunch in the Arnie Palmer Tavern at the Treesdale Golf and Country Club with a group including Joey Porter, linebacker coach of the Pittsburgh Steelers, when Ben Roethlisberger, the Steeler quarterback, stopped over and asked, "Did you hear what Harrison did?" Then Ben told the story.

Harrison's two sons came home from school with trophies. Dad asked his boys why they won trophies? Everyone got one, they answered. That triggered the NFL football all-star. He marched back to the school with sons and their participation trophies, announcing to a school administrator that he was returning the trophies so his sons are not taught that they're entitled to something just because they tried their best. "Sometimes your best is not good enough and you have to work harder to stand out in life. That should drive you to want to do better, not cry and whine until somebody gives you something to keep you happy."

Boom.

Now that's great parenting and a great reminder for all of us. Harrison was the youngest of fourteen children and was never given anything unless he earned it. He was a walk-on at Kent State university and through hard work and grit become an NFL all-star.

Now let's look at the economy and how it can affect happiness. No matter where we work, or if we are retired, the economy will affect our WHH continuum.

Most people do not have a plan to deal with downturns in the economy and how to deal with the stress and worry this would ultimately incur. The stress and worry will negatively affect health and happiness. Do not wait for these business cycle bumps in the road to happen. Know they will happen and prepare accordingly with WAS and RIA's.

On average, the U.S. economy has had a recession every six years since 1948. A recession is typically defined as an economic decline manifested as a period of negative economic growth. The National Bureau of Economic Research, a non-profit presumably nonpartisan organization, looks at economic statistics to determine if we are in a recession. Gross domestic product output, unemployment levels, level of inflation, and other metrics are measured over time.

You have heard of Bull and Bear markets. Investors define a Bull market as a prolonged growth rate increase of 20% or more in a stock market index or individual stock. A Bear market is a decline of 20% or more. The economy is constantly moving in and out of Bull and Bear markets. Similarly, the economy is constantly moving in and out of recessions over time.

"In a recession," Fidelity Brokerage Services notes *from Fidelity.com 2024,* "the economy shrinks, which can lead to lower levels of employment, worsening corporate performance, deteriorating stock market results, and higher borrowing costs for both consumers and companies."

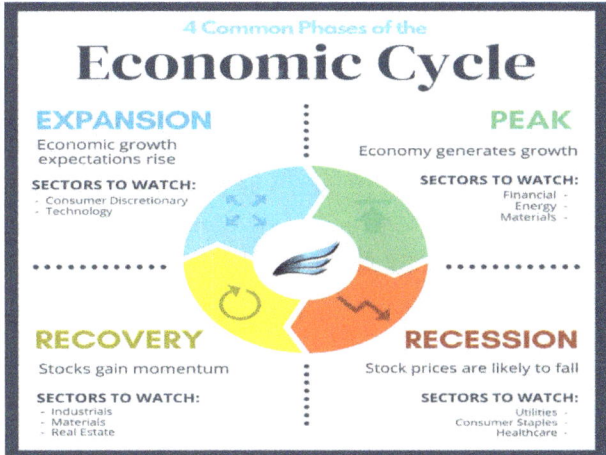

The diagram above is a hypothetical illustration of the business cycle, the pattern of cyclical fluctuations in an economy over a few years, which can influence asset returns over an intermediate-term horizon. There isn't always a chronological, linear progression among the phases of the business cycle, and there have been cycles in which the economy has skipped a phase or retraced an earlier one."

To maximize the WHH continuum, gain the knowledge of how to counteract or plan for downturns through Wealth Advisory Services (WAS) and Registered Investment Advisors (RIA) and Certified Public Accountants (CPA), who provide clients fiduciary based advice. Your stress and worry will subside and your health and happiness will increase.

BEST Success Practice #35 to maximize the WHH continuum:
Proactively plan with your WAS/RIA/CPA, to develop what-if scenarios to deal with financial and emotional aspects of inevitable market down turns.

In every country I have traveled and immersed myself, I saw varying levels of happiness. How do other countries define or experience happiness? How can we relate to and appreciate how other countries approach happiness?

Happiness is relative to a person's circumstances and to their culture, which can vary dramatically from one country to another. As I reflect on my travels around the world, India stands out from most of the rest. Few places exhibit such a range of people, religions, culture, and wealth.

In most of the major cities, such as New Delhi, Mumbai, and Chennai, each major street intersection struck me as its own ecosystem. On any given day the cacophony of organized chaos at the intersection was astounding to this "Gora" (white guy) from America. It was my first experience with the traffic. No were else, except in Indonesia, had I seen bumper stickers on many trucks and service vehicles that plead, "SOUND HORN PLEASE." Where most of us grew up, honking your horn is an abrupt and startling event. In India, it is considered a courtesy to sound your horn as you attempt to pass by a slower vehicle. I could not distinguish between slow or fast, as everyone seemed to be sounding their horns and going at the same speed. As a side note, most vehicles had their side mirrors either knocked off or removed, limiting their drivers' ability to see behind them as they traveled. The various horns beeping and tooting with different musical pitches every minute of every day became background noise well into the night.

My first trip to India was to New Delhi. I remember one major intersection in particular. I asked my driver to drop me off, so I could immerse myself in the life of the streets. It was not uncommon to see in one part of an intersection an elephant pulling a huge cart loaded with what looked like hay or straw. At the opposite end of the intersection, there might be a Mercedes with tinted windows, its horn blaring as it tried to maneuver around a three-wheel motor bike with almost flat tires spewing black diesel smoke. Why were the tires almost flat? There were seven people either sitting or standing on this diminutive motor bike, smiling, just happy not to be walking. Those who were on foot dodged the non-stop stream of traffic. Jay walking was the norm at these New Delhi intersections.

In the middle of the intersection was an Indian traffic cop on a platform, directing traffic as if he were directing the Boston Symphony, a fusion of rock and Hindi music, and a ballet—all at the same time. I could not discern any semblance of order. I imagine there was, but I could not see it.

Roman Russo, who authored *Optimal Happiness 2021* (2021), discussed happiness in India: "I'm sure every single Indian kid has heard the phrase, 'Log Kya Kehenge,' meaning 'What will the people say?'" Whether you grew up abroad, as the child of parents who have immigrated from India, or if you grew up in India, you have most likely been affected by this concern for the opinion of others.

There is tremendous social pressure to conform to traditional social rules in India, including those relating to the extended family, elders, and society as a whole. Failure to conform is seen as shameful. In other words, even when I—an outsider in the country—wanted to conduct myself in my own way, the local culture forced me to consider the reputation of my family and therefore to behave in line with *Log Kya Kehenge*. Thanks to Indian culture, people are extremely concerned about what society might think of them. Families want to uphold their honor by following what society deems as the right path for them and their children. For example, many parents want their child to follow a certain career path, which is the reason for all the "engineer, doctor, lawyer" memes among Asian kids.

Geographically, India is about half the size of the U.S. lower 48 states. India's population estimated at 1.4 billion, however, dwarfs the 345 million American population. From an American point of view, Indian cities may seem overpopulated, noisy, polluted, and two thirds of the Indian population may live in poverty, but, as Roman Russo writes, "some of the poorest people really know how to be happy in certain areas of their lives. These people value true relationships over materialistic objects. They are happy even with having very little because they are mindful of their surroundings and live in the present moment, while appreciating genuine relationships the most."

I wanted to take a break from ten straight hours of meetings held inside a five-star hotel in New Delhi India. The SOUND HORN PLEASE buzz was heard even through the concrete block auditorium walls. It was twilight as I started my walk. What I saw was unexpected, even shocking. As I crossed the street, the sidewalks became populated with people claiming a space to spend the night. They were positioning themselves so that people walking on the sidewalk were able to step over them rather than stepping on them. The best way I can describe it was like looking at railroad ties.

I stopped and watched this scene unfold as if it had been choreographed and rehearsed for years. Very politely and without missing a beat or looking down at the people getting ready for "bed," pedestrians stepped over them. The walkers had no choice but to use the sidewalks as the traffic in the streets was heavy at the time. I followed suit. What was both inspirational and hard to believe, as I looked at the people I was stepping over, some who were not yet sleeping, looked up at me and smiled--not all of them but most of them. They were smiling at me!

I could not comprehend the smiles until I asked an Indian colleague the next morning about it. She said because I looked at them and they were happy to have found a spot on the sidewalk for the night. These were some of the more premium spots, as they were up off the street and cleaner than the gutters. If they did not secure a sidewalk spot, they would have to sleep in the gutter.

Happiness and smiles is relative to one's circumstances not just in India, but everywhere.

Happiness is often thought of as the ultimate destination, an aspiration or goal meant to be attained. But what if happiness were not something we pursued only in moments of peace and abundance? What if it were something we actively chose or emanated, even in the midst of hardship or a hard loss? Speaking of smiles, on a recent trip to the Philippines, I witnessed a powerful example of happiness borne out of adversity—something deeper than simple acceptance of their tragic lot. It was a joy forged in hardship, then passed down through generations, becoming a symbol of hope and resilience. In Bacolod City, dubbed the "City of Smiles," this embodiment of happiness is most flamboyantly displayed during the MassKara Festival, an event that has come to represent the triumph of the human spirit despite the tragedy that befell their capital. Bacolod City lost its main economic engine when artificial sugar was invented in the late 1970s. Over 75% of the city's gross domestic product flowed from natural sugar farms, and the trickle -down monies they generated. As you would expect, the city deteriorated with the collapse of the sugar industry. But today, the city is a thriving tourist mecca. It is the ultimate turn-around story, complete with smiles.

As we in the United States build our wealth and plan to transition to future generations, we can learn from examples in other countries as other countries can learn from us. Can the distant past provide hints and clues for future generations while preserving our legacy? Can we avoid the same mistakes and enhance the adaptations as they did in Bacolod City?

I asked **Rita Galila**, of Makati City, Philippines, a Filipino entrepreneur, author, and life-long resident, to share her perspectives and research of multigenerational wealth, health and happiness. Here is what she said…

THE SUGAR BARONS OF BACOLOD, PHILIPPINES

The rich heritage of the sugar barons of Negros Occidental begins not only with the sugarcane business but also stems from the volcanic origin of the island's soil, being sun-drenched year round. Having this topographic advantage its inherent agricultural potential, it was only a matter of time that the key people and innovators influx Bacolod, forever changing the city. By late 19th and early 20th centuries, it became an emblematic hub on this boot-shaped Visayan island, transitioning from relative obscurity to immense wealth--a specific type of prosperity that only a few could even imagine. For these sugar barons, wealth was not merely material; it represented a way of life, a reflection of their newfound status, and for several generations, the center of their happiness and health.

I want to transport you, the readers, back in time to an era of opulence and grandeur, examining the lives of the most prominent sugar families—the Marinos, Gastons, and Lacsons—and reflecting on how their extravagant lives eventually transformed with the rise and fall of the sugar supremacy.

THE RISE OF THE SUGAR ARISTOCRACY

By the turn of the 20th century, Bacolod City, the capital of Negros Occidental, had become the sugar capital of the Philippines. Sugarcane was the province's main star, fueling a sprawling industry that enriched landowners, many of whom hailed from affluent Spanish or mestizo (a local intermarrying a Spanish descent thus spawning half-breeds) background. As the demand for sugar soared worldwide, particularly from markets in the United States, Negros Occidental emerged as an absolute goldmine. Bacolod's society burgeoned as quickly as its affluence, expanding its economic influence in no time. By the early 1900s, the sugar industry accounted for nearly all of the province's economic output, and it was in this environment that families like the Marinos, Gastons, and Lacsons rose to unimaginable wealth.

DON MARIANO LACSON AND THE "TAJ MAHAL OF NEGROS"

One of the can't-miss attractions is Talisay's historic The Ruins. The mansion symbolizes an era where undying love was central to its existence, and money served as a mere tool to construct a lasting memorial. A task sworn by Don Mariano Ledesma Lacson, often called the "Taj Mahal of Negros" as a testament of his love for his deceased wife. Built in the early 1900s, it was commissioned in memory of his Portuguese wife, Maria Braga, who died tragically while pregnant with their 11th child. The Italianate mansion was constructed with the finest materials imported from Europe, featuring Neo-Romanesque columns and surrounded by vast sugarcane fields overlooking the coastal scenery of Negros. For years, the house stood as a living testament to the Lacson family's immense fortune, their tragic love story, and the almost mythical image of a sugar baron's lifestyle.

For the Lacson family and others like them, wealth was not merely measured in money or land but in the ability to design their distinguished families lasting legacy—a privilege granted only to the select few during those days. Their fortunes allowed them to live luxuriously and shaped the identity of their descendants, though, as we shall see, it came at a cost in later years.

VICTOR GASTON AND THE FRENCH ARISTOCRATIC HOUSE OF GASTON:

While the Lacsons built opulent homes left and right, the Gaston family—another pillar of the sugar aristocracy—maintained its status as one of the oldest and most influential sugar dynasties. Their wealth story began with Yves Leopold Germain Gaston, a Frenchman who introduced sugar refining techniques to the island. His entrepreneurial acumen in engaging in sugar cultivation on a commercial level laid the foundation for an empire that spanned generations.

Yves's eldest son, Victor Gaston, inherited the mantle and helmed the expansion of the family's sugar operations. Under his leadership, the Gaston estate in Silay City, just outside Bacolod, flourished into a prosperous center for sugar production. Silay became known as the "Paris of Negros," a hub for art, culture, and social life all funded by the sugar wealth that poured in from the estates' earnings.

The Gastons built elaborate palatial mansions with of colonial-style architecture, while the interiors were adorned with custom-made French Creole furniture hosting extravagant soirées that rivaled the social gatherings of European nobility. Their homes, with ornate woodwork, sprawling gardens, and imported chandeliers, were emblems of prestige. The f amily's wealth afforded them not only physical comfort but also access to global culture, with many of their children studying abroad in Europe or the United States.

Yet, beyond the walls of these mansions, a different reality loomed. For all their wealth's worth, the sugar barons relied heavily on a labor force of sacadas—seasonal sugarcane laborers particularly from neighboring islands such as Panay and Cebu—faced significant hardships and discontent under the rule of the hacenderos (landowners) who toiled against unfair labor practices and oppressive conditions. While the aristocracy enjoyed their wealth and health, the laborers who worked their fields lived in poverty, often housed in makeshift quarters with inadequate food, water and sanitation. The sacadas suffering became symbolic of the social and economic inequalities that plagued the whole country during the Spanish colonial and post-colonial period. This resistance highlighted a societal divided so deep that it later became one of the main factors in the decline of the sugar industry.

THE MARINO FAMILY LEGACY

Among the elite sugar families, the Marinos also climbed to prominence in Bacolod, their wealth spanning multiple generations. Like the Gastons, the Marinos were deeply embedded in the province's high society. They were known for their lavish parties and conspicuous consumption. Don Marino, in particular, made headlines with his sprawling estate, which rivaled if not surpassed, some of the most grandiose homes in the Philippines during his time. His influence extended beyond the sugar industry, shaping local politics and commerce in the region.

However, despite their wealth, the Marino family's health and happiness were often fragile. The pressures of maintaining such vast estates, coupled with the volatile nature of sugar prices plus a global market collapse due to oversupply and the rise of alternative sweeteners severely cutting the profits of the haciendas, which heavily relied on exports. To sustain a lavish lifestyle and to keep their plantations running despite negative margins, most of these barons took on enormous debts. When sugar prices plummeted further, they were unable to repay these loans leading to foreclosures and bankruptcies. As these economic and social challenges compounded, they eventually took a toll on these elite families. While they could afford the best doctors and medical treatments, the stress of preserving their empires weighed heavily on them, sometimes leading to premature deaths or chronic illnesses. It was as if the very wealth they had amassed came at a steep price. The burden of expectations, upkeep of their lifestyle and the great power they wielded came with an equally insurmountable responsibility—one that rarely few could evade.

WEALTH'S DOWNFALL IS CONVERSELY A REBIRTH OF NEW HOPES AND NEWFOUND RESILIENCE

As the global sugar market shifted in the 1980s, with the rise of artificial sweeteners and increased competition from other countries, the sugar industry in Negros Occidental began to collapse. For the families that had relied on sugar for generations, this was a devastating blow. Sugarcane fields once buzzed with activity became idle, and the mansions that had once hosted glamorous social gatherings stood empty or in saddening state of disrepair and abandonment.

The Gaston family, for example, faced the sobering reality of selling off their land hectare by hectare, as Melissa Gaston, the great-grand-niece of

Victor Gaston, later recounted. What had once symbolized of immense wealth had become a burdensome inheritance. Like many descendants of the sugar barons, Melissa struggled to maintain the family's heritage; her wealth now more theoretical than tangible. The land passed down through generations remained millions worth on paper, but selling it posed its own challenges—fraught with legal complexities, market fluctuations, and the emotional toll of parting with a family legacy. The stakes were now higher but Melissa's resilience shone through as she engaged in active conservation projects, driven by her family's passion to preserve whatever remained of their estates and its lasting memories---the very land that silently witnessed the rise and fall of its ancestral gentry.

Pursuit of Wealth, Health and Happiness Can also Be a Double-Edged Sword

The ascendance of the sugar aristocracy was a gilded era for the sugar barons, where vast plantations and immense wealth was a source of pride for the select few to an almost regal status, ruling over their domains with unquestioned power and a penchant for lavishness. Little did they know that this privilege was also precarious--- a misfortune waiting to unfold. During those times, they enjoyed unparalleled opulence, their health was maintained by access to the best resources and their happiness reflected in their social stature. But as the industry declined, so too did their fortunes, forcing them to confront and accept a new kind of wealth—one that was intangible, rooted in the preservation of history rather than in their former status as a sugar powerhouse basking in its erstwhile glory.

The health of the sugar barons, both physical and mental, also deteriorated with the industry's decline. The stress of maintaining crumbling estates, coupled with the loss of social status, weighed heavily on many of the successors. Happiness, once thought to be solely derived from material wealth, once again became an elusive pursuit. Factors such as meaningful relationships, personal fulfillment, health and a sense of purpose emerged as key components of genuine happiness. As time passed, the descendants of these barons developed new skills to adapt to the changing course of their lives. They came to realize that even a vast wealth and resources alone could not guarantee lasting happiness. A more nuanced understanding of what constitutes a fulfilling life emerged---one that goes beyond what is immediately visible, particularly in the context of their struggling haciendas.

AN EVOLVING LEGACY: A TIMELESS STORY OF RESILIENCE

Today, Bacolod's sugar barons are but a memory, and their descendants no longer wield the same power they once did. Yet, some has survived and retained considerable wealth and influence, though their fortunes have greatly diminished. A few of the grand mansions remain, some preserved as heritage sites, while others crumble into ruins, as if waiting for a savior to one day restore them. The once thriving sugar industry has become a distant memory, though the legacies of families like the Marinos, Gastons and Lacsons endure though their kin.

From the perspective of both foreign and local tourists, the remnants of this golden era are still visible today. Heritage houses, like the Gaston family home, serve as reminders of a time when sugar was king and the barons lived like royalty. But for their descendants, wealth now takes on a different form. No longer tied to the prosperity of sugar, their happiness lies in preserving their family's rising-above-the-adversity stories and their rightful place in Philippines historical map as the "Sugar Bowl of the Philippines"—that they were once upon a time, a cornerstone of the local economy for over a century.

And for rest of the heirs, lessons learned mean that wealth is no longer just about grand mansions or fine clothes for random family socials. It's about preserving heritage, demonstrating resilience, and adapting to a changing social status. Their approach to life now reflects a more mindful, more modest existence—an intentional lifestyle that starkly contrast with the extravagant way of life the sugar barons left behind.

One of the heirs to the famous Bacolod sugar plantations is Melissa, who embodies the City of Smiles persona. I asked her why she is always smiling and happy. "We have a choice to be happy or sad, I choose to be happy," she explained.

I met her while she was training for the Ironman competition in Kona, Hawaii. The competition consists of a 2.4-mile swim, a 112-mile bike ride, and a 26.2-mile marathon, a total of 140.6 miles. Even some of the best of the best who qualify for the Kona competition, often but cannot finish within the allotted time frame—or at all. "Time does not matter. People crawl to the finish line to complete their goal," Melissa told me.

Melissa started training for triathlons at age forty-seven. She did not know how to swim, never rode an event bicycle, and was even excused from gym class in high school due to her lack of athleticism. By age fifty-three, she qualified for and finished the Kona Hawaii Ironman. She has maximized Happiness through physical fitness, diet, and an infectious smile. The lesson I took away was never to give up on your goals.

As I bounce around Asia, let's go back to India.

India's diversity of wealth was on full display the evening a group of us were invited to a contractor's home for dinner. Our driver passed slum after slum until, right around the corner on the edge of the last slum we passed, was a gate. As it opened, we were greeted by a number of servants, crisply dressed in bright white. The home was palatial and had a large swimming pool in the basement. Among the guests were the wife and two daughters of the Russian ambassador. Three servants set out course after course of food. After dinner, one of those daughters stood up and sang for us. As it turned out she, was a Fusion rock star, twenty-two, and quite the performer.

After dinner and the entertainment, I spoke to the host over a scotch, no ice. His biggest worry and stress was how he could maintain his business legacy. In his mid-fifties, his physical health did not appear to be at its best. He seemed stuck. Neither of his two daughters were interested in taking over the contracting business he had built from scratch. The family had no wealth transition plans. He was not in a position to maximize WHH.

As an aside, most non-Indians will have issues with food and drink consumption while visiting most of Asia. The New Deli contractor wonderful hospitality included the best food, and thankfully no New Deli belly issues.

BEST Success Practice #36 to maximize the WHH continuum: For gut health, never drink the native water and always peel any fruit skin before consumption in a foreign country.

The next day after the dinner with the New Deli contractor, a colleague ordered a whiskey at a five-star hotel bar in India. It was our last evening of one of many trips to India. He asked the bartender to place one ice cube into the double shot glass. His logic was the alcohol would kill any germs. During the seventeen-hour flight back to the USA he was in the airplane bathroom for most of the flight. When he arrived in his hometown, he was admitted to the emergency room for a number of issues. He lost 24 pounds in two weeks—not a recommended weight-loss program for a wiry guy, given the pain and suffering endured, quite possibly caused by one small ice cube.

Let's look at another example of the Wealth Health and Happiness Continuum, this one from the opposite side of the globe.

I was traveling with the vice-chairman of our board to see our top global customer. This was my first time alone with the vice-chair, so I took advantage of the opportunity to get to know him as a person. Before I could start a meaningful conversation, however, his phone rang. I could only hear one side of the conversation as we traveled on the noisy highway, but it was clear that the fifteen-minute conversation involved a significant level of conflict involving a family member. After he hung up, he was silent. Finally, he announced: "I have a disease." He paused. "I am never satisfied."

Now here was a person earning in the neighborhood of $20 million dollars a year. One of his homes was a penthouse suite in Chicago filled with investment-grade art and collectibles. His next-door neighbor was Oprah Winfrey. Beyond question, he was a wealth-accumulation success, clearly ticking off the W box in the WHH Continuum.

"What do you mean you are never satisfied?" I asked him. He did not answer.

In fact, I had personally experienced what he meant in numerous staff meetings over the past year. For instance, we had a blowout quarter, hitting every financial metric in one of the businesses for which he was responsible.

His response?

"Not good enough." He pointed to another business in his portfolio, which had not met its goals. "Why didn't you anticipate this? Why didn't you help the other business?"

For me, it was even more personal. Each of his staff members was given personal goals in support of the business we ran. In my case, for that calendar year, I was assigned fourteen goals. At review time, I had met thirteen of the fourteen metrics and was feeling confident of a a solid bonus. What I received was a rating and bonus that not only reduced but downgraded disproportionately.

After hearing one side of the conversation, it was clear to me that his "never being satisfied" affected his happiness at home and at work. He never discussed his family problem with me, he did not speak of the phone call, and I lost the opportunity to get to know him as a person. As a businessman, his performance was in the upper decile. Yet it was clear that his WHH continuum was out of balance. Over the years, I have interacted with more than eight hundred CEO and Director level suite corporate leaders globally. Such an imbalance is an all too common trait among this group of high performers. They sacrifice happiness and health to attain monetary wealth in support of their teams.

Over time, I have done a series of informal surveys about happiness. Most of the people I interviewed were strangers, some were acquaintances, and others are friends from age seventeen to ninety-six. I did tend to weight the interviewees toward the older side, since they had ample life experiences and reflection perspectives we can learn from. They are not just point-in-time resources but embody an amalgamation of a lifetime of moments. The main question I asked in the interviews was "What is happiness?" Not "What is happiness for you?" but "What is happiness?"

Here are some of the results of the non-scientific interviews. Answers ranged from a few words to a 143-page anthology describing the individual's happiness and life journey. (I'll get back to that response shortly.) Some people answered in brief compass, taking an average of fifteen minutes. One person spent over four hours with me. Surprisingly (to me), many people could not or did not want to answer the question. The answers that follow are in no particular order.

JOSEPH

A retired teacher and principal, Joseph, ninety-four, WWII war hero, answered the question as posed by his sons: "Dad, are you happy?"

"Happiness, happiness, everyone is worried about being happy. Can I get you a lollipop? Just go live your life and do the right things. Happiness will follow."

CAPTAIN TOM TAYLOR

Captain Tom Taylor was flying his last flight after 34 years. The American Airlines 787 Flight #102 from Honolulu to Dallas redeye was under his command. His career started as a U.S. Navy Top Gun and then a Top gun instructor. After his military career, he flew with American Airlines, advancing within the pilot hierarchy through every size and type of airplane in the fleet. We learned this during a flight from the head flight attendant, who proudly listed Captain Taylor's accomplishments in a flight announcement before take-off. When she concluded, the passengers gave a long round of applause. His wife, sitting in coach on the plane with us, beamed.

About 2:00 am, I got up and headed to the galley to stretch as most people were asleep. I could never sleep on airplanes. Captain Taylor walked into the cabin, his calm stride, demeanor, and his voice bespoke the quiet confidence of experience and competence. I introduced myself and asked him, "After everything you have accomplished, how would he define happiness?"

He looked at me as to say *Why you are asking me the question?* I did not wait for him to actually ask me but explained that I was writing a book. He took a few moments before answering. "Happiness is having the choice to take stress out of my life. The stress of work is a different level of stress than self-induced stress. Many of us are the sandwich generation with needs to fulfill for elderly parents and children. Happiness is being financially able to reduce stress for my family. Family is happiness."

JENNIFER (BY LETTER)

Jennifer Powers Iacobucci, Esq..... Senior Principal Law Clerk to Hon. Stephen K. Lindley
Appellate Division, Fourth Department
50 East Avenue
Rochester, New York 14604

Happiness is a sense of purpose and service. That purpose can be anything and can change over time. Teenagers' "purpose" is to study, get good grades and set up a life of stability and security via colleges, trades or other employment. As a teenager, my purpose was just that. In my 20s, my purpose was to finish law school and get a job as a prosecutor, so all my goals were related to that. I graduated a year early from college and graduated with honors from law school. I was happy and, while I did not get a job in a coveted big city office, I got a job in a small county in upstate New York. I was happy. I had to waitress on weekends to pay my student loan debts, so I rarely had a day off, but I was happy and fulfilled. While working there, I met my "second parents." They instilled in me a sense of service. Like many young adults I had stopped attending church and just figured that I was a believer who did not need a building to practice my faith. Bob and Julia Rodger helped me reconnect with my chosen house of worship – the Episcopal church, and I started attending regularly, and I did so from then until now. In my 30s, my purpose was to have a family – having lost my mother when I was just 33. I gave birth to three wonderful children and, since their birth, they have been my everything. As the oldest is set to graduate high school on June 22, 2024, I have learned that I must have a purpose beyond them, and I recently reached out to the Catholic Church where we belong to see about shifting my focus from purpose to service. Unfortunately, the Catholic Church does not allow me to hold certain roles, but I will find a position of service. Have I always been happy? No. There have been dark times, and times when I felt completely alone, but it was my purpose that got me through those times for my family. During those time, I fell back on my career as my sense of purpose. For almost 30 years, I have worked in a profession I love, and I have been fortunate to serve the State of New York as a court attorney for three separate and amazing judges. I am in the shadows, anonymous, but I can work from home, which was incredibly important during years that my oldest had significant health issues. I serve the People of the State of New York, and I feel incredibly honored to hold that position and to be a part of our justice system. I have loved the law since I was 5 years old, and I am so grateful for the opportunities my job has provided to create a work-life balance of purpose and service. In a nutshell, my "happiness" is a result of my family, my career in the shadows of the court system, and my faith in God.

EDWARDO

I spoke to a fifty-one-year-old Italian Ethiopian now living in Honolulu named Edwardo, who made a living as a cowboy until he was injured. I saw him sitting at the bar of the Equus Hotel downtown Honolulu, wearing an Australian bush hat, during what turned out to be his day off from working at a local restaurant.

What caught my attention were two things. One, it was 7 am Hawaiian time and, second, his unique, big, hardy, long laugh. I just had to meet him.

We had a cigar together on the H1 street outside of the Equus bar. We met Mike Dailey, the owner, who is in his seventies, in tremendous physical shape, and still competes in polo matches. The Equus is the only family run hotel left in downtown Honolulu we learned.

I asked Edwardo what is happiness? He took a few long draws on the Perdomo Esteli Habano I had given him. He said if I gave him ten minutes he would have an answer.

"Sure," I said.

True to his word, he went back to the bar and started to write on a scrap piece of paper. Then he brought it back to me.

"I wrote a poem about happiness."

He handed me the paper:

"Mountain high are a cheerful Hi,....resurrected from a rotten seed...today see I did to your hands ....caress.... as your words express...
my sails are at rest."

After reading the poem, I told him I didn't understand it.

"I was trying to get the attention of the bar tender I like. I hoped she would notice that I was writing a poem and would find me interesting." He went on to explain that, if she did notice him, he would find happiness. "I have no money, but I have hope."

I thought to myself that he was not helping his cause by pounding down beers at 7:30 in the morning, but I looked at the bar tender. Edwardo did have good taste in bar tenders.

A SIXTY-SEVEN-YEAR-OLD WOMAN

A sixty-seven-year-old woman born in Tanzania, who moved to the Netherlands, then to California, and was now living in Kona told me: "Happiness is being able to wake up in the morning to hear the birds and the wind in the trees and feel the sunshine or rain, to be able to walk and connect to heart space, knowing that everything happens for a reason and that nature does not hurry yet everything gets accomplished. Happiness is feeling the deep compassion for the people we love and all around. Feeling content and gratitude deep inside for LOVE that can fill us up if we allow it to happen."

MELISSA

I spoke with a fifty-four-year-old female Ironman competitor from the Philippines, Melissa Gaston Puey. She was training at the grand-daddy of all Ironman venues, on the dock in front of the King Kamehameha Hotel in Kona, Hawaii. Every year the best of the best triathletes qualify to compete in the Kona Ironman race. It's the most grueling cumulative 2.4 mile swim in ocean currents, a 112-mile bike ride and a 26.22-mile run. Many people do not finish the race. Melissa won her age group. She started to train and reinvent herself when she was forty-seven. She changed her eating habits and sleep patterns. She said she became more joyful. Amazing focus and dedication to her sport exuded from her. I asked, "What is happiness?"

"Happiness is the balance between being a blessing to others and to yourself. I can maybe expound later but now I must swim."

A THIRTY-EIGHT-YEAR-OLD FEMALE PART OWNER
OF A DINER IN KEY WEST

"Happiness is being content with your surroundings. It's the joy of little simple things. Every moment and scenario can be different … before kids, with kids, after kids. It is a very difficult question to answer."

JIMMY FANTIN

A fifty-six-year-old male mortgage banker and business owner, Jimmy, started by telling me a story:

> There is a very successful dealership in New York that sells Bentleys, BMWs, and other high-end vehicles. The owner fired the GM after a series of poor results. Since he was driving a company vehicle and was no longer an employee, I was assigned to drive him home to Connecticut.
>
> He was sitting next to me and said, "Jimmy, do you know what happiness is? It's seeing the dealership in the rear-view mirror!"

Jimmy went on to tell me, "Happiness is a state of mind. People make a choice each day they awaken to be or not to be happy, depending on the circumstances. A man was in a wheelchair suffering from cerebral palsy. One of his legs had fallen off the footrest of the wheelchair and he asked me to lift his foot back to the rest area. After I did this, he smiled and said, "Thanks for making me happy! I am happy to call you my friend.""

WILLIAM

William, who retired from a Big Eight (now Big Four) global accounting firm, had this answer:

> Let me share with you from when I was eight years old. I got my first job from my immigrant grand-father who owned a butcher shop in Newark NJ. At that time, that was happiness. I saved my money and bought my own shoes and clothes at age eleven. I did not have to depend on anyone, but my parents were my backstop. That was happiness. My parents taught me to don't always follow what my friends were doing. Don't get pressured. When I made the right choice to not follow, that was happiness. I remember we never locked our doors at home or for the car. That feeling of security and safety is happiness.
>
> We had four boys that are all successful. That is happiness. We never spent beyond our means. We never went into debt. We go to church every Sunday. Values and morality are important and instilled. That is happiness. Hearing my wife pass on wisdom to our grandkids saying, Do not have a stupid day! That is happiness.

RETIRED PAPER-PACKAGING EXECUTIVE

A retired seventy-three-year-old paper packaging executive, who had lived in twenty-seven different locations worldwide, told me: "Happiness cannot be defined as every day is different."

HAROLD

Harold, a Canadian about to retire at sixty-two as a corporate executive with global responsibility, told me: "Happiness is a finished to do list. I have worked all my life and ignored my health. All my financial bucket lists are complete. I have all the money I need, now I can spend the necessary time to focus on me. It is for me, a state of mind where nothing is eating at me. No stress or adverse pressure. But family is true happiness, for the most part."

DAVE

A sixty-four-year-old sales executive from Wisconsin, Dave defined happiness for him "as God, family and friends. In that order."

AM EIGHTY-EIGHT-YEAR-OLD GREAT-GRAND MOTHER

"Oh that's easy," she said. "Family is happiness."

DICK

Seventy-five-year-old Dick retired from corporate America at fifty-two, earned his brokerage license, and today works thirty hours a week with a wealth advisory service in support of charitable trusts and a few friends. This is what he said to me:

When I was in my late forties, I realized working as an executive for a Fortune 100 company was hurting my family due to the travel. The out of balance state was consuming me. Also, the travel on airplanes caused a chronic sinus condition. I was in poor health. Happiness was making the commitment to pivot to a local work lifestyle.

I graduated with an electrical engineering degree. My dad influenced me with these words: Engineers figure out how things work and how things are built. After earning my MBA years later, I now could see how to build wealth.

Having loving parents, good social relationships work for me to maximize happiness.

TWENTY-FOUR-YEAR-OLD WAITRESS

A twenty-four-year-old working as a waitress as she pursues her double major in aerospace engineering and mechanical engineering from Embry Riddell University defined what is happiness: "I don't have enough life experience to answer. It is a journey not a destination." After an hour, she circled back to me and said, "I have given your question more thought. Happiness is being surrounded by people who love me and I love them."

JULIO

An unemployed sixty-year-old from Puerto Rico, Julio, told me: "Happiness is having faith and good health." Months later, he told me that he had accepted an offer to manage major building projects in New Jersey.

THIRTY-ONE-YEAR-OLD PARKING VALET

I was at a swanky restaurant in Jupiter, Florida, and after dinner, was waiting at the valet parking stand. A young man walked up.

"How are you doing? I asked.

"I am great!" he said with unmistakable sarcasm. When I asked him what happiness is, he said, "I am a white guy under forty years old. I have no chance at happiness."

As I was getting into my car, I started to drive off but stopped, got out, and went back to the valet. I asked if I could walk with him as he headed to the parking lot. He said sure. I felt compelled to learn more about him but given that I had maybe a minute of time, I just asked if he wanted to be a millionaire. He laughed, and then I explained the Rule of 72. He took out his phone and wrote down notes. I then told him to look around the parking lot. We saw a $300,000 Bentley, a $400,000 Lamborghini, countless other high-dollar cars. People he was interacting with and driving their cars were most likely wealthy and successful. Many were business owners or, at the very least, had connections and influence.

I coached the thirty-one-year old parking attendant to be the best valet attendant he could possibly be. Do something of service for the car owner....wash the windshield...be positively memorable...stand out in a good way. Use this approach, and you will have doors open up for you. Someone in that parking lot of expensive cars will notice you and approach you with an opportunity.

Now maybe he's an addict or can't hold down a steady job or just does not care to be responsible. I never found out his life story. But at that moment in time he looked me in the eye, gave me a firm hand shake, smiled, and said thanks as he got into a customer's $200,000 Mercedes-Benz G-Wagon.

FATHER GALLAGHER

This eighty-four-year-old Roman Catholic Priest in Cranberry Township, Pennsylvania, told me: "I think happiness comes from living a meaningful life. If you asked Jesus on the cross if He was happy, He would have said no. But if you would have asked Him if what He was doing was meaningful, he would have said yes. Happiness is a product of a meaningful life! Hope that helps."

ART FIOCCO SR.

Ninety-seven-year-old Art golfs twice a week. This is what he had to say to me:

My life is blessed. I was drafted out of high school by the Army. I wanted to follow my cousins who joined the Marines. So, I ignored the Army and was on my way to Paris Island with the Marines, when the Army MP's came to my parents' house looking to arrest me. Happiness for them was finding out I was in Paris Island and was not going to be arrested. While in basic training, we were not allowed to go to church. I did not like that, as I am a man of faith learning from the Apostles and what they did.

I graduated from the University of Miami with a starting pay of $6,000 per year. I was rolling in dough. I remember someone saying, a new car would cost $10,000 some day. I said, "No way would that ever happen." In my mid twenties and thirties, I was able to make a sufficient paycheck to support my family. When I was in my mid thirties to my forties, I drank too much. Quitting was happiness.

Despite my wife, a son, and a daughter dying before me, I am happy to have two sons who are living and very successful.

I golfed with Art, who would walk from the member tees to the up-front red tees on every hole. He is in amazing physical health--and works at it. He shot a 98 that day but regularly shoots his age or less and has the ultimate in golf, a hole-in-one. His son, Art Jr., is a 7 index and one heck of a golfer. Like father like son, he has had numerous hole-in-ones.

NEETA P

She is a thirty-seven-year-old doctor from Palo Alto, California, with two children under the age five. "Happiness right now is eight hours of sleep in a row," she told me.

DOMINIC M

A ninety-three-year-old retired maintenance superintendent from north-western Connecticut, Dominic spent an hour with me. He said:

Happiness depends on your timing. Early in life while in college, my college roommate introduced me to his cousin who I married. We were married for sixty-five years. I still remember when we first met. Happiness.

Another happy moment in time is when I was able to pay $2000 cash for a lot in northwest Connecticut in 1963. That was a lot of money back then. Now all I had to do was build the house. I got bids from two reputable companies. They wanted $60 to $65 thousand to build a five-room 1500 square foot house with an unfinished basement. I was driving home from work and saw two guys building a stone wall. I stopped and asked them if they built houses. They said yes. They gave me a price of $13,000, if I would do the electric, plumbing, and interior finish work.

"Are you sure? $13,000!"

"Yes."

I talked to a buddy, who told me I'd better get that in writing. So, I did. Once I received the one page "contract," I said I would need to go to the bank for a loan.

So that's what I did. The banker liked me and said he would take a risk on me as this was my first loan ever. He said I was an honest guy. A year and a half later, I had a new home. As it turns out, the guys building the wall that I hired to build the house...It was their first house they built. They did a great job. I even spent another $1,800 dollars for a brick front and sides to give it some class. The house still stands today. That was happiness.

The most happiness is having a good family and faith in God, and my health to enjoy it all.

A SIXTY-TWO-YEAR-OLD RETIRED IT EXECUTIVE FROM A GLOBAL TRANSPORTATION COMPANY

When I asked her what is happiness, she replied curtly: "Let me know when you figure it out." I think she was irritated by my question.

A SEVENTEEN-YEAR-OLD

A seventeen-year-old who works at a restaurant to-go pick-up counter told me: "Happiness is having a new baby sister in a few months. I can buy her clothes and presents. I have two younger brothers, and now I have a baby sister to dote on, and I hope she will see me as her favorite. I also like to do good things for people, so someday they will return the favor."

PAUL

Forty-seven-year old physician Paul told me "Happiness is helping others."

FRANK

Eighty-six-year-old Frank, who came to America from England, said, "Happiness is drugs, sex and rock and roll." To look at him, you might have expected that response. He stood at five-foot five, had a long white beard with a pony tail painted blue. He had a cigar wedged between his missing front teeth and proudly proclaimed it a Cuban cigar. As I got to know him, I asked him again what is happiness. He gave it about ten minutes of time and said, "I graduated from college in England and when I legally"—he emphasized "legally" and launched into a detailed tangent, which we need not go into here—"came to this great country years ago, I was hired by what people now call a software engineering company. We were a subcontractor to IBM. My job was to decode, recode, and work with the mainframe hardware. So, to answer your question, Happiness for me is to do what you do, but do it exceptionally."

EDGAR

Edgar, a sixty-seven-year-old retired professional skier from Western Canada, told me, "What is happiness has many answers. It depends. Like, right now I want to be able to play better golf. In all seriousness, it's good health and good relationships."

BILLY

Billy is an eighty-one-year-old retired New Jersey businessman, who recently had two major brain surgeries. His doctors told him he should not have survived. This is what he said this about happiness:

I have no expectations as I live my life. Thirteen years ago, my mother gave me a miraculous metal. Ten years ago, I started to wear it twenty-four hours a day as a reminder of my mom who had passed on. Now this is going to sound strange, but I was awakened from a dream I had last year. In the dream, my mom told me to go to the hospital. I had been experiencing slight dizziness and balance issues over the prior month but just attributed it to getting older.

That morning, I drove myself to the emergency room. After a series of tests, they admitted me with what had been a slow brain bleed that, as it turns out, caused an infection. They did life-saving surgery the next day. They had to remove part of my skull cap … well you get the point.

My illness created happiness manifested as the miracle of the dream I had. I have always tried to be in service of others. I have no doubt being God- and spiritually-centered allowed me to overcome my life-threating illness. Oh, and my Mom in my dream.

MASSACHUSETTS BUSINESS OWNER

A eighty-two-year-old third-generation floor product and services business owner from Massachusetts said, "Happiness is other people. People equal happiness to me. I am transitioning the business over to my daughter as I finally retire. Seeing how she treats the customers with kindness and patience brings me joy. She does not see them as dollar signs but as people who need our expertise."

JILL S

Jill was a forty-three-year-old CFO of a startup company gone bust and is now a mortgage lender and consultant to a university in Colorado. "Happiness," she said, "is experiencing joy from a variety of ways. The lack of fear and pain gives me happiness. Laughter with others makes me happy."

SONNY BAHRI

A recently retired fifty-nine-year-old doctor, Sonny is building a tent lodge business in the Serengeti, Tanzania Africa. As a physician, he had been responsible for the clinical radiation oncology and cancer care departments of multiple hospitals.

I have dealt with death and dying all my adult life. At times, all I could do was slow down the inevitable. Having to tell patients and their family members they were going to die and witnessing their initial reactions to my carefully chosen words was excruciating for me.

Some of their reactions surprised me. Many were happy for the time left after the initial shock of the news delivered. Many families were drawn closer to each other. Hospice nurses speak of how a level of peace and calm transitioned as patients and family except the reality. Death is inevitable.

I have been an atheist up until recently. As a student in pre-med and med school, we were trained to be scientists not theologians
Reflecting over my life and the experiences I have had globally, they speak to a logic of a supreme being. I have been studying Bhagavad Gita and its readings gives me happiness.

Bhagavad Gita is the song of God or "song of the Lord." It is a poem written in Sanskrit thousands of years ago and part of the Hindu religion, just as the Bible is for Christians, the Torah/Talmud is for Jews and the Quran is for Islam.

The Bhagavad-Gita is a doctrine of universal truth and a book of moral and spiritual growth. Its message is sublime and non-sectarian. It deals with the most sacred metaphysical science. It im- parts the knowledge of the Self and answers two universal questions: Who am I, and how can I lead a happy and peaceful life in this word full of dualities and dilemmas?

It's a timeless book of wisdom, like the Bible, that inspired Thoreau, Emerson, Einstein, Oppenheimer, Gandhi and many others. The Bhagavad- Gita teaches how to equip ourselves for the battle of life. A repeated study with faith purifies our psyche and guides us to face the challenges of modern living leading to inner peace and happiness.

Dr. Bahri's Safari Tent Lodge in the Serengeti, Tanzania, Africa

BILL LEVANT

Seventy-nine-year-old Bill Levant compiled a 143-page "Collection of Life Stories" for his daughter-in-law using a series of questions she had developed for family patriarchs and matriarchs to answer over a six-month period. At first, Bill found the work a chore, but, wanting to please his daughter-in-law, he began to write down the answers to the questions she asked. Soon, he realized what a great history and walk down memory lane it was. Happiness transformed the chore into a pleasure. Here is a sampling:

What was your Dad like when you were a child?

My dad was a big man, about 6'2", 270 lbs, all muscle, solid and no fat. My high school coach thought he was a professional football player and why I was not as big. He was a trailer truck driver for Ballantine beer. His deliveries consisted of kegs of beer for which he was known to lift the full keg over his head. A keg weighed over 165 lbs back then.

He loved us, but in those days especially with men, his affection toward us was not shown outwardly. In his silent way he demonstrated his love. He was strict and instilled in us good manners, etiquette and ethics. Later in life, I heard comments from his friends about how proud he was of me and my accomplishments. I did not hear it from him."

How did you get your first job? Tell me an adventure you've been on? What inspires you? Have you ever doubted your faith? Have you ever sleep-walked or talked? How did you get to school as a child?

What was one of the most expensive things you've ever bought?

One of the most expensive things we purchased was our beach home in Avalon NJ. Reflecting back on it, it was one of the best decisions we ever made. Both from an overall family, as well as a financial perspective. (Authors note…purchased for around $300,000 many years ago, now valued at just under $4,000,000.) It acts as a catalyst in keeping the family close. Our son's, daughters-in-law, grand and great grand-children have formed special bonds. We all make it a point to attend the Avalon home on the 4th of July together. Swimming, boating, crabbing, clamming, fishing, jumping off the dock etc are a reflection of the great time we have together.

What has made your faith in God stronger? Have you pulled any great pranks? What was your first boss like? What were you like when you were 50? How did you decide to get married? What makes you Happy?

Happiness can be defined in many ways: being loved, blessed, health, faith, prosperous, success etc. However, taking all of these items into consideration and consolidating them, the most significant form of Happiness for me is sitting back and reflecting on my most precious assets, my loving wife and family. Throughout my entire life I have been truly blessed. My wife Juanita has been the staple of my life, the key ingredient in developing our loving family and our collective success and well-being. I reflect on the loving family I have, how well they get along and the success they have achieved in their own right. I continue to be grateful for their strong religious faith and love of God.

Happiness is not materialistic things, it is what is articulated above and the continued love I receive from my wife and collective family.

What is really an eyeopener for me and should be for the rest of us is how this anthology can be used as a template for anyone, no matter what our age. I revert back to Steven Covey's "begin with the end in mind" philosophy. What if we all started a collection of life stories as we are living life, not in retrospect at the twilight of life. Will this make us appreciate our lives and the lives of others? Would we be happier as we live in the moment instead of reflecting back in time?

> **BEST Success Practice #37 to maximize the WHH continuum:**
> **Initiate a family narrative history, starting with the oldest member.**

Here are a few more of my interview results:

FEMALE ENTREPRENEUR AND HER MOTHER

A twenty-nine-year-old female entrepreneur from Jensen Beach, Florida, who owns two businesses responded to my question with "I really don't know." Her mother, who was working on this particular Sunday and overheard my question, said, "I can answer that question. "Happiness is having healthy children and grandchildren. Nothing else matters to me."

RICHARD

A sixty-six-year-old Welshman now living in the USA responded to me with "Let me think about your question. As I think about my response, I am having difficulty. Walk with me."

Now, let me tell you about this Welshman. I have seen him walking in our community for many years. As it turns out he walks twenty miles a day. Twenty miles a day! He has been doing this for years. When he said walk with me, I felt panic and stress.

As we walked, he said that he had been promoted by an Electrical Engineering company and was transferred from Wales to Florida. The hectic pace of being a new general manager caused weight gain and stress. His parents died within six months of each other, causing great sadness. He said he retired and now consults for a few hours a week. Then he told me: "Happiness is being out in nature and enjoying the beauty. When I walk at night, the moonlit sky is beautiful. The sounds at night are peaceful. During the early morning, the area comes alive with the sounds of morning, birds chirping, the wind through the palms. I really love it here. I say a mantra when I am not listening to music when I walk."

"What do you mean?" I asked. "Do you pray?"

"Yes, because I am blessed. I used to be heavy and lethargic. I started to walk, and one step led to another, and now I walk twenty miles a day. I take a day off once in a while."

ADAM BAILEY

A fifty-two-year-old super lawyer and best-selling author in the Connect-icut-New York-New Jersey tri-state area, Adam Leitman Bailey (he gave me permission to use his name) said, "Good health is your foundation. To have a meaning in life, something to strive toward …Goals …some should be almost unattainable. When I was in the seventh grade, I wanted to be an NBA basketball player. I am five foot nine. Thank God for my God-given mind and high energy level." He went on to say that "my beautiful wife and our kids provide immense joy and happiness, as I hope I provide them."

He built his law firm from scratch and has grown it to the point where he is a regular on major news networks and interviewed by other major news media. Not bad for having graduated near the bottom of his class. "I am never satisfied," he went on to say. "Aim high and fall short and try again. Winston Churchill said something like, 'As you go through Hell… keep going.'" He continued: "I get more from criticism than praise. When I was eighteen, I read every motivational book I could find. I finished reading them all by the time I was twenty-two."

What an education! Adam the super lawyer represents billionaires and shared some of his conclusions about this experience. "Many billionaires are not motivated by money but use it to keep score. Many are the oldest child in their family, eccentric, and different. They have given up their personal lives. Their meaning of life and happiness is work."

Adam grew up poor and said it was the "best thing to happen to him." He also represents people who are less fortunate and donates to charity all the proceeds from the books he has authored. In one of his award-winning books, he has shared how children can be successful even though they are poor, like he was.

ELIZA

A twenty-three-year-old grad school student from Akron University, Eliza responded to my question: "Interesting you should ask me what is hap-piness, as I have been asking myself lately. I think at this stage of my life happiness is coffee and writing." She is studying creative writing while working at a coffee shop thirty hours a week.

STEVE

Steve, sixty-six, is a Rotary Club officer in northeast Ohio and an executive with the Bally Sports network. "Happiness is, family and friends." Twenty minutes later, he added: "I had a small biological family growing up, but my wife was one of thirteen children. She was always so happy, and I longed to have a big family dynamic. My father was adopted, and we did not have any relatives. This motivated me to make friends later in life. I have four best friends from high school. We are inseparable, meeting every week. We all go on vacations together. We have all weathered life's roads together. Happiness is remaining friends."

BRANDON

Twenty-seven-year-old Brandon manages a coffee shop in Cuyahoga Falls, Ohio, named Yada Yada. (No, it's not the Seinfeld sitcom phrase, but the Hebrew word *to know*). He defined happiness as "Finding contentment with the Lord. I felt a call to ministry when I was about eighteen years old. I have been bouncing around from job to job searching what to do. Nothing felt right." Earlier this year, an opportunity through a mentor connected him to Chaplain training school for the U.S. Air Force. He explained that he will be away from his wife and family for months in training. Once he is done, he will finally be content that he is doing what he was meant to do. His wife has agreed to the sacrifice of being away from each other.

MARLY

Marly, sixty-one years old , is a woman from the Azores, She told me that "happiness is to have no stress and have peace in my family." Her husband, Joe, died in her arms several years ago. She is now dating Manny, who grew up on the same island when she was young. He recently lost his wife to cancer. One family member is not happy with the arrangement, and this has caused stress.

CLAUDIA FERRARI

I recently meet Claudia Ferrari who immigrated from Peru to the USA as a 21 year old. She came to the USA with $700 dollars and on her own. Her father said she would not last 6 months and would be back to Peru. She has been in FL for 30 years. Her mother was from Italy and instilled a high level of spiritualism despite a lack of religiousness. Her father was a pragmatic man who was a master motivator as described by Claudia. He was a lawyer and congressman in Lima. He would say "Your will is your Power." She tells the story of how he taught her to swim. As she was swimming across the pool and barely reached the end, he was waiting for her and as she was gasping for breath, he said "you made it, to reach is easy, to go back is difficult, now go back!" And Claudia did.

She is a self-made woman, who has a successful business and owns several properties. She has a wealth accumulation philosophy. She calls it 5/5. Fifty percent of her wealth accumulations goes toward investments and fifty percent to happiness accumulation. She said "I want to give back now and not wait as God does not guarantee tomorrow."

`Given the inextricable link of health and happiness, I asked her to compare the Peruvian people's healthcare system to that of the USA given her healthcare business perspective. In Peru, 65% of the 34 million people (2025) population are poor and 5% are wealthy. The political history of Peru has been maligned and peppered with socialism and communistic style governments over the years. Ollanta Humala, a socialist leader who aligned with Victor Chavez of Venezuela is one example. In the past, the China communist model of Mao Zedong or Maoism was adopted and gained control and influence with the poor rural areas first and then poor urban areas. Corruption became a common entrenched occurrence.

Claudia shifted gears and went on to say "materialism is so minimal in Peru and such a fixation in the USA, causing higher levels of stress and anxiety." She explained the USA healthcare system is the best in the world. Many of the top doctors in Peru come to the USA to practice and become citizens draining their homeland of top-level talent for the opportunity.

I asked her what is happiness. She thought about it for a few minutes and said, "When you know who you are and you have lived or had many experiences, you realize love is happiness. God, Emanuel, Jesus all are a light that exudes positive energy, good feelings and balance." She quoted Mark Nepo, "Like the ocean, the surface of what we're living maybe choppy and disturbed, while the depth of life that hold us, is calm and deep."

Claudia has faced the choppy adversities you would expect a single woman immigrating to a foreign country to experience. Her positive light shined through it all and has been a proud productive citizen of the USA.

MOTHER MARY

We all can't reside on a mountain top, live completely free from life's burdens, and always be euphoric. But there are many places in the world where monetary wealth does not exist or is shunned, places where there are different priorities to pursue, including joy, peace, reverence, and contemplative practices. In the Greensburg, Pennsylvania, countryside is a Benedictine nun's monastery, Saint Emma's, run by Mother Mary. Her goal is to pray for others formally from 5:20 a.m. to 7:30 p.m., with an hour off during midday as the nuns pursue spiritual perfection. They have fund raisers, a bed and breakfast, a gift shop, and many volunteers who help maintain the shrines, buildings, and grounds.

What does this have to do with maximizing WHH? There are some places where we can go on "retreat." Some retreats are silent for days at a time, with no technology allowed. St. Emma's Monastery is a place for spiritual renewal in support of our life's work. Call it a counterbalance to societal stress. Contemplative mediative efforts are not as successful without direction and practice. If you have never been on a multi-day silent retreat…you are in for a detoxification. Remember, *silent* includes no technology. I went nuts the first twenty-four hours. Medical studies abound that correlate stress reduction with physical health increases and happiness. Spiritual coaches to help us increase our spirituality and are a blessing. The nuns sacrifice their-lives so others can unwind. The positive stress they incur in constant prayer and a spartan lifestyle become our opportunity to "de-stress" within the confines of this sanctuary.

BEST Success Practice #38 to maximize the WHH continuum:
Pray, meditate and go to Church/Synagogue/Temple/Mosque and
congregate with others. Help others. Stay active. Detox from technology
for a few days through a retreat.

Let's start with happiness and unhappiness rankings of countries and work our way to individual and state-of- mind happiness.

Nick Routley Chief Product Officer at Visual Capitalist published "Charting the Relationship Between Wealth and Happiness, by Country" (September 2023). In it, he analyzed Credit Suisse data, which breaks down the average wealth per adult in various countries around the world. I summarized the top ten and where the USA ranks.

WEALTH and HAPPINESS Metrics *Source: Credit Suisse Bank 2023*

Rank	Country	Medium Wealth per Adult	Happiness Score
1	Finland	$73,775	7.8
2	Denmark	165,622	7.6
3	Iceland	231,462	7.6
4	Switzerland	146,733	7.5
5	Israel	80,315	7.4
6	Sweden	89,846	7.4
7	Norway	117,798	7.4
8	Netherlands	136,105	7.4
9	Luxembourg	259,899	7.4
10	Austria	91,833	7.2
14	USA	79,274	7

Then I summarized happiness, by country. The optimum space is the right upper section called happiest and wealthiest. Conversely the bottom left section is the unhappiest and poorest.

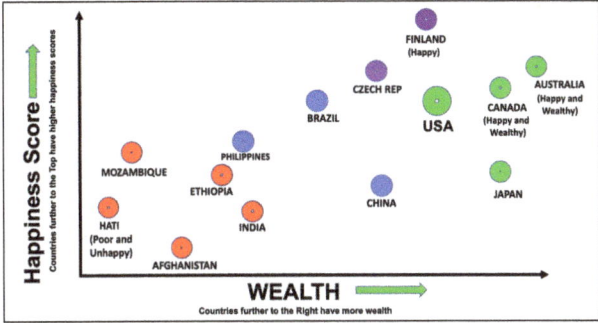

I researched happiness by country to determine macro traits and trends. One source is the *World Happiness Report 2024*, which lists the countries that have trended toward unhappiness since 2010:

The Average happiness score for all countries is 5.5 with the USA 6.7 points down from 7.3. The reasons? Political upheaval, population shifts, inflation, and crime.

COUNTRIES BECOMING UNHAPPIER

	COUNTRY	2010	2023	DECLINE
1	AFGHANISTAN	4.2	1.6	-2.6
2	LEBANON	5.5	2.2	-2.3
3	JORDAN	5.7	4.2	-1.5
4	VENEZUELA	6.9	5.6	-1.3
5	MALAWI	4.6	3.4	-1.2
6	ZAMBIA	4.7	3.5	-1.2
7	BOTASWANA	4.6	3.6	-1
8	YEMEN	4.6	3.6	-1
9	EGYPT	5.0	4.0	-1
10	INDIA	5.0	4.1	-0.9
11	BANGLADESH	4.8	3.9	-0.9
12	DRC	4.0	3.3	-0.7
13	TUNISIA	5.1	4.4	-0.7
14	CANADA	7.5	6.9	-0.6
15	USA	7.3	6.7	-0.6

These are the top 15 countries out of 146 with the greatest happiness score declines as tracked by the *World Happiness Report 2024*

The USA, in 2024, dropped out of the top 20 for the first time since the happiness report has been tracked in 2010. The USA fell from fifteenth happiest country to twenty-third.

While the results don't definitively point to monetary wealth being necessary to happiness, there is a strong correlation between wealth and happiness across the board. Broadly speaking, the world's poorest countries have the lowest happiness scores, and the richest report being the most happy.

The Happiness Research Institute, based in Denmark, uses the Gallop Poll as the basis for its *World Happiness Report*. The research leverages six key factors to help explain variation in self-reported levels of happiness across the world: social support, income, health, freedom, generosity, and absence of corruption. Governments are increasingly using this analysis to orient policies toward happiness. Argentina presents an especially eye-opening history. In the early 1900s, its economy was arguably among the top ten. In the 2023 World Happiness Report it ranked 52nd in happiness and 69th in economic prosperity terms.

Why? Socialism exacerbated by decades of Peronism, widely considered to be a variant of left-wing populism although some have described it as a Latin American form of fascism instead. Call it what you want but, the prosperity of a nation declined as its wealth generating form of capitalism was slowly milked for social spread the wealth programs.

In November of 2023, Argentina elected a new President, Javier Milei. He immediately initiated steps to lower inflation and cut government regulations/spending that were hindering economic growth in favor of social programs without the ability to pay for them.

In a little over a year the Argentina Milei government went from a significant deficit to a positive surplus.

Why?

"The fact that you have a president, head of state, who is defending the free market, who is defending the role of entrepreneurs and business as creators of value and just defending deregulation when the tendency in Latin America and much of the West has been to regulate the economy . . . I think that's very positive, not only for Argentina, but for the region as a whole and maybe beyond," Daniel Raisbeck, a policy analyst at the CATO Institute, wrote.

Raisbeck stressed that Milei's primary measure of cutting spending has proven highly effective, while arguing that the significant deregulation in other parts of the economy has helped it revive.

Prior to Milei, "Argentina was one of the most regulated economies in the world," Raisbeck said. "So, when you have a very well-thought-out package like the one that they introduced . . . and you get rid of as many of those regulations as you can, then it's very positive."

This is a commentary on how Nations as well as individuals, need to balance their WHH continuum. High debt and inflation equals human misery and unhappiness. What is happening in Argentina is proof yet again that 1976 Nobel laureate Milton Friedman's application of economic stimulation through free markets works! Sadly, many countries, including the United States recently, follow the British economist John Maynard Keynes or Keynesian economics. The new 2025 administration in the USA, is going back to our Constitutional Republic and Democratic roots with a focus on Milton Friedman economic applications to minimize regulations and big government in support of free market Capitalism.

At Providence College we were mandated to study Western Civilization and other courses including Logic. Logic?

History has taught us the absence of logic and polylogism (multiple logics) have caused great societies and countries to go astray. Illogic and polylogism can threaten our liberties and ultimately our happiness. Polylogism, in the strictest sense is the absence of a uniform logic of fact. It's a divide and defiler of what is truth. Let me explain. Logic helps remove emotional supposition and inculcates clarity not just perspective. When Karl Marx and socialism came to prominence, he advocated a series of conflicts between people's religion, race, gender, and language. All for the good of a classless society. Illogic. What was true for one class of people was false for the other in attempts to cloud what is logical truth.

Without truth we cannot maximize our wealth, health and happiness. He drafted the "Communist Manifesto" to inject, among other ideas, a conflict between free market Capitalism and the worker. Logic says with no Capitalism you cannot employee workers except through the government.

With Capitalism, jobs are created for workers who in turn create value, foster entrepreneurship, and create other companies, all while funding the government with tax dollars. Very Logical.

BEST Success Practice #39 to maximize the WHH continuum: Constitutional Republic and Democracies with free market capitalism and low historic inflation produce more WHH than non-democratic, non-free-market countries. Limiting government-funded programs adds to the long-term stability of the economy. Individuals contribute to stability by limiting their credit card debt.

GDP is not a Measure of Income Equality/Inequality or Happiness

Luca Ventura, in *Global Finance Magazine* (May 2024, gfmag.com) reported:
  If we simply consider a nation's gross domestic product (GDP)—the sum of all goods and services produced by a country during one year—then we would have to conclude that the richest nations are exactly the ones with the largest GDP: United States, China, Japan, Germany. But how could the economies, for example, of Singapore or Luxembourg ever match that

of such powerhouses when they are no more than small dots on the world map?

Another problem with GDP is that it does not measure income inequality, that is, how a country's riches are distributed among the population. That is why a more accurate representation of people's living conditions begins with dividing a nation's GDP by the number of people that live there: per capita GDP and its growth rate tell us much more about the social wealth potentially available to each person and whether this wealth is either increasing or decreasing over time.

However, using per capita GDP still poses a problem: the very same income can buy very little in some countries and go much further in others where basic necessities—food, clothing, shelter, or healthcare—cost far less. To gauge how wealthy a country's citizens are it is necessary to understand how much they can buy. That is why, when comparing per capita GDP across countries, GDP should be adjusted for purchasing power parity, which helps us take into account the inflation rates and the price of goods and services in each given place.

When considering happiness, is it better to be rich in a poor country or poor in a rich country? Studies show the best chance of enjoying a superior standard of living is to reside in a richer nation no matter where a person falls on the income distribution scale. Then again, wealth for some without a good measure of equality for everyone is problematic, to say the least. The coronavirus pandemic proved it most strikingly. Low-income workers, often migrants, living in some very wealthy nations suddenly found themselves unemployed, homeless and stranded without much of a safety net. Many less affluent nations, in the meantime, bent over backwards to take care of all those in need during the crisis.

Because energy and food are essential goods with few substitutes, higher prices are particularly painful for low-income households. It is easier for families to cut down or eliminate spending on electronics, clothing or entertainment when prices surge, but when it comes to food, heating or transportation—crucial to both live and earn a living—this becomes much more difficult. As a result, an inflationary scenario can often pose a threat to economic and social stability.

This is why, in the long run, it is better not only to be rich but to be egalitarian as well. Too much economic inequality stifles growth for all, political instability is more likely, healthcare care costs and mortality rates are higher, and so are crime and corruption rates. Being rich in a poor country also has costs.

Typical economic inequality is witnessed historically and today in countries that are run by dictators, or where communism, fascism and socialism abound. Free market capitalism-based republics and some democracies have a better chance of maximizing WHH for the population as a whole.

Executive Summary from Long and Happy Lives

In 2022 the Happiness Research Institute utilized data from the United Nations, Organization for Economic Co-operation and Development (OECD). In addition they implemented their own surveys the results of which produced insights on how to live longer and happier lives.

Ventura compiled and summarized the salient points below.
  ◆ 5.8 million good life years are lost to moderate loneliness 5.6 million good life years are lost to severe loneliness 6.4 million good life years are lost to depression
  ◆ 6.2 million good life years are lost to financial distress
  ◆ million good life years are lost to physical inactivity 1 million good life years are lost to divorce

Here are the top ten losses of well-being adjusted life years per the study:
1. **Loneliness is the most burdensome condition for adults over 50 years old.**
50+ year-olds experiencing severe loneliness lose 28% of their potential wellbeing in Denmark, and 25% in Europe. On a societal level, moderate and severe loneliness are responsible for more wellbeing lost among older adults than almost any other condition under consideration.

2. **Depression also poses a substantial threat to wellbeing in later life.**
50+ year-olds with depression lose 17% of their potential wellbeing in Denmark, and 18% in Europe.

3. **Experiencing loneliness in childhood increases social and economic risks in adulthood. Older adults who were lonely in childhood are, for example, more likely to become depressed or get divorced later in life.**

4. **Diseases have differential impacts on quality of life.**
Some health conditions like high blood pressure and high cholesterol

predict relatively small declines in wellbeing, while others like Parkinson's and Alzheimer's have substantial impacts on quality of life.

5. Over time, older adults are able to adapt to some adverse conditions more easily than others.

While losing a spouse or having a heart attack can have substantial short-term impacts on quality of life, many adults are able to adapt in the long-term. However, adaptation to loneliness and depression is much less common.

6. Individual wellbeing burdens can have substantial spillover impacts on loved ones.

Partners of patients with Alzheimer's disease, for example, often experience even larger declines in wellbeing than patients themselves.

7. Older adults with low life satisfaction are major consumers of healthcare services and public assistance.

In Denmark, 50+ year-olds with below average life satisfaction are 23% more likely to be admitted to a hospital, 58% more likely to experience a health problem limiting their ability to work, and 72% more likely to receive some form of public assistance two years later

8. Low wellbeing in later life can cost up to 200,000 extra bed days in hospitals per year.

50+ year-olds with below average life satisfaction are more likely to spend extra nights in the hospital two years later. In Denmark, if the proportion of older adults with low life satisfaction remains constant, it could result in 200,000 additional overnight hospital stays per year by 2050.

9. Population growth is expected to exacerbate wellbeing burdens among older adults.

By 2050, the societal wellbeing burden of depression in Europe is expected to increase by 21%, and the burden of severe loneliness is expected to increase by 40%.

10. By preparing for demographic aging, we can support not only longer, but also better lives.

Longer life can have a number of societal benefits. Older adults can participate in civil society, care for others, and contribute to economic prosperity. Yet if we do not adapt to demographic aging and provide for wellbeing in later life, we may face a much more uncertain future.

OECD (Organization for Economic Co-operation and Development) is inter-governmental with 38 countries founded in 1961 to measure happiness.

There are many governmental, clinical, scientific, mathematical and spiritual entities over the years who are measuring happiness. OECD is one and I have summarized their 275-page report using the following chart:

A simple model of subjective well-being

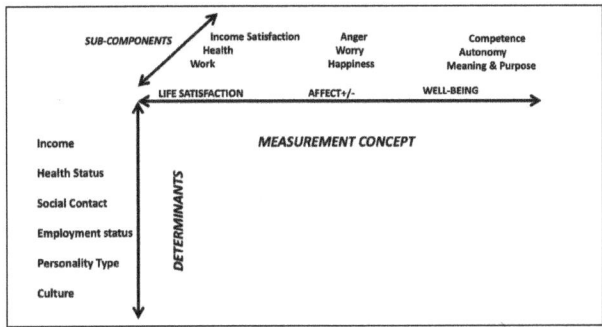

OECD Guidelines on measuring subjective well-being 2013

A summary of crucial elements point to why people within a country can be happy or not. Here they are...

Employment status – employment status is known to have a large influence on subjective well-being, with unemployment in particular associated with a strong negative impact on measures of life satisfaction (Winkelmann and Winkelmann, 1998).

Health status – both physical and mental health are correlated with measures of subjective well-being (Dolan, Peasgood and White, 2008), and there is evidence that changes in disability status cause changes in life satisfaction (Lucas, 2007).

Work/life balance – there is significant evidence that aspects of work/life balance impact on subjective well-being, in particular commuting (Frey and Stutzer, 2008; Kahneman and Kruger, 2006), and time spent caring for others (Kahneman and Krueger, 2006). Relevant measures include hours worked (paid and unpaid), leisure time, perceived time crunch as well as information on how time is used.

Education and skills – education and skills have obvious interest both as variables for cross-classification and because there is good evidence that education is associated with subjective well-being at a bivariate level (Blanchflower and Oswald, 2011; Helliwell, 2008).

Social connections – social contact is one of the most important drivers of subjective well-being, as it has a large impact both on life evaluations and on affect (Helliwell and Wang, 2011b; Kahneman and Krueger, 2006; Boarini et al., 2012). Although only some elements can be measured well in the context of general household surveys, measures of human contact, such as frequency of contact with friends and family, volunteering activity, and experience of loneliness, should also be collected where possible.

Civic engagement and governance – trust in others as well as more domain-specific measures of neighborhood and workplace trust are crucial factors when accounting for variation in subjective well-being (Helliwell and Wang, 2011b).

Environmental quality – environmental quality is inherently a geographic phenomenon, and integrating datasets on environmental quality with household level data on life satisfaction is costly. Nonetheless, there is some evidence that noise pollution (Weinhold, 2008) and air pollution (Dolan, Peasgood and White, 2008) have a significant negative impact on life satisfaction.

Personal security – security is important to subjective well-being. Living in an unsafe or deprived area is associated with a lower level of life satisfaction, after controlling for one's own income (Dolan, Peasgood and White, 2008; Balestra and Sultan, 2012).-

See table below from OECD guidelines on measuring subjective well-being 2013. Many of the outcomes and charts are driven by data collected in surveys. Many of the surveys are driven and funded by government entities or the United Nations. I don't know about you, but I tend to be leery of surveys by the government. It's one of the many reasons in the USA, people are not willing to talk to census takers as the survey questions are invasive to many people. People do not trust strangers with their personal information or data. There are also inherent bias by country and their methods to collect data and the interview process. There are interpretive error rates normally associated with data collection. Survey's have error rates but represent data sets and conclusions we can learn from.

Table 4.3. **Mean net affect balance by activity, from Kahneman et al. (2004)**			
Activity	Percentage of sample	Time spent (hours)	Net affect[1]
Intimate relations	11	0.21	4.74
Socialising after work	49	1.15	4.12
Dinner	65	0.78	3.96
Relaxing	77	2.16	3.91
Lunch	57	0.52	3.91
Exercising	16	0.22	3.82
Praying	23	0.45	3.76
Socialising at work	41	1.12	3.75
Watching TV	75	2.18	3.62
Phone at home	43	0.93	3.49
Napping	43	0.89	3.27
Cooking	62	1.14	3.24
Shopping	30	0.41	3.21
Computer at home	23	0.46	3.14
Housework	49	1.11	2.96
Childcare	36	1.09	2.95
Evening commute	62	0.62	2.78
Working	100	6.88	2.65
Morning commute	61	0.43	2.03

1. Net affect is the average of three positive adjectives (enjoyment, warm, happy) less the average of five negative adjectives (frustrated, depressed, angry, hassled, criticised). All the adjectives are reported on a 0-6 scale, ranging from "not at all" to "very much". The "time spent" column is not conditional on engaging in the activity. The sample consists of 909 employed women in Texas.
Source: Kahneman, Krueger, Schkade, Schwartz and Stone (2004), Figure 2, p. 432.

After researching Scale distortion theory, specifically by S.W. Fredrick, Yale University and D. Mochon, University of California, San Diego in their publication, " *A Scale Distortion Theory of Anchoring*", there are psychological inuendo as well. How the scale construct is created and presented in a survey will also bias the outcome. The scale method of 1-10, the Cantrill ladder, or point total approach are linked to the issue of scale anchoring. Is the scale intended to be unipolar (i.e. reflecting a single construct running from low to high) or bipolar (running between two opposing constructs)? The weather, time of day, month of the year, all have an effect on the person answering surveys.

All of this speaks to imperfection rates, but represents the best available cumulative data gathered.

The surveys listed in this book and their sources represent some level of fact at the time of the survey. Point-in-time surveys do not necessarily reflect a holistic outcome. One of the reasons I surveyed or reported on past interactions of over 800 people was to attempt to codify researched surveys.

One popular Methodology referenced in many surveys adopted by many countries is Cantrill Ladder.

Imagine a ladder with steps numbered from zero at the bottom to ten at the top. Suppose we say that the top of the ladder represents the best possible life for you and the bottom of the ladder represents the worst possible life for you.

If the top step is 10 and the bottom step is 0, on which step of the ladder do you feel you personally stand at the present time? We can pick holes at this widely adopted approach. How one feels is subjective and time based and can be skewed.

Now to understand what happiness is, we have to understand the antithesis of happiness. How do we avoid being unhappy? It is not possible. We are human and we will and do have bad moods and days. How we overcome bad days or circumstances is problematic. We'll share some examples as it relates to the WHH continuum.

Many motivation coaches and therapists researched, have methods to get us

back on the happiness track. A summary of their approaches are in the next Best
Success Practice.

BEST Success Practice #40 to maximize the WHH continuum:
• Exercise Set Goals (see chapter on Goal setting methods)
• Act on goal identification achievement
• Socialize in person and share why you are unhappy (loneliness kills)
• Understand you can't be happy or motivated all the time

Research indicates that many wealthy individuals are neither happy nor unhappy
but manage through it all.

Donnelly Hobson, G. E. Zhen, E. Haisley, and M. I. Norton, authors of *Million-aires and Happiness* (2018), wrote:

… how the wealth of high earners (millionaires) corresponds with overall
life satisfaction, and whether or not a millionaire's source of wealth plays
any role is explored.

The researchers analyzed data taken from respondents who had a net
worth ranging from $1.5-$15+ million US. A 7-point scale was used to
assess the overall life satisfaction of the respondents where 1= "strongly
agree" and 7="strongly disagree" to the statement "All things considered,
I am satisfied with my life." Respondents also indicated the source of
their wealth, allowing the researchers to calculate the percentage of earned
versus unearned wealth.

Results showed those with a net worth of $3-$7.9 million US
dollars were no more satisfied with their lives than those with a net worth
of $1.5-$2.9 million US dollars. It wasn't until net worth climbed to
$8-$14.9 million US dollars that respondents reported higher life satisfaction. Lastly, those with a net worth of $15+ million US dollars reported
being marginally more satisfied than the lower tier millionaires.

In terms of wealth source, respondents who earned their wealth reported higher ratings of happiness than those whose wealth was
unearned. The apparent psychological benefit of earning your wealth
seems to align with existing research suggesting there is an inherent love
in labor. It's found that the amount of value we place in something
corresponds strongly with the work we put into acquiring it."

Wealth Altruism and Transition Maximize Joy and Avoid Heartache

Wealth transition must be done right to produce maximum WHH for all. An immigrant came to the USA and worked the night shift as a cleaner at a Dunkin Donuts. Thirty -five years later, he owned five DD franchise locations and was worth millions. He worked until his untimely death from a heart attack at age seventy, leaving the business to his son with no conditions or stipulations. His son was forty-one, and dad had provided for him and his sisters throughout their lives.

What did the son do?

Within a year of his dad's passing, he sold the five units and the buildings that housed the five Dunkin Donut locations with the exception of one. The one property that was retained produce rent payments that go to his mother for her retirement. The son who inherited the fruits of his dad's self-sacrificing life of hard work "retired" at age forty-two. He spends his time riding his motorcycle and doing as he pleases.

Was the WHH continuum maximized for all? No, of course not.

Why is it that many of the wealthy give away their fortunes? Is it guilt? The imposter phenomenon—which causes you to feel that you are a fraud undeserving of your wealth? Have they achieved so much, they want to implement meaningful legacy change? Is it peer pressure from other wealthy friends and family?

Should we make a charitable donation and receive a tax write-off, pass wealth onto family, or just give it away?

Most people who donate a large percentage of their wealth have lived life and accumulated tens of millions of dollars. When they give, it makes the national news. Think Warren Buffett, Charlie Munger, and Bill Gates. They have been in the public eye all these years and have created charitable foundations to expedite the transfer of billions for causes that are meaningful to them.

To give billions to a legitimate and worthy cause or to purposefully continue a legacy is admirable. In contrast, data suggests that second-generation wealth, inherited without condition or stipulation, tends to be less appreciated, less valued, and even squandered, as in the Dunkin Donut example.

If you have earned substantial wealth, you need to devise an orderly plan for its transition. There is no one size that fits all. Each of us has different circumstances and dynamics.

> **BEST Success Practice #41 to maximize the WHH continuum: When transitioning business or personal wealth, plan at least ten years prior and use a professional (WAS, RIA, CPA, knowledgeable attorney) to customize your plans, knowing they will likely change over time.**

In every family dynamic, certain skills, personalities, and experiences determine who takes the lead relating to finances, taxes, and wealth management. It is rare to see a collaborative effort between the family members. The next story, which I call "The Coach's Wife," is all about how not to achieve the correct balance of WHH.

With the best of intentions, the Coach did all he could to shelter his wife from many of life's realities. His approach and intention were the product of his love. He did not want her to worry or be burdened. He was aware that she was both a worrier and a procrastinator. The problem was that, after decades and decades of sheltering, Mrs. Coach had no idea of how the family finances had been or should be managed. All she knew is that she had everything she needed and wanted. And so, she was happy.

Time passed, and life was good.

Coach grew fifteen years older, his health began to fail, and he developed Alzheimer's. His wife began spending all her time caring for him. They had discussed finances and the details before his memory loss became severe, but Mrs. Coach was more concerned about her husband's health, care, and comfort than she was about money matters. She did not pay as much attention to the issue of wealth as she should have.

Many years prior, the Coach set up a donation of $1 million dollars to support Alzheimer's research. He set up, with an estate attorney and financial planner, all the right and responsible solutions should he die before his wife. It was an example of altruistic love.

Now, flash forward to his passing. The Coach's wife is an emotional mess. At age sixty-seven, for the very first time in her life, she is struggling to understand the investments, bills, banking, and tax consequences that are now hers. She has to learn how to live alone. Her step-children are no help. She is not religious, and she does not have a circle of close friends.

Her mental health begins to fail. After a memorial celebration of this great coach, some of his former players reach out to her and recommend grief counseling. That is a kind thing to do, but she also needs help with the proper stewardship of what are now her finances.

Her situation is one that is played out every day. As difficult as it may have been for him, the Coach should have involved his wife in managing family matters, even though she wanted him to "handle everything." His own controlling demeanor and personality were no help. A better balance of WHH would have made the transition easier and reduced her mental anxiety. Knowledge is power. Well-meaning as he was, the Coach should have coached his wife in an essential aspect of the family's welfare.

BEST Success Practice #42 to maximize the WHH continuum: Be certain that more than one family member is knowledgeable about the legal, financial, and health management aspects of the family's personal and business wealth as well as the future intentions for these matters

4

How Your Personality Can Be Integral to Your Success or Failure

Are we born with our personality, is it in our genes, or is our personality formed over time by the environment in which we live? Doubtless, this timeless question requires more than a simple either/or answer. But we have all heard "he's a natural born leader" or "you can tell she is a born salesperson."

But why and how did he emerge as a leader and she start a successful enterprise that made her a multi-millionaire? Why do we succeed or fail? Personality certainly matters. Ego drive and empathy play a big part in shaping our WHH. We can assume that an important aspect of personality is genetic, but surely environment must play a part as well. A person may be born with a "tall" genotype, but if this individual grows up undernourished, it is unlikely that the genotype will be fully expressed in the phenotype. The person we see before us will not be tall.

We all have a predisposition or leaning toward certain behaviors and other characteristics. Some of us are outgoing, or grumpy, or loud, or quiet. Some people always smile. Some always frown. Is their attitude a gift or curse of nature or of nurture? Does the happy person have ample reason for joy? Does the sad person face pain or other issues?

There is an array of recognizable patterns of behavior, which researchers have determined are linked to personality types. Some of these types are principally genetic, but most are influenced by how we grew up, our experiences, and whom we associate with. These personality types develop over time. Your personality is unique to you. Social sciences have categorized us into groups based on a number of traits, including temperament, energy level, how we react to outside stimulus, and how we respond to various situations. All influence the creation of personality over time, but no two people are exactly alike.

Successful professional Texas hold 'em poker players are intuitively aware of their opponents' actions and reactions. They can "read" behaviors to determine if their opponents are bluffing or truly have a good hand. They can deduce what type of personality they are opposing. They look for physical reactions and, combined with the psychological, they can make a call to go all in or fold.

In 1998, seven of my colleagues and I were recruited away from Siemens-Westinghouse Corporation to start an electrical engineering services division for Eaton Corporation. As we were in our own recruitment stage of grow our Eaton Electrical Engineering Services business, we intuitively sought engineers who would be able to work well on a team. We found that most engineers were singularly focused to solve problems by themselves. They generally did not fit into our team dynamic. We learned from trial and error that we needed a different search approach. We concluded that we needed to hire amiable engineers willing to get their hands dirty. We modified our hiring target approach to identify good team members capable of adapting to the *group* personality we were creating.

This approach followed education researcher Dr. Ron L. Pinnell's "An Investigation of the Relationship Among Teachers' Personality Typologies and Perception of Organizational Climate In Secondary Schools" (1989), which revealed evidence of group as well as individual personalities. Pinnell adopted a group personalities concept that is a social system of interacting personalities bound together by social relationships. This group personality is characterized by interdependence of elements, differentiation from its environment, complex networks of social relations, individual actors motivated by their personalities, and a distinctive unity that goes beyond its component parts.

Pinnell concluded: "A school system can be considered a group dynamic with its own collective of individuals forming its own group personality." We concluded that any group can have its own personality, made up of individual personalities. This is germane to maximizing the WHH continuum, because individual personalities can change over time through interaction with the personality of a group in which they are a member.

Years ago, I witnessed how the personality of an aluminum manufacturing customer of mine metamorphosized over time. He had been a Marine with a tough "jarhead" can-do personality and a true conservative politically. He graduated from engineering school, married, and was hired by a Fortune 1000 company, where he advanced into senior management. His children thrived and were very successful in their own right. He retired early with millions. Life was good until his wonderful wife died in his arms after battling cancer, at age fifty-six.

After this, he took bicycling alone thousands of miles, from coast to coast for months at a time, camping on the side of the road as he struggled with her untimely death. He focused on his health, lost weight (he had been 20 pounds overweight), and seemed to be overcoming his grief. Eventually, he remarried. His new wife was the opposite of his first wife, very liberal and self-centered, and in less than a year his personality changed, mimicking hers. He also became sedentary and drank too much. It was living proof of how the environment we live in and the people we associate with, can change our personality. Who we team with, socialize with, and work with affects our individual personalities potentially creating positive or negative outcomes.

In my opinion, one of the more useful studies on if we inherit our personalities or is it influenced overtime by who we associate with, where we live and what experiences we accumulate is…

Heritability of the Big Five Personality Dimensions and their Facets; A twin Study. Kerry L. Jang and W. John Livesley *University of British Columbia and University of Western Ontario*

I have summarized the salient points of the Heritability (observable variation in a population) study as follows:

The genetic and environmental etiology of the five-factor model of personality as measured by the revised NEO Personality Inventory (NEO-PI-R) was assessed using 123 pairs of identical twins and 127 pairs of fraternal twins. Broad genetic influence on the five dimensions of Neuroticism, Extraversion, Openness, Agreeableness, and Conscientiousness was estimated at 41%, 53%, 61%, 41%, and 44%, respectively. The facet scales also showed substantial heritability, although for several facets the genetic influence was largely nonadditive. The influence of the environment was consistent across all dimensions and facets. Shared environmental influences accounted for a negligible proportion of the variance in most scales, whereas nonshared environmental influences accounted for the majority of the environmental variance in all scales.

Jang and Livesley go on to say, "Our results suggest that genetic and environmental effects are not uniform across all facets of a dimension. For example, our data suggest that not all facets of Conscientiousness are influenced to the same degree by genetic factors. Individual differences in Order, Self-Discipline, and Deliberation appear to be largely determined by environmental influences."

My conclusion: There is minimal genetic effect on personality and more outside influences over time.

Have you ever wondered if some people are predisposed to success and others to failure? Do different personality types have an effect? Freelance writer Charlotte Grainger, sheds some light on this subject in "The Five Personality Traits of Self-Made Millionaires" (*True You Journal,* truity.com, July 23, 2024). The key word is "Self-made":

Why are the rich rich? Maybe it's luck. Or, maybe it's their personality traits.

We've all pondered one of life's deepest mysteries: What is it that makes a self-made millionaire or Billionaire? We all know who they are. Why is it the select few go on to become self-made millionaires while others simply fall short?

Leg-ups, lawsuits, and mastermind songwriting abilities aside, the super wealthy could share more than just a ton of cash. Yes, they may have similar core personality traits, too. How do the rich score on the Big Five personality test?

Before we go any further, let's cover the basics. You may already be familiar with the Big Five personality test. Despite being less famous than Myers and Briggs and other systems, the Big Five is thought to be the one of the most scientifically sound personality models and is the one that researchers tend to use when assessing personality.

According to Grainger:

The Big Five is a *trait* model of personality, rather than a *type* model. Most popular ways of describing personality talk about personality types, such as Type A or Type B personalities, or Myers Briggs' INFPs, ENTJ and ESTJs [they identify sixteen different personality types]. Although type models are easy to understand, they are not scientifically sound, as people don't neatly sort into categories. The Big Five describes people in terms of traits on a spectrum, and as such, is a valid and evidence-based means of understanding personality.

The Big Five model has its roots in a theory called the lexical hypothesis—the idea that we can create a sort of taxonomy of individual differences by examining the language we use to describe each other. Early researchers took an inventory of words that describe personality traits, such as "friendly," "helpful," "aggressive," and "creative." They then attempted to organize these words into related clusters. For instance, a person who's described as friendly is also likely to be described as gregarious, talkative, and outgoing. Researchers consistently found that trait-related adjectives tended to cluster into five groups, corresponding to the five traits in the Big Five.

Today, the Big Five model is the basis of most modern personality research, and as such has been used to illuminate everything from how much of our personality is inherited.

Grainger continues:

As the Big Five name suggests, the model uses five verticals — each distinct — to measure an individual's personality: Openness, Conscientiousness, Extraversion, Agreeableness and Neuroticism. The concept rests upon the idea that we each have different levels of these traits, which can be measured through a series of questions.

Personality traits of the super wealthy would be helpful to understand, so that we might see how many of these traits we are applying in our own lives.

Grainger continued her investigation, asking

What do self-made millionaires have in common — aside from the size of their bank accounts? That is the question that German researchers set out to answer. To get to the bottom of the conundrum, the team took a deep dive on data looking at 20,000 citizens. The data included each individual's scores on the Big Five personality test and what their net worth was. It also looked at whether their wealth was inherited or self-made.

The study found that rich individuals, i.e. people with a net worth of more than one million had a distinctive personality profile when compared to the non-rich. Overall, they tended to be more risk-tolerant, open, extraverted and conscientious than the rest of the group.

The study also found that these individuals tended to be less neurotic than others. Let's take a moment to break down what each personality trait looks like in real terms.

Grainger continues with a five-step summary in conjunction with Niloufar Esmaeilpour of the Lotus Therapy & Counseling Centre. She cites Esmaeilpour:

1. Risk Tolerant

Making serious money is oftentimes risky business. Whether it's making the right call or taking that all-important leap of faith, self-made millionaires rise to the challenge.

"Business ventures, investments and other avenues that lead to significant wealth often come with inherent risks," explains Niloufar Esmaeilpour, who is associated with the Lotus Therapy & Counseling Centre. "Those who can navigate these uncertainties without becoming overly stressed or anxious might be more likely to reap the rewards."

As a disclaimer, that's not to say that top-earners throw caution to the wind when it comes to their decision-making. "It's also important to note that risk tolerance doesn't necessarily mean recklessness. It can imply a calculated approach to uncertainty," adds Esmaeilpour.

2. More Open

Making it big can often mean spotting something that others may have missed. Rather than fostering a closed mindset, self-made millionaires are more likely to keep it open. This approach to life—and, of course, business—could help them to reap financial rewards.

"Being open to new experiences and ideas is a hallmark of the trait known as Openness. This quality might be particularly advantageous for the wealthy, as it often correlates with a readiness to adopt fresh business approaches, ventureinto novel investment opportunities, or swiftly adapt to the ebb and flow of economic trends," says Esmaeilpour.

3. Extroverted

Big earners often have big personalities to match. Since networking is central to any type of business, it's logical that a person who exhibits extraverted traits would do well here. After all, if you love connecting with others and being sociable, you're already onto a winner.

As Esmaeilpour puts it, "Extraverted individuals might find it easier to create and maintain valuable connections, negotiate deals, or lead teams, all of which can play a role in accumulating wealth."

4. Conscientious

Scoring high on the Big Five trait of Conscientiousness means that you dedicate yourself to your work and ensure that you follow the optimal processes. So, it's no real surprise that people who have the ability to knuckle down and be productive end up making more money.

"Conscientious individuals are typically organized, responsible, and persistent. Such traits can be advantageous in managing finances, planning long-term goals, and ensuring tasks are completed efficiently and effectively," says Esmaeilpour. "It's not hard to see how these attributes might correlate with financial success."

5. Less Neurotic

The final piece of the puzzle that makes up self-made millionaires is a low score on Neuroticism. Yes, those who make it to the top of the financial charts are more likely to be emotionally stable and show fewer neurotic traits than the rest of us. Who knew?

"Neuroticism is associated with emotional instability, anxiety and mood swings," says Esmaeilpour. "Lower levels of neuroticism among the wealthy might suggest that they're less likely to be hindered by excessive worry or negative emotions, which can be barriers to clear decision-making or sustained effort in business ventures."

How to Change Your Behavior and (Maybe) Become Wealthier

By this point, you should have a clear picture of the traits that the ridiculously rich share. But if your personality doesn't quite align with all the above, don't panic. It's not game over.

Personality traits typically stay the same throughout life, that does not mean one cannot change behavior. In the spirit of continuous self-development, let's take a look at some expert-backed habits. The following advice could help you to become a millionaire or at least increase your income.

BEST Success Practice #43 to maximize the WHH continuum:
Learn to take calculated risks

Risk-taking may not come naturally to you. That's perfectly okay. However, if you want to push beyond your comfort zone, you can change your perspective. Doing your research ahead of time could make those big decisions feel less like gambling.

"While it's important not to be reckless, taking calculated risks is often necessary to achieve significant gains," says Esmaeilpour. "Understand the risk-to-reward ratio and make informed decisions."

BEST Success Practice #44 to maximize the WHH continuum:
Practice being more social in person

Spoiler Alert: Not everyone loves social situations. And few of us enjoy stuffy networking events. But if you're looking to get ahead, you should adopt a "fake it 'til you make it" approach. I am not suggesting you lie or deceive. Just try to step out of your comfort zone.

Of course, if that doesn't work and you still have trouble socializing, there is another option. Find someone who will do the hard work for you. This could be a friend, business partner, or simply an associate you can piggy-back off. The choice is yours.

BEST Success Practice #45 to maximize the WHH continuum:
Create a solid routine and be more conscientious

Conscientiousness may not be a card you've been dealt. However, you can counteract this shortcoming by learning to structure your time effectively. Whether you use a calendar app, a time-blocking approach, or just an old school diary, this change could literally pay off. Time management works.

"Successful individuals often have daily routines that help them stay productive. This could be in the form of morning rituals, regular exercise, or specific work routines," explains Esmaeilpour. "Discipline is essential to maintaining routines even when motivation wanes."

BEST Success Practice #46 to maximize the WHH continuum:
Make time management a priority

Staying up to date matters more than you might imagine. Since self-made millionaires tend to be inherently open and curious, they are likely to do this by sheer accident. However, the rest of us mere mortals have to work hard to make learning new things a real priority.

"Wealthy individuals often emphasize the importance of ongoing education, be it in the form of trades, books, courses or seminars. Always seek knowledge, especially in areas you're investing in," says Esmaeilpour.

BEST Success Practice #47 to maximize the WHH continuum Success:
Adopt a growth mindset

Of course, your perspective is the key to your success. You don't have to be a genius to make that connection. Here, Esmaeilpour points to the advice of Dr. Carol Dweck, renowned psychologist, who is famed for emphasizing the importance of having a growth mindset.

"This means believing that abilities and intelligence can be developed with effort, time, and the right strategies," says Esmaeilpour. "By adopting this mindset, you'll be more open to challenges, resilient in the face of setbacks, and dedicated to learning — all crucial elements in the path to wealth."

Becoming abundantly wealthy doesn't tend to happen by accident. The select few who make it often have a variety of advantages, including an excellent education (formal/trades/life experience), background stability, and core personality traits. While you can't change your starting point in the race of life, you can still look to get ahead. One approach is to emulate the behaviors to the super rich and successful, which I have shared with you.

Myers-Briggs is another suitable personality indicator. You can access this diagnostic tool at mbtionline.com.

In 2020, Amy Keyishian of LearnVest, researched and summarized Ray Linder's book *What Will I Do with My Money?* He looked for and found correlations between personality types and traits and various investment actions.

Keyishian reported:

He also consolidated the Myers-Briggs 16 types into four broader categories: Protectors, Planners, Pleasers, and Players. But he's careful to point out that there's no right or wrong place to be within the 16-category universe. Rather, the purpose of figuring all this out is to capitalize on your type's natural assets—as opposed to shame yourself or beat yourself up.

Amy interviewed Linder to hear more about his four Ps—Protectors, Planners, Pleasers, and Players:

PROTECTORS

Myers-Briggs Types: ESTJ, ESFJ, ISTJ, ISFJ

"These people are, by nature, very conservative," says Linder. "They think ahead, make sure their future is taken care of, buy the same brands, and shop at the same stores," he adds, noting that they are careful caretaker types who often end up working in the banking system—though not the Wall Street community.

It may sound like this is the ideal way to be, but the case that first interested Linder in the study of personality types was actually an extreme Protector, "a conservative guy financially, but he got very emotional at the idea of spending anything here and now," Linder explains. "It was difficult for him to let go of this idea of a perfect future, even to take advantage of minimal-risk investments or schedule a vacation."

This, he points out, can lead to all sorts of problems, not the least of which could be marital discord. According to Linder, Protectors make up about 38% of the population.

If You Are a Protector

Although it may seem like being a Protector is a recipe for success, this personality type can have a lot of trouble with unanticipated change—and make bad decisions out of sheer panic.

Prepare for the unexpected by having a full emergency fund, which should cover at least six months of net income.

PLANNERS

Myers-Briggs Types: ENTJ, ENTP, INTJ, INTP

"These types will be more into longer-term investing—they're better able to take risk with contingency plans," says Linder. "I could give a Planner all of the probabilities and long-term goals, but what he wants to know is exactly what he will have every day, and then he'll track that with utmost certainty."

Planners like to see themselves as competent—the smartest guy in the room—and they make up about 12% of the population.

If You're a Planner

You're great at big-picture thinking, but you can become so focused on the forest that you overlook the trees. In other words, Planners may be living so much in the future that they miss opportunities in the here-and-now. Linder calls this "analysis paralysis."

Choose a portion of your income to divert immediately to long-term savings and set up another account specifically for "mad money" to use on indulgences today.

PLEASERS

Myers-Briggs Types: ENFJ, ENFP, INFJ, INFP

These folks take money personally—as an extension of themselves—and "how they spend it is an expression of their identity," says Linder. They approach the idea of "pleasing" in two different ways—pleasing themselves or pleasing others. But Linder says that pleasing is different from planning because "a planner wants to make sure that you've got shoes on your feet and a safe and comfortable environment. The Pleaser is more about the emotional, relational needs of themselves and others."

Pleasers see themselves as "caring," and make up about 12% of the population.

If You're a Pleaser

A Pleaser can be subject to financial abuse at the hands of individuals who may take advantage of the Pleaser's desire to put others' needs above their own. And even when they're taking care of themselves, Pleasers can abuse their own good natures by overspending "because I am worth it." Bottom line: Steer clear of toxic friends, who can manipulate your best intentions.

PLAYERS

Myers-Briggs Types: ESTP, ESFP, ISTP, ISFP

Players love having the freedom to merely react to the moment: One of them even told Linder that "currency equals current-cy." Since they're characterized by a tendency to be compulsive, and are unlikely to think long-term, Players are "often the ones at the highest financial risk," says Linder.

Obviously, Players see themselves as "carefree," and comprise about 38% of the population.

If You're a Player

You belong to a class whose members are going to be overly impulsive and optimistic about risks—and carefree about planning. It's worth noting that there's also an upside to the Player type: resourcefulness and a can-do attitude are invaluable to any entrepreneurial experiment.

HOW TO USE YOUR RESULTS

Across all categories, Amy Keyishian goes on to say, Linder believes the point to understand is that it's not about the money, but what money means to you and any family or business partners. If your Protector partner says, "We can't afford a vacation," he might really be saying, "I'm worried that you will be left bereft if I don't watch every penny." Meanwhile, as a Pleaser, you may be thinking, "What's the point of having that comfortable old age if we have no great memories to share and look back on together?"

So, the important thing to do is validate the feelings and impulses around your attitude toward money—and budget in a way that's both responsible and doable. This doesn't mean that you should just give in to feelings and impulses, nor does it mean that you should power up to fight them. Rather, you should acknowledge them without judgment, so you can move forward in a way that's realistic, given your tendencies.

When people feel validated, says Linder, they're more likely to reach for their goal because "when you stop reacting, you can begin acting on your own behalf."

LINKING PERSONALITY TYPES TO MONETARY WEALTH

Studies abound linking personality types to how much money you are likely to earn. Some personalities consistently earn more than others.

In *"The Income Effect of Personality Type,"* published in 2024, Truity Psychometrics explains:

How much we earn depends on many factors, most of them fairly obvious. We all know that pursuing education, gaining on-the-job experience, and demonstrating leadership skills can boost our paychecks. But did you know that how much you earn may also depend on your personality type?

Multiple studies have demonstrated a link between income and personality traits such as extraversion, goal orientation, and the willingness to put one's own interests ahead of the interests of others. In this report, we will outline the results of our research on income and personality type, as described by the theories of Isabel Myers and Katharine Briggs. Although Myers and Briggs' theory is not widely used in academic research, it is the personality theory most familiar to the general population, and so allows us to describe the associations between personality and earning potential in a way that is easily understood.

From my own past Myers-Briggs tests and myersbriggs.org website data, I will take a deeper dive into the Myers-Briggs detail. Myers and Briggs proposed four major dimensions of personality, each of which is described in terms of two ends of a spectrum:

- **Extraversion vs. Introversion** describes how a person gains and manages their energy: through interacting with others, or by being solitary and quiet.
- **Sensing vs. Intuition** describes how a person processes information: with a concrete and matter-of-fact style, or through imagination and inference.
- **Thinking vs. Feeling** describes how a person makes decisions: based on logic, or based on moral and personal concerns.
- **Judging vs. Perceiving** describes how a person organizes their life: in a structured, orderly manner, or a looser, more spontaneous manner.

A person's scores on each dimension are combined to create 16 distinct personality types, each coded by the initials of the four preferences. Thus, a person who prefers Introversion, Intuition, Feeling, and Judging would be called an INFJ.

ISTJ: INTROVERSION, SENSING, THINKING, JUDGING
- Tend to be more quiet and serious
- Realistic, responsible and practical
- Earns success by being dependable and thorough
- Enjoys order and organization

ISFJ: INTROVERSION, SENSING, FEELING, JUDGING
- Quiet and conscientious
- Committed to meeting obligations
- Friendly, loyal and considerate of others' feelings
- Values order and harmony in their home and work environments

INFJ: INTROVERSION, INTUITION, FEELING, JUDGING
- Concerned with serving the common good
- Insightful and eager to learn others' motivations
- Tends to seek meaning and connection in relationships and ideas
- Committed to their values

INTJ: INTROVERSION, INTUITION, THINKING, JUDGING
- Original thinkers who are motivated to achieve their goals
- Identifies patterns in events to determine an explanatory perspective
- Skeptical and independent
- Maintains high standards for themselves and others

ISTP: INTROVERSION, SENSING, THINKING, PERCEIVING
- Quiet, sensitive and kind
- Committed to their values and people who are important to them
- Enjoys being alone and working at their own pace
- Conflict-averse

ISFP. INTROVERSION, SENSING, FEELING, PERCEIVING

- Tolerant, flexible and logical
- Quick to find workable solutions for problems
- Interested in cause and effect
- Values efficiency

INFP. INTROVERSION, INTUITION, FEELING, PERCEIVING

- Idealistic, curious and adaptable
- Loyal to their values and people who are important to them
- Eager to understand others and help them reach their full potential
- Seeks to live a life that aligns with their values

INTP. INTROVERSION, INTUITION, THINKING, PERCEIVING

- Theoretical, analytical and skeptical
- Interested in developing logical explanations for things that interest them
- Values ideas over social interaction
- Problem solvers

ESTP. EXTRAVERSION, SENSING, THINKING, PERCEIVING

- Spontaneous, lives in the moment
- Prefer action when problem-solving over theoretical explanations
- Enjoys aesthetics and material comfort
- Learns by doing

ESFP. EXTRAVERSION, SENSING, THINKING, PERCEIVING

- Enjoys working with others
- Spontaneous and easily adapts to new people and environments
- Realistic, outgoing and accepting
- Learns best while trying a new skill with other people

ENFP. EXTRAVERSION, INTUITION, FEELING, PERCEIVING

- Warm, enthusiastic and imaginative
- Desires affirmation from others
- Eager to offer appreciation and support
- Spontaneous, flexible, able to improvise

ENTP. EXTRAVERSION, INTUITION, THINKING, PERCEIVING
- Smart, outspoken and stimulating
- Resourceful when solving problems
- Good at reading other people
- Finds routine boring, often finds new ways of doing things

ESTJ: EXTRAVERSION, SENSING, THINKING, JUDGING
- Practical, decisive and organized
- Values achieving results in the most efficient way possible
- Quick and forceful in implementing plans and decisions
- Maintains clear and logical standards for themselves and others

ESFJ: EXTRAVERSION, SENSING, FEELING, JUDGING
- Cooperative, conscientious and kind
- Values harmony in their environment
- Desires appreciation for their contributions
- Enjoys working with others to complete tasks efficiently and accurately

ENFJ: EXTRAVERSION, INTUITION, FEELING, JUDGING
- Empathetic, responsible and loyal
- Attuned to others' emotions, needs and motivations
- Often acts as a catalyst for individual and community growth
- Responsive to praise and criticism

ENTJ: EXTRAVERSION, INTUITION, THINKING, JUDGING
- Enjoys long-term planning and goal-setting
- Often well-informed, well-read and eager to share their knowledge with others
- Skilled problem-solvers
- Readily assumes leadership, forceful in sharing their ideas

Thanks to previous research investigating similar personality factors, we can expect that Myers and Briggs's four dimensions of personality will have a clear impact on income. For instance, academic research has shown that higher earners tend to be more focused on long- term goals, a trait that Myers and Briggs would classify as part of a Judging preference. In interpreting these effects through Myers and Briggs' popular theory, I hope that the analysis can provide you with an accessible and actionable understanding of how personality traits may be impacting earning potential.

I conducted this research using data provided by 72,331 respondents to online TypeFinder® personality assessment from late 2018 to early 2019. (The source for the chart below is www.truity.com)

The TypeFinder personality assessment is a measure of personality type based on the theories of Isabel Myers and Katharine Briggs. The assessment has been shown to be valid and reliable. It assesses preferences on each of the four major dimensions of personality as well as 23 more detailed facets of personality, which allow more insight into specific traits and characteristics.

To examine the connection between personality type and income, Truity summarized and sorted hundreds of thousands of personality tests.

This analysis showed that income was highly variable from one personality type to another, with some types much more likely to achieve high earnings. Extraverted and Thinking types dominated the top of the earnings charts, with ENTJs earning the highest salaries of all.

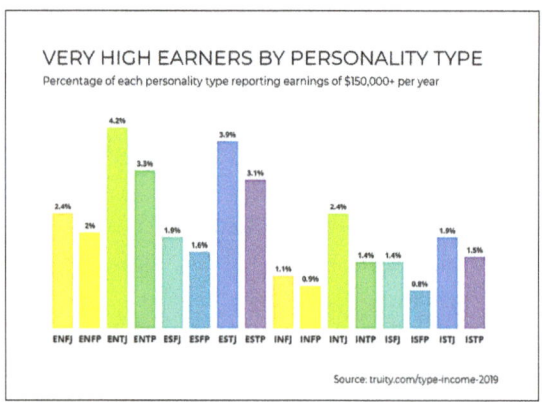

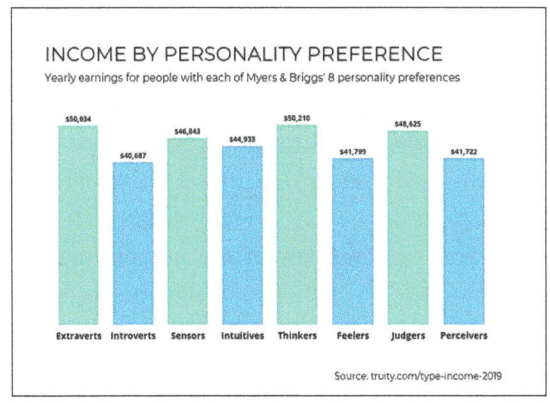

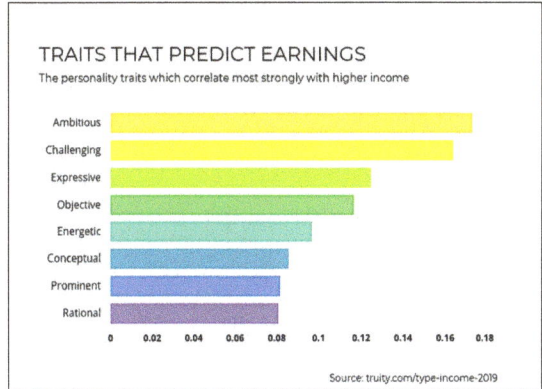

Average Incomes by Personality Type and Age Group data table

Type	Under 18	18-21	Twenties	Thirties	Forties	Fifties	60+
ENFJ	$7,102	$11,772	$32,787	$52,875	$61,837	$65,982	$57,637
ENFP	$6,628	$9,887	$28,860	$47,868	$58,447	$60,520	$46,824
ENTJ	$6,208	$13,029	$39,403	$70,632	$79,845	$78,579	$84,114
ENTP	$6,458	$11,813	$32,938	$62,246	$88,926	$83,505	$75,152
ESFJ	$6,279	$10,167	$34,182	$51,812	$59,343	$54,311	$60,233
ESFP	$6,838	$7,874	$33,297	$47,247	$51,948	$59,763	$62,773
ESTJ	$11,271	$11,489	$36,599	$62,883	$77,564	$72,804	$69,229
ESTP	$13,879	$14,905	$37,739	$60,511	$66,500	$74,277	$59,275
INFJ	$3,427	$5,679	$26,514	$45,898	$59,805	$62,252	$44,425
INFP	$1,643	$5,268	$22,991	$37,440	$54,485	$52,039	$39,475
INTJ	$8,409	$10,774	$29,231	$57,131	$73,676	$74,956	$54,128
INTP	$3,341	$6,692	$24,458	$44,365	$64,408	$72,488	$54,189
ISFJ	$5,601	$7,438	$28,164	$46,676	$52,510	$54,797	$45,943
ISFP	$3,416	$6,181	$27,933	$39,317	$39,089	$42,589	$29,060
ISTJ	$5,642	$9,144	$33,273	$55,825	$65,897	$62,435	$49,420
ISTP	$6,835	$5,390	$26,852	$45,595	$60,757	$61,030	$67,674
All	$6,359	$9,128	$30,059	$51,919	$64,075	$64,034	$55,788

DiSC

Another personality typing tool is called DiSC.

You have heard of the White Coat Syndrome? Certain personality types are negatively affected by just the thought of going to the Doctor. Their blood pressure goes up and their pulse increases driven by a worry of a poor prognosis even though they are perfectly healthy. Nurse friends of mine tell the story of how they have taken blood pressure readings days before and after the actual Doctor visit. The results are normal. When the patient actually goes to the Doctors office, the readings become abnormally high. Some patients blood pressure readings go up just seeing the actual Sphygmomanometer cuff. Interestingly, some patients when taking their own readings go back to a normal result. This human behavior is controlled by outside entities and situational construct coping. Who is in control is also a determinant.

The *DISCprofile.com* explains:

DiSC° measures dimensions of your personality. It does not measure intelligence, aptitude, mental health, or values. DiSC profiles describe human behavior in various situations—for example, how you respond to challenges, how you influence others, your preferred pace, and how you respond to rules and procedures. It measures tendencies and preferences, or patterns of behavior, with no judgment regarding value or alignment with a skill set or job classification. DiSC is a tool for dialogue, not diagnosis.

At its broadest, DiSC measures four aspects of personality: dominance, influence, steadiness and conscientiousness .

1. **Dominance (D):** Direct, competitive, decisive, authoritative, and confident; can be too blunt, demanding, or aggressive
2. **Influence (I):** Social, emphasis on relationships, optimistic, collaborative, and convincing; may not speak directly, lacks follow-through, and fears loss of influence/friendship/social status
3. **Steadiness (S):** Calm, cooperative, stable, patient, and deliberate; values group acceptance; may be indecisive, fear change, or overly accommodating
4. **Conscientiousness (C):** Independent, objective, cautious, systematic, diplomatic, with an emphasis on accuracy and quality; may fear criticism, fail to delegate or compromise, or not join teams or engage in social events

If you complete a DiSC, in your profile, you'll read about your unique behavioral style, your tendencies, needs, preferred environment, and strategies for effective behavior.

There are no preferred styles. Some styles produce more Wealth or Happiness or Health outcomes long term. Yes, you might be given a label as a high S or a Di, but there are no value judgments in that label. Your style does not indicate that you'll be good at one type of job over another, for example. Each style has the potential to flex or stretch into other styles when needed. It might just take extra energy or some practice.

Statistically, and scientific studies prove certain personality types will earn and save more money than others.

You're not either this or that. Sometimes people get worried that they will be seen as being one way in all circumstances. Everything DiSC reports use a dot within a circle of styles to show that everyone exhibits traits of all four major styles. The adaptive testing method makes it even easier to discover your innate style, but innate never means exclusive. For example, the *Everything DiSC Sales* profile is based on a salesperson being able to adapt their style to complement or match the style of the buyer.

Scoring is done electronically for Everything DiSC profiles. Each of the eight DiSC scales is measured, but these scores do not show on the profile report. Instead, a person's dot placement is displayed in a circular image. This has proved to be more engaging, memorable, and informative than a series of numbers or graphs.

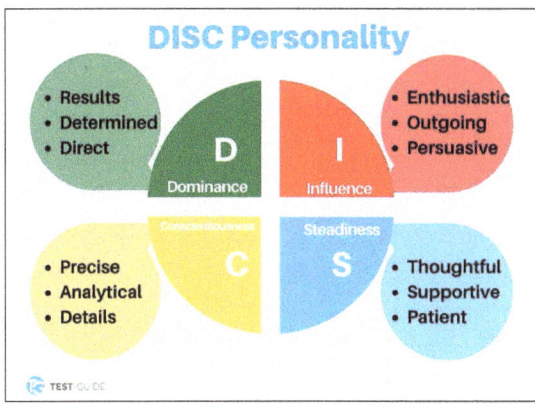

Personality and Health

We have discussed how personality can affect wealth. Can it also affect health?

Yes, it can. Here is what Kendra Cherry reported in *"How Your Personality Type Affects Your Health," a 2022 publication medically reviewed Amy Morin LCSW*:

Could your personality type be harming you, or is your personality actually helping you live a longer life? Our personalities play such an important role in determining our behaviors and habits, so it is little wonder that personality type has a connection to your health. Everything from how often you visit the doctor to how you deal with stress is connected to your personality.

Philosophers, physicians, and researchers have long tried to find connections between personality and physical health. During the time of the ancient Greeks, Hippocrates and Galen suggested that there were four humors (or personality types) and that each was connected to susceptibilities for certain physical or mental illnesses.

Interest in the topic persists to this day and research *has* found that personality traits can be important health predictors. Researchers have found that the personality traits exhibited during childhood are linked to later health and are tied to other key health markers including overall longevity.

TYPE A

The classic type A personality is often characterized as hard-driving, controlling, and perfectionistic. People who exhibit characteristics of this personality type tend to be more competitive, impatient, tense, assertive, and even aggressive.

Type A's are often seen as hard-driving workaholics who will do anything to get ahead. They often feel a need to dominate, both at work and in personal interactions, and may derive their feelings of self-worth and self-concept from their perceived achievements.

This personality type has been a subject of interest since it was first described in the 1950s and research has associated it with a number of negative health outcomes.

Some studies have shown a relationship between the Type A personality type and hypertension, increased job stress, and social isolation.
Older studies suggested that there was a connection between the Type A personality type and heart disease, but subsequent research has complicated these findings by failing to confirm the link. Type As do tend to experience

more hostility, a characteristic that has been tied to an increased risk of heart disease.

The initial research conducted more than 40 years ago suggested that Type A personalities were at a 7-fold increased risk of developing coronary artery disease. But more recent studies suggest that the real culprit behind the increased risk of heart disease is likely related to anger and hostility. So what can you do to reduce your health risks if you have a Type A personality?

- **Understand what you can change**. Even if personality type is linked to increased health concerns, some have suggested that there may be little patients and doctors can do to mitigate these risks. However, some experts suggest that personality change is possible and that even if you don't necessarily change your personality, there are steps that patients can take to minimize the potential health consequences of their overall personality type.

- **Focus on the negative traits**. If you tend to have some of the more negative features of the type A personality, such as a tendency to be stressed out, hostile, and socially isolated, explore things that you can do to lower your chances of developing hypertension and other health problems.

- **Practice coping and stress management**. Effective stress-management techniques can help you learn how to better cope with daily life stress. Learning how to manage feelings of anger and hostility can also help. And looking for ways to improve your social connections can help improve your well-being both now and in the future.

MORE LAID BACK

People with a laid-back personality, often referred to as a type B personality tend to be much more relaxed and easy-going than their Type A counterparts. In contrast to Type As, Type Bs are typically less stressed and less competitive.

These individuals are apt to be more focused on performing tasks for the enjoyment of doing so rather than being so driven by a need to achieve, win, or dominate. That isn't to say that Type Bs do not value accomplishment. They work steadily toward their goals but also enjoy the process and experience less stress if they do not win.

People with the Type B personality type may also be more attracted to careers and hobbies that are more laid back and creativity centered, such as becoming an artist, writer, actor, or therapist. There are still health implications associated with the Type B personality. If you are Type B:

- **Maintain healthy behaviors**. Being laid-back might mean taking a more lackadaisical approach to your health. Being relaxed can be great, but don't slack on your healthy habits.
- **Focus on the positive.** For Type Bs, the news is mostly good. If you have this personality type, you probably have a lower risk of developing health issues related to anxiety. You tend to enjoy life, are pretty good at coping with stress, and likely have a good quality of life. All of these factors may mean that you are less likely to experience negative health outcomes that are linked to stress, anger, and anxiety.

PEOPLE-PLEASERS

People with an "eager to please" personality type tend to be accommodating, passive, and conforming. This personality type can have its health upsides and downsides. On one hand, they're eager to please nature means that they are more likely to follow their doctor's orders.

Because of their passive nature, people pleasers may be more likely to feel hopeless or helpless in the face of a negative health event.

They may also be less likely to seek help when something is wrong, instead feeling that they don't want to be a burden or inconvenience to others. When faced with a diagnosis, they may simply throw in the towel and assume that nothing they do will make much of a difference. So what can you do to protect your health if you tend to be a people-pleaser?

- **Focus on your needs.** People-pleasers sometimes place their own well-being last. Being conscientious of others can be a positive trait, but be sure to take time for your own health as well.
- **Take an active role in your health.** In can be easy to fall into thinking that your health is out of your hands, but taking a more internal locus of control may help you feel more in control of your current and future health. Instead of focusing on the external influences that affect your health, pay attention to the things that you can change through your own actions.

WORRYWARTS

If you tend to have a neurotic personality, you may respond to feelings of loss, frustration, and other stresses with negative emotions. Experiencing intense emotional reactions to relatively minor life challenges is common.

Researchers have found that this trait can be a predictor of a variety of physical and mental disorders, including overall life longevity.

One research review found that those who were higher in neuroticism and lower in other OCEAN or Big Five traits (extraversion, agreeableness, openness, conscientiousness), particularly those lower in conscientiousness, tended to be less healthy than their less-neurotic peers. Those who are high in neuroticism may also be more likely to experience physical health problems such as cardiovascular disease, irritable bowel syndrome, and asthma.

Neuroticism has been associated with generalized anxiety disorder, depression, panic disorder, antisocial personality disorder, and substance use. Are there any strategies you can follow to help minimize the possible health risks of a neurotic personality?

- **Use preventative strategies**. Being a worrywart can have health risks, but the upside of better understanding your personality is that you can take steps to engage in preventative care.
- **Control your worry.** Excessive worrying can be troubling, so finding ways to control your thoughts and replace negative emotions with more positive ones is important. Strategies such as distraction, talking to a friend, and relaxation techniques can all be helpful if you find yourself overcome with neurotic feelings.

DISTRESSED

The type D personality was first introduced in 1996 and is characterized by "distressed" traits such as being more prone to negative emotions and a lack of self-expression. Stress, depression, anxiety, anger, and loneliness are also associated with the Type D personality. It can also come with serious health consequences.

So what are the possible health implications of having a Type D personality? One study suggested that people with Type D personalities are at a four-fold risk of death compared to those with other personality types. According to another study published in the journal *Circulation: Cardiovascular Quality and Outcomes*, people with this personality type are at a three-fold increased risk of heart problems, including heart failure.

Approximately 20% of American adults have the Type D personality, with an estimated 50% of patients with heart problems exhibiting characteristics of this distressed personality type.

So what should you do to help mitigate the potential health risks of having a Type D personality?

- **Talk to your doctor.** Some experts hope that screening heart patients for these traits would allow doctors to connect those at risk with behavior and cognitive counseling.
- **Practice good stress management techniques**. Self-help approaches such as practicing good stress management techniques and reframing events to focus on more positive emotions may also be helpful.

INTROVERTS

One study found that people who tend to be more extroverted, conscientious, and agreeable also tend to be healthier. This is due, in part, to the fact that people who exhibit higher levels of these traits also tend to be more likely to communicate more effectively with their doctors.

A 2009 study found that social support was linked to physical health outcomes including healthier behaviors, better coping skills, and observance to medical routines. Doctors and other health experts have long understood that quality social support and connections can have an important protective effect on both physical and mental health. So what can you do if you are not an extrovert?

- **Build social support.** Even if you tend to have a more introverted personality, seeking out strong social support is one way to help lower potential health risks associated with your personality type. Lack of social support has been linked to a variety of ailments including decreased immunity and an increased risk of heart disease.

WHAT IT ALL MEANS

While research indicates that personality type clearly plays a role in health and well-being, certain ailments are more likely to be influenced by psychological characteristics. Heart disease, for example, is more strongly linked to personality type than cancer.

So why does personality have an impact on health? Why are certain traits so tied to certain ailments? The answers are not clear, but one potential explanation is that personality impacts behavior and lifestyle choices.

People who are more conscientious may be more likely to make healthier choices while those who are high in neuroticism may be less likely to seek medical help or have weaker social support systems.

Just because you tend to have a certain personality type does not doom you to a future of acquiring certain ailments.

As with many things, your individual risk of developing a health problem can depend upon a variety of factors beyond your personality, including genetics, environment, lifestyle, and behaviors.

Understanding your personality might be a great way to help determine what sort of health choices or changes you need to focus on making. By being aware of the potential hazards you may face, you can work with your health care professional to come up with a plan to minimize the dangers.

Of all the studies I researched, the most involved, salient and comprehensive includes Jacqueline M. Gilberto, Meghan K. Davenport and Margaret E. Beier titled *"Personality, Health, Wealth, and Subjective Well-being: Testing an Integrative Model with Retired and working older adults." 2020.*

Here is the authors' summary of their conclusions about wealth and health correlation:

Research suggests that personality promotes behaviors that help or hinder adjustment throughout adulthood (e.g., neuroticism and alcohol abuse; Soldz & Vaillant, 1999). Retirement scholars have framed retirement adjustment in a similar way, suggesting that personality variables should be considered antecedents of personal resources in retirement (Wang, Henkens, & van Solinge, 2011). For example, people who are highly extroverted may be more successful than others at accumulating social benefits and health.

Evidence suggests the Big Five personality traits are related to physical health outcomes. Specifically, in later life, the health behaviors of a lifetime accumulate to impact older adults' health and mortality (Bogg & Roberts, 2004). Because neuroticism is negatively related to health-related coping behaviors and other health outcomes, we hypothesized that neuroticism would negatively correlate with health (Lahey, 2009, Smith et al., 2002). Conversely, as conscientious people are less likely to be unhealthy.

We expected wealth and health to be positively correlated, in part because wealth affords the opportunity to access preventative health services; if wealthier people's health is compromised, they are more likely to have the means to seek treatment (Pollack et al., 2007). We also hypothesized that wealth and health positively predict well-being as both health and wealth afford people the opportunity to "maximize their quality of life" with fewer restrictions on their behavior (Diener et al.,)

This study used existing data collected through the ongoing Health and Retirement Study (HRS). The HRS is a National Institute on Aging funded (grant number NIA U01AG009740) longitudinal study administered by the University of Michigan. It examines how older adults' health, finances, work experiences, and individual differences, including personality, are related to health and retirement outcomes in late life. The HRS comprises a nationally representative sample of over 37,000 U.S. adults.

To paraphrase Ozer and Benet-Martinez in their 2006 review, our study demonstrated that "personality has consequences" (p. 401). Specifically, our results suggest that personality affects individuals' personal resources and subjective well-being in late life, regardless of retirement status."

I researched many of these personality study correlations as they relate to WHH. What was surprising to me that people are not necessarily "born" with their personality. It develops over time. Earlier in life, we are more malleable and adaptable. We have an increasingly difficult time adapting our personality as we age. If you don't find your personality type listed among those most likely to succeed and maximize WHH, don't fret. You still have the ability to modify your type.

The DiSC or Meyers-Briggs or Big Five OCEAN (Openness/Conscientious-ness/Extroversion/Agreeableness/Neuroticism) personality models are not infallible but represent indications at a point in time. All models have flaws. Nevertheless, if we look at personality models, we create more awareness about ourselves, family members and work colleagues.

The Takeaway

I have researched for you the main personality traits and types, using the most effective methods available. So, what is the takeaway? How can this help maximize your WHH continuum?

First of all, if you or your family or colleagues have not taken at least one of the principal tests discussed here, do it! The most commonly used is Myers-Briggs, which is not a perfect test but a very useful indicator.

All the tests we discussed capture a moment in a lifetime, not an entire life. Here is an example. Twelve of us on our president's staff were introduced to the Myers-Briggs personality test by our Human Resource team at Eaton. They did a great job introducing our corporate division staff to the approach. Many of us were skeptical, but we filled out the details and sent off the completed tests to be analyzed. After a short time, we received our personality types with descriptions.

Months later, our president said, let's take the test again! He was skeptical and wanted to see if his staff would have the same results and personality type outcome. The twelve of us completed the questionnaire for a second time in three months. Surprisingly to our president, eleven of us had pretty much the same score. But one staff member had the direct opposite of what he identified three months ago. Human Resources asked him if was having a bad day when he took the test? He responded that when he completed the first-time test, he was upset at having to take time from his busy day to go through the process. If that is the definition of a bad day, then yes, he had a bad day. He was asked to take the test a third time a few months later. He scored yet a different "personality."

These personality tests are not 100% infallible.

Conclusion: Personality impacts Wealth, Health and Happiness outcomes. You can adapt or tweak your personality to secure a more favorable outcome over time. You can influence others in the pursuit of personality focus to maximize their WHH.

BEST Success Practice #48 to maximize the WHH continuum:
Determine your personality type with one of the methods identified.
You can adapt or change your personality over time.

5

Ego Drive and Empathy Application

Know that you will at times have to adjust your ego to be more empathetic. Conversely, you may have to adjust your empathy and inject more ego drive. Envision a straight line with Ego on the left and Empathy on the right. In the middle of the line is a fulcrum point. As you encounter a situation with another person, you have choices. Let's use an example. You are running a business you founded many years ago. You are successful, but recently the downturn in the economy has you behind on your goals. You have a meeting to close a large order with a new customer. The long-term "deal" is worth millions.

As you are traveling to the customer site, you strategize on how to win the business. Your proposal is rock-solid, and you believe you can execute on the order. You worry about the competition, however, as they have done business with this customer before. Now you think, how can I walk away with the order commitment today? You need this job to make or break the year's profitability.

As you arrive at the customer site, you learn that the executive decision-maker is going to be late for your appointment. You think, great, they are putting me on ice to get an advantage as we negotiate--a common practice among some customers.

You sit in the lobby for what seems like an eternity. Patience is not one of your personality traits. Time seems to have stopped as you look at the clock ticking one second at a time on the wall. Your mind drifts to your family and how much you need this order. After about fifteen minutes, the executive secretary comes out and offers you some coffee. You accept, thank her, and inquire about your appointment. The secretary says the executive is dealing with a situation and it will be another thirty minutes.

Great.

Now you begin to think you're not the favored supplier, and maybe you are being used to leverage the incumbent supplier.

Finally, you are led to the executive's office. Introductions are made and you are seated. As the executive begins the review of your proposal and asks a few questions, you notice he is glancing at his watch. Now you believe the customer is just using you and your bid to fulfill a "we need at least two bids" policy. You begin to get angry about this waste of time and resources. After the executive looks at his watch again, what do you do?

Let's say you are more ego-driven than driven by empathy.

If your ego drive is in the 100% UP mode, and empathy is in the zero percent DOWN mode, you ask the executive, "Why do you keep glancing at your watch, sir? You seem to be going through the motions, and you are not giving me a fair chance to earn your business! I am a busy man and if you are just using my company as a check on the other supplier, just tell me and I can be on my way!"

If your empathy is in the 100% UP mode and you ego drive is in the zero percent DOWN mode you would say, "Sir, I am so sorry for interrupting you today. I will step out and schedule another appointment time with your executive secretary."

Of course, neither is an effective response to the situation at hand. As this is a real-life example, let me share what actually happened.

I was the sales engineer waiting in the lobby. The executive customer, Russ, was the VP of Purchasing, an electrical engineer by training, for the largest aluminum smelter in America at the time, Alcoa, in Massena New York. Here is what happened. I asked him, "Is everything okay?" I tilted my ego drive more toward empathy on the scale.

"Why do you ask?"

"Our meeting was delayed, and now I noticed that you were glancing at your watch."

He asked me to close the office door. I don't know why at that point in time he confided in me, but he told me why he was very pre-occupied. His wife, he explained, had called earlier. Her doctor's visit that morning in Massena identified a major problem with her pregnancy. The doctor said the baby was not gaining weight and was most likely going to be born prematurely. He explained that he was especially concerned because he was new to the area and had discovered that the local hospital did not have an extensive track record for premature baby care. With that, he apologized and suggested we meet latter this afternoon to review the bid.

Again, I tilted my approach toward empathy. "We are headquartered in Pittsburgh, which has one of the best neonatal care hospitals in the country. Let me use your phone"—this was in the pre-cellular days—and, with your permission, I'll call this hospital's head of engineering, who happens to be a customer. I'll ask him to connect us to someone who can help schedule your wife for admittance. Is that okay?"

He handed me his phone, and by the end of the day they were scheduled. At that point he clearly could not focus on Alcoa or himself. He was concerned about his wife and unborn babies health.

By not leaping into either extreme of 100% ego drive versus 100% empathy, you can engage people far more effectively to meet their needs. Meet their needs, and yours will most likely be met as well. Worst case? You will at least find out the real reason for the other person's behavior in the current situation.

By the way, after a difficult pregnancy and three months in the hospital after delivery, the baby boy went home to Massena. He grew up to be a successful businessman. The Alcoa executive had stayed in touch with me and the company I represented until he retired nineteen years later. We stayed in communication well into his retirement years. My company earned millions of dollars in orders over those years, providing exceptional service and products.

Here are some Ego Drive/Empathy scale examples:

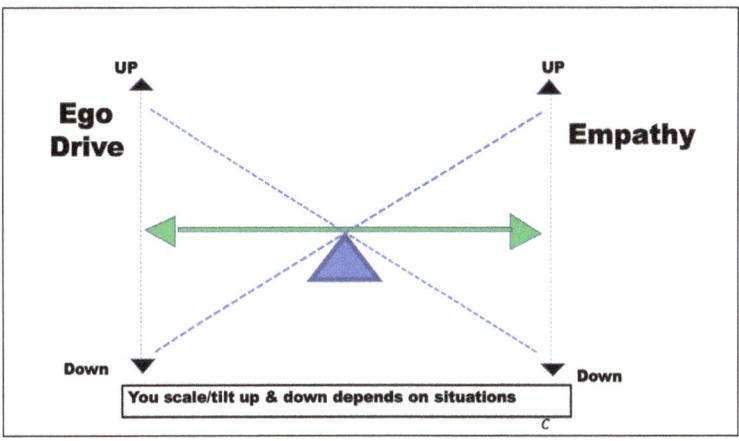

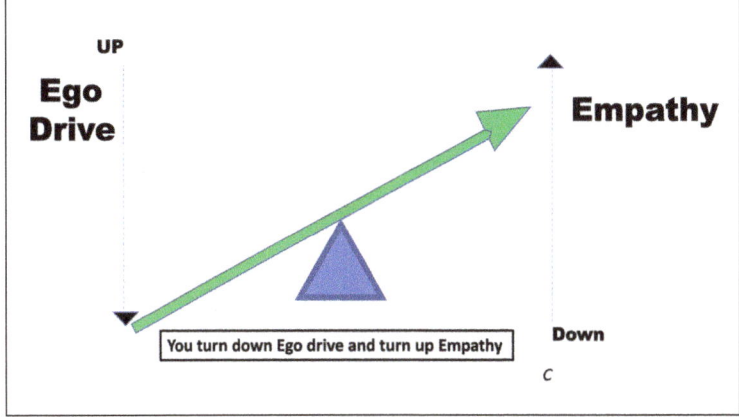

More Empathy applied.

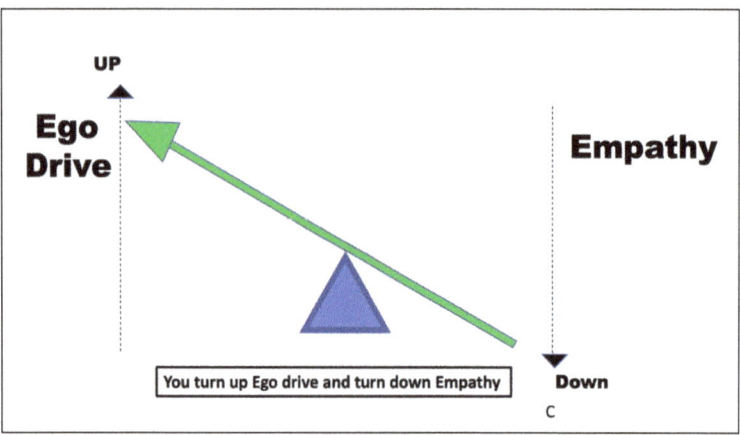

You can adjust or tweak your ego and empathy. It is not a binary, all or nothing issue, but, as the charts depict, an adjustable balance. It teeter-tots up and down on the blue fulcrum point.

Happiness involves both our ego and empathy. How we balance these determines maximum happiness for ourselves and those who come into contact with us.

BEST Success Practice #49 to maximize the WHH continuum:
Adjust your Ego drive and Empathy as conditions warrant.

6

Time Factors

"Everything has been figured out, except how to live"
—**Jean-Paul Sartre**

WHH is inextricably linked to time and the effort to use time. Why is the old adage of "give a busy person more to do and they will get it done" still true today? Have they mastered time travel? Are they exceptionally driven to succeed? Do they maximize the use of time?

Time management is a constant to be used as a tool to maximize WHH.

Have you ever slowed down time? Let's explore how you can slow down time even though time passage is a constant. One of my favorite artists is Salvador Dali, and one of my favorite Dali works is *Melting Clocks*. My Mom, who was a wonderful artist for sixty years, got my brother, sisters, and me involved in art. I tried to create my own version of *Melting Clocks*. Even with my Mom's expertise, lets just say I did not possess her talent, let alone Dali's. My rendition could be called *Flopping Clocks*. We all interpret works of art differently. My view is that Dali was trying to slow down the passage of time as it slips away.

World-class athletes in all sports speak about how they slow down time with "attentional focus." Great pitchers, golfers, and basketball players perform the impossible. I reference these specific sports not to exclude the others, but to be able to speak to my experience playing them and observing firsthand.

When a pitcher threw the perfect strike and won the game, his success is often described as a state of mind. Despite high-decibel screams from the opposing team's fans, the opponent trying to steal third base, the batter stepping in and out of the box, the world-class pitcher throws the strike to win the game. When asked how he accomplished the feat, despite all the distractions and pressure, the pitcher usually says something to the effect that he did not hear the crowd or see any distractions. "I slowed down my mind and blanked out all distractions. I trained my mind. Time seemed to stand still."

We all have mechanisms or a "swing key (the golf trainer's term) to employ when time is a factor or pressure is at the highest. Ever give a speech to a thousand people in an auditorium? If you are prepared and you are waiting to go on stage, what does time do? It drags on and on. You are pumped up, the adrenaline is pulsating. You are ready and want to perform *now*!

What if you are not prepared and your next on the stage in fifteen minutes? That quarter-hour races by. Before you can blink, you are being introduced to the podium. *Oh S%&^T! I am next,* as you stumble out onto the stage with cotton in your mouth. Which fifteen-minute period went by slower?

Let's use a ridiculous example of how time is slowed in ancient Eastern cultures to foster discipline and focus. Imagine sitting on a wooden bench with no back support. Next to you is a gong and a person with a hammer. No it's not the hit song, "Get it On," from the 1970s *Bang A Gong* album by the English Rock band T.Rex .

Now, as you are sitting, the person hammers the gong every two seconds for an hour. Bang! Bang!! BANG!!! Sounds like torture to me. The pain of the wooden bench, the loud sound of the gong piercing your ears.

Now, contrast that Bang a Gong scenario with sitting on that same wooden bench, holding hands with a loved one, on a mountain top overlooking a serene meadow and a beautiful lake with the sun setting in the distance . No gong. My guess is time flew by faster than the Bang a Gong example. Which hour actually went by faster? Neither. Both were an hour.

Nevertheless, the unpleasant hour is perceived as longer than the pleasant hour thanks to "psychological affectation. Psychological affection is made up of three dimensions; affective, behavioral, and cognitive. State of mind and emotion play into how we can "slow down time" or how "time fly's by." We can be trained to use state of mind and emotion to our advantage, just as a world-class athlete does. And we can apply the technique to maximizing WHH.

When we were very young, one of the hits shows on TV was *Leave it to Beaver*. Created by Joe Connelly, Bob Mosher, and Dick Conway, it aired from 1957 to 1963. Reruns are still being shown. The star was a kid named Beaver Cleaver, played by Jerry Mathers. The story line is not important for purposes of WHH. *Leave it to Beaver* is a benchmark example for how most of the TV shows were filmed and produced at the time.

Now, flash forward in time, from *Leave it to Beaver*, to when Music Television, or MTV, debuted in 1981. It was the first time a cable TV show linked music with video of the band. MTV was a gamechanger for how TV shows would be produced and filmed going forward.

What was one of the salient differences between *Leave it to Beaver* and MTV productions? Time sequences.

When the audience watched *Leave it to Beaver,* the video time interval between screen shots was 4 to 5 seconds. When MTV produced a show, the interval between screen shots was 1.2 seconds, on average. This was akin to watching the difference between a golf match and a playoff hockey game. Golf is slow and precise. Hockey is constant motion and speed. The MTV show seemed to go by quickly while *Leave it to Beaver* was slower. With MTV, your mind was blitzed every second with a new image to comprehend. When I watched MTV for the first time, time went by so quickly that I found myself wanting more. I felt energized. Watching *Leave it to Beaver*-era shows seemed to drag on and on by comparison. But, there was a level of calm and relaxation. Your mind slowed. With MTV time sequences, I would forget to breathe, given the non-stop action.

If *media* can condition our minds, then *we* can condition our own minds as well.

Why is this important for the WHH continuum? The conditioning of our minds, resultant attention spans, and ability to focus are determinants for decision-making. To maximize the WHH continuum, we must train our minds at various times to slow down time or to speed it up. Let's see an example.

Your financial advisor has just presented you with a new investment option. It has long-term implications for your wealth. You experience a level of stress as you contemplate the recommendation, even though you trust your financial advisor.

You want to slow down time and limit your stress in support of your Health. You budget your time management, make the decision quickly, and go forward. This is a simple example of how to balance your ability to garner wealth but not at the expense of your Health and Happiness. WHH is maximized.

Here is another example of how the time factor can affect your WHH.

A friend's colleague was faced with making a major life-changing decision. He was approached to sell his business. You can imagine the stress. He built the multimillion-dollar twenty-five-year-old business from scratch. He felt responsible for every one of his sixty employees and their families. The company looking to buy was a Fortune 100 public corporation with tens of thousands of employees globally. His company value proposition and customer base were financially and demographically attractive to this global company.

His financial and accounting advisors did the multi-month due diligence, and the parties began negotiating the terms of the sale. The emotional aspects of this potential wealth transition were staggering for the small business owner and founder. He did not sleep much. He worried about how his employees would be treated inside a Fortune 100 company. He did not eat well. He gained weight. He just did not feel well, suffering under the burden of his success. Time passed slowly, and the stress mounted. The Fortune 100 company made an offer that all his advisors said was a great deal, but there was one aspect the founder could not accept. There were no long-term employment guarantees for his sixty employees. Welcome to the public company quarter-over-quarter drumbeat. As time went by, the founder's procrastination and anguish continued.

In the end, the deal closed. The founder sold the company after agonizing over the decision. Everyone involved said it could have moved faster. Time is money. He would stay on as an employee and advisor in support of the backlog of business expectations. The private company's orders and revenue forecasts, used to help value the company purchase price, was also set as a claw back mechanism if expectations were not met. Money from the purchase price was set in escrow based on meeting the performance over a timeline.

During year one, the two company cultures clashed as the integration continued. Big company politics and policies stifled the creative and nimble aspects of the small private company. The styles of operation clashed. The sales team Integration was a bigger challenge than expected. A reorganization occurred. People were transferred out of the acquired company into headquarters of the Fortune 100 company. Frustrated employees quit. Such is the way of some acquisitions. This was expected and was built into the proformas as a cost detractor from earnings.

You can guess how this affected the founder's WHH continuum before, during, and after the deal. There is a need for analytical rationalizations. Emotional and psychological affectations aside, the need can be managed. What I mean by this is that the founder could have done a better job to maximize WHH outcomes. Here's how. Negative overload on the Health and Happiness aspects abounded. The founder did not take into consideration how his procrastination caused his Health and Happiness to decline. He slowed down time for a financially beneficial outcome at the expense of his overall WHH.

What could the founder have done differently to maximize WHH? His training as an engineer and propensity toward minutiae slowed the negotiation process.Knowing his personality type and traits, he should have proactively planned to minimize his involvement. However, some people cannot change, even when they understand logically that their actions are counterproductive and even harmful.

A more rapid due diligence timeline would have limited the founder's stress. Rip off the band-aid! The founder should have realized his level of emotion was going to be excruciating. His business broker and accountant should have pushed back when he wanted to micromanage every detail. The buyer was on the verge of walking away as timelines were missed. Duration and the quarter-over-quarter metric expectations are the norm for publicly traded companies. They have a fiduciary responsibility to the shareholders to make profit quarter after quarter, while minimizing any surprises.

For the founder, his business was family. For him and his family (business and biological), the acquisition was a negative experience. No matter how hard you try to shelter them, family and friends are affected. In this case, the experience could have been managed more appropriately to maintain a balanced WHH approach. The best way to manage it would have been to do so proactively by having in place a business wealth transition. Planning for the future is a best practice that reduces stress and improves health.

Steven Covey, in his *Seven Habits of Highly Successful People,* coined the phrase, "Begin with the end in mind." Plan for an exit transition suited to succession and personal wealth.

Many years ago, twenty of us spent four hours with Covey, during which he pre-announced his Eighth Habit, which he called "Inspiration and Leadership." My takeaway was that people can be trained on how to change for the better. We can be leaders of transition and transformation.

How many times have you said or heard, "I am so busy, I don't have any time to do anything else except what I am already doing"? To maximize WHH, we will need to find the time to implement positive change. Priorities must change.

I was on a flight to Charlotte, North Carolina. I was seated in the exit aisle row with five people in their mid to late twenties. Every one of them had their heads down and fingers flying on smartphone keyboards, playing games or doing puzzles during most of the flight. It seemed to me a waste of precious time.

We have seen an increase in distractions and time stealers—games and digital shopping on phones, iPad games, sports betting, legalized gambling. These are all addictive to some extent, as are loads of cable TV channels, YouTube, and podcast choices running the gamut from sports, entertainment, education, and silliness. The pressure people feel to stay up to date on social media wastes time. And then there are the online opinion and propaganda outlets that pose news programs. They suck away yet more precious time. Many states have legalized some drugs, which also steal time and focus, but technology addiction is even more widespread.

We all have the need to relax and wind down, but addiction is not the answer. When people tell you they are busy and don't have time, just realize that minimizing addictive distractions will give them more time. It is all about priority and goal setting. Why can't we find one hour a day to apply what we learn on how to maximize WHH? We could, through conscious goal setting and time management techniques.

BEST Success Practice #50 to maximize the WHH continuum:
Avoid time distractions and find one hour a day to maximize your WHH.

The WHH continuum is an awareness method and tool for change.

Let's circle back to that founder and his family business. After year two, he recovered from the experience. He took off thirty pounds he didn't need and shed some medications that were no longer necessary. He started sleeping much better, aiming for the seven to eight hours per night. His biological family spends more time with him, as he has cut his work week back significantly, running a small consulting business to keep his mind active. He has always tried to maintain his spirituality throughout his life, but lately he has stepped up his efforts, thanks to his new-found time.

BEST Success Practice #51 to maximize the WHH continuum:
Sleep 7-8 hours per night.

With his net after-tax proceeds from the sale of his business, he has set up charitable giving trusts and is more altruistic. His WHH continuum is now in proper balance.

Since worrying is a human condition, he still worries about his new earned financial wealth transition. He has interviewed six WAS companies so he can pick two to delegate his wealth transition and investment strategy. He plans to stay involved knowing he can't completely abdicate the responsibility.

7

S.M.A.R.T. Goal Setting

"Awareness is one thing... formulating action and change
due to awareness is another... " —Anonymous

I understand how valuable your time is. I spent the time necessary to provide a WHH continuum pathway for you to follow or, more important, to adapt. Maybe you are practicing all the right behaviors and have maximized WHH on your own. For you, I hope my extensive research and experience have validated your own best practices.

As I did the research, I intuitively saw a correlation with WHH. The pages of this book reveal how the three components of WHH are inextricably linked. Too much of one, too little of the others make for a less robust and less fulfilling life for you and others.

Let's wind down our exploration with some *actions* for you to consider taking. Some of the success traits and profit patterns discussed in this book are basic. As Vince Lombardi, the Hall of Fame football coach, once said, "You never have to get back to basics if you never leave!"

Your first action is to read each one of the WHH best practices list every day for a few weeks. Become familiar and refamiliarize yourself with each one. If you don't set goals, you are less likely to achieve the outcome you are looking to accomplish.

Your second action is to choose a few of the most applicable best practices to implement immediately.

There is a method to goal setting I have used with 501c3's, business plans, teaching, and for my personal life. It is called S.M.A.R.T. Goals. Many of you in the business world have heard of this and even used the approach. To maximize your WHH life experience you must set goals. It is a time-tested success method. S.M.A.R.T goal setting works.

> **BEST Success Practice #52 to maximize
> the WHH continuum: Set SMART Goals.**

S is Specific…not general.

M is Measurable. If you can't measure your progress or lack thereof, you will not improve or adjust.

A is Achievable. This is the more difficult part of S.M.A.R.T goal setting. Our Human nature sometimes overrides logic. Start small and build up. Don't say you will save $1 million dollars in two years when you earn $75,000/year.

R is Relevant. Make sure the goal achievement outcome is meaningful to you and your situation.

T is time-bound. You cannot set a goal with no time limits to be effective. You must have a time constraint. If you miss it, fine. Reset and go forward, Never give up.

Now that you read and re-read the WHH best practices list every day for a week, it's time to pick one that is most applicable for you to "actionate." (Yes there is no such word, but I like it). Base your choice on your priorities. How do you accomplish this? Stack rank the WHH best practices. Take all the WHH best practices and, beginning with the best of the best, rank them in descending order. The first is the one most appropriate for your specific wants and needs. If you don't have time to stack rank, pick the top five out of the list.

When you have completed this, move to setting goals.

Here is an example of one WHH best practice using the SMART Goal approach. Let's say you picked the WHH best practice to test your water for toxicity and impurity from the WHH Best Success Practice success list.

> **BEST Success Practice to maximize the WHH continuum:
> Test your water. Purchase and install the best water filtration system you
> can afford and change out the filter as required.**

S....Specific: FIRST—Identify three water test companies to test your water source.

M...Measurable: SECOND—Pick one company based on their solutions offered, price, and your needs. Run the test. If the results are negative, your are done. If there are toxins present, move to the R

A...Achievable: FOURTH—Have the system of your choice delivered and installed.

R...Relevant: THIRD: Choose a system, making sure it meets your needs before its installed.

T... Time bound: FIFTH—The total project should be completed in two months.

You now find yourself at an intersection, not the New Delhi India intersection shared earlier and filled with chaos, but one that is quiet and traffic free. This is you with a choice to make. You can do nothing and wait for the traffic and chaos to show up. Or go forward.

What if you set SMART goals, and you worry you will fall short?

Author Victor E. Frankl was a holocaust survivor who wrote dozens of books. He saw death every day in the Nazi camps. He watched people give up their will to live, and he saw others make it through against all odds. Most of his reflections center around psychotherapy based on man's motivation to search for the meaning of life. Frankl's premise is that, because we are human, we cannot avoid suffering. We must figure out how to cope with loss and failure and move on. Don't let the past define you, but do learn from it.

My father, a WWII hero who served in the 15th Infantry, Third Division, engaged the enemy face to face in hand to hand combat. It was kill or be killed for two solid years. A purple heart, a silver star, a bronze star, and other metals were awarded in the same foxholes as WWII's most decorated hero, Audie Murphy. My father's philosophy, which he shared with me much later in life, was, "I am like an arrow moving toward a target. I don't worry what is on my periphery or behind me. The past is the past, move forward."

Same thing applies if you miss your SMART goal. Stay motivated as all goals are not always achieved. Wipe out negative thinking with a positively structured goal. If you fall short, learn from the miss and set a new SMART goal. Adaptive adjustments are to be expected over time. Positive habits will form through repetition.

Move forward like that arrow toward the target. If you follow through and "actionate" what has been presented to you, consistently over time, you will achieve Maximum Wealth, Health and Happiness.

Turns out that breaking bad habits or starting new good habits is not easy…. No kidding.

As humans, we become our own worst enemies when we what to implement change. We will have confirmation bias as we try to implement some of these best success practices. This is when we seek out information that confirms our pre-existing beliefs learned or experienced from long ago, while ignoring or dismissing positive contradictory evidence. Prior to my research for this book, I needed to remove my confirmation biases. We also have cognitive dissonance. We experience discomfort when we hold conflicting beliefs or when we are making a decision that contradicts our thoughts and experience from the past. Said another way, our ego does not want to allow us to admit we made a prior mistake.

The other success killer? Procrastination. Don't wait to get started.

I have done the research for you…now the rest is up to you. Go forward and do something.

8

Wealth Health Happiness Effort by Age Group©

Optimum effort ratio if you are 20-30 years old ©

100% Wealth Health Happiness

To maximize your WHH lifetime continuum, 75% of your time and effort toward Wealth acquisition, 20% Health and 5% Happiness©

The chart above and those that follow assume one starts the lifetime journey in their twenties or thirties and continues throughout their life. Good habits are formed and continued into the forties, fifties, and beyond. Stay the course.

In general—this is statistically proven—most twenty-to-thirty-year-olds are healthy and happy compared to the ratio of monetary wealth acquired. Said another way, most twenty-to-thirty-year-olds have not accumulated much wealth, if any at all, and need to focus on saving and investing.

By sacrificing early in life, the optimum WHH can be achieved in the longer term. You may have to work overtime or two jobs to meet your savings goals. You may have to start a business and have to sacrifice your home life or "party" life. You may have to delay that new car purchase or dinner out once a week. The effort to maximize health is minimal, as most twenty to thirty year olds are generally healthy if they eat right, exercise, and minimize vices. Consequently, a large percentage of time can be dedicated to Wealth acquisition.

This hypothesis and theme are not without faults. For instance, some twenty to thirty year olds are unhealthy and unhappy and should spend more time getting healthy and happy and less time on wealth acquisition.

The research and facts reported in this book show that positive happiness and health outcomes follow wealth creation. There is very little supporting evidence that 100% time spent on health outcomes will produce wealth, or 100% time spent on happiness acquisition will produce the required monetary wealth.

The percentage of WHH in the charts are a suggestion, and there will be months or even years where no percentage of time will be spend acquiring wealth. Maybe 100% of time available will be spent on seeking better health outcomes after a poor diagnosis. There is a level of fluidity required, as life's journey is dynamic, not static.

What I have concluded after all the research and studies is that the percentage of effort I suggest will provide you with the best WHH continuum and balance. Wealth is relative. You don't have to be a millionaire to be wealthy if you have income coming in with no expenses. But how many of us have no expenses?

The pursuit of and the act of wealth acquisition is a leading indicator of health and happiness future outcomes.

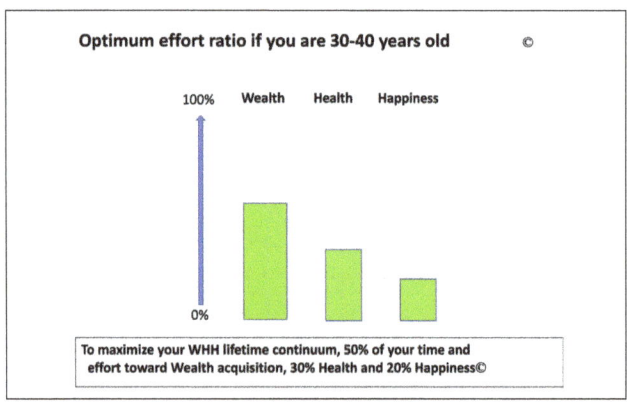

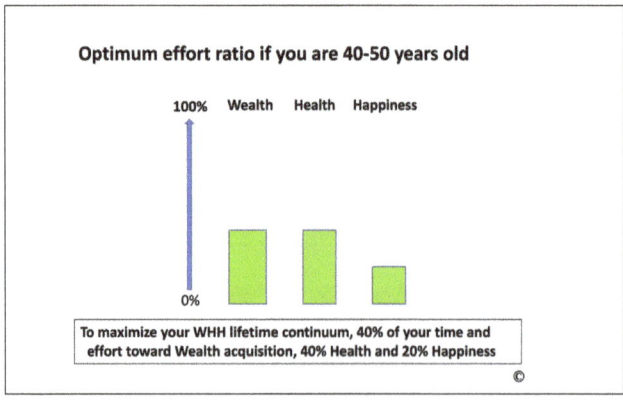

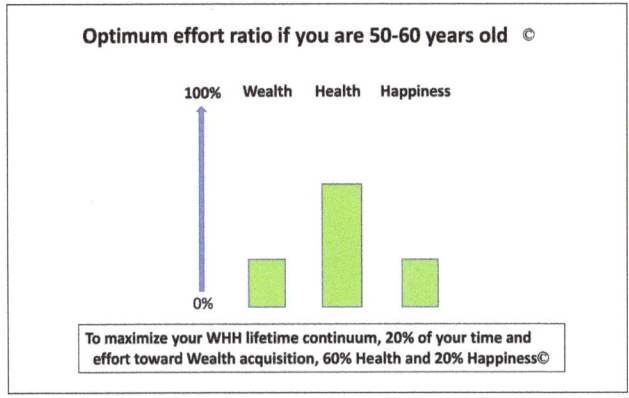

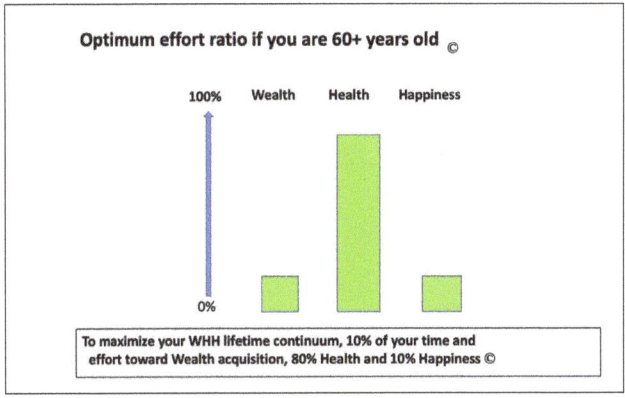

Now you find yourself in the sixty-plus range of life. Because you have followed the WHH plan from an early age, you have wealth and wealth managers supporting you. If you have not followed any of the WHH patterns of success outline, you still can improve the situation for yourself and your family. The time spent on wealth acquisition converts to cash flow management, wealth preservation, succession planning, and estate planning.

If you're a business owner, wealth transition is in full swing once again with the help of RIA/WAS/CPA/attorneys. If you are past sixty years of age, more time and money is spent on health and happiness approaches.

Spirituality is an overlay on all WHH. How we pursue wealth is as important as the wealth we accumulate. If we acquire wealth through illicit or illegal means, we eventually cause unhappiness for others and ourselves.

All the research and studies from thousands of years ago to the present suggest pursuing spirituality in tandem with WHH is doable and even produces higher levels of health and happiness.

We should not pursue wealth in a self-centered, me-first way or for the love of money.

You may question why so little time in the age brackets listed above is spent on proactive happiness acquisition. It does seem counterintuitive. After all, who wakes up in the morning with a goal to be unhappy?

All the research suggests that if you nobly, legally, and ethically pursue Wealth and Health, Happiness follows. A lower percentage of time and effort is needed for the Happiness outcome. Take care of your wealth and health, and happiness follows in tandem.

What if you have not started the WHH continuum effort in your twenty to thirty age bracket and find yourself behind in all the averages and categories? What can you do?

No matter what your stage of life, adopt and implement the recommendations outlined in the book. You will improve your situation. If you are below the average in wealth accumulation, or your health is poor, and happiness is periodic at best, there is still hope.

Let's say you are fifty years old and, like about 50 percent of the US population, you have zero savings. Since time is against you, what can you control? You can control your savings rate and, to a lesser degree, the return rate on your savings. A fifty-year-old saving $1,900 a month for twenty years, earning an 8 percent return, can get close to a million dollars in savings. To maximize your returns, save in a 401K, 403B or IRA instrument. Hire a WAS/RIA to support your goals. Statistically, people who invest on their own earn 2 to 3 percent less than people who hire a WAS/RIA. Don't go it alone. Hire a professional.

Wealth, health and happiness maximization takes effort. Set small SMART goals and give it a try. All research points to improvements for you, if you start and act on the recommendations I have shared with you.

9

Summary of Wealth Health Happiness Best Practices, Success Patterns, and Actions©

1. BEST Success Practice to maximize the WHH continuum:
Constantly acquire and apply knowledge.

2. BEST Success Practice to maximize the WHH continuum:
Learn, apply and teach the rule of 72 as early as possible.

3. BEST Success Practice to maximize the WHH continuum:
Save money for retirement first. Do not buy a car, or house or any large purchase. Open a Roth IRA and invest in a low-cost Standard and Poors 500 index/ETF first and add to it each month. Diversify your portfolio to minimize inevitable corrections.

4. BEST Success Practice to maximize the WHH continuum:
Do not isolate yourself from others that you love or trust. Set a SMART goal to become a millionaire by a certain age. Share your commitment to become wealthy with family and friends.

5. BEST Success Practice to maximize the WHH continuum:
If you are in your twenties and thirties, work as many hours per week as possible, save as much as possible. Work two jobs, if you are physically able.

6. BEST Success Practice to maximize the WHH continuum:
Re-evaluate where you live and determine if you can move to a lower cost and lower tax area to invest and keep more of your money.

7. BEST Success Practice to maximize the WHH continuum:
Measure and record all your expenses in the year prior to retirement. There are many free budget templates on-line you can customize tor your specifics. Include an inflation rate 2 above ABOVE the government reports. Increase your estimated budget by 20 percent per year for your first five years of retirement. Do not do your budget estimates in a vacuum. Include input from advisors, family, and friends.

8. BEST Success Practice to maximize the WHH continuum:
Team with your WAS/RIA/trust attorney to run Monte Carlo simulations to mitigate your risk of wealth longevity and withdrawal rate issues.

9. BEST Success Practice to maximize the WHH continuum:
Build a safety net emergency savings account to reduce stress and minimize the need for credit card usage.

10. BEST Success Practice to maximize the WHH continuum:
 To minimize illness, during your late thirties and early forties, schedule an "executive" physical every year with a physician, preferably one who is not employed by an insurance company or affiliate). See your dentist twice a year starting in your twenties. See your eye doctor every year especially if you are past fifty years old.

11. BEST Success Practice to maximize the WHH continuum:
Develop and work to keep an in-person social network throughout your life to minimize loneliness and increase health and happiness. This should be in-person, not online.

12. BEST Success Practice to maximize the WHH continuum:
- Physical activity
- No alcohol abuse and no smoking
- Mature mechanisms to cope with life's ups and downs, stress reduction
- Enjoy a healthy weight
- Have a stable marriage.

13. BEST Success Practice to maximize the WHH continuum:
Choose Healthier organic meals over fast food and keep meals down to 40 percent carbohydrates.

14. BEST Success Practice to maximize the WHH continuum:
Break the sedentary lifestyle, always be moving. Example: If you find your-self sitting down to hold a meeting, stand up. You will burn more calories, and the meeting will be more productive, saving precious time

15. BEST Success Practice to maximize the WHH continuum:
Minimize your emotional stress to extend your life by avoiding "crazies"

16. BEST Success Practice to maximize the WHH continuum:
Change your surroundings or go outside

17. BEST Success Practice to maximize the WHH continuum
Get Some Uninterrupted Sleep

18. BEST Success Practice to maximize the WHH continuum:
Ditch the electronic devices before bed to enhance your quality of sleep

19. BEST Success Practice to maximize the WHH continuum:
Cardio exercise thirty minutes a day combined with attention to diet can extend your life by six to nine years.

20. BEST Success Practice to maximize the WHH continuum:
Use the Black AXIS Foam roller to provide spine therapy and overall proactive spine health.

21. BEST Success Practice to maximize the WHH continuum:
Drink less alcohol, smoke less, eat less meat, stay hydrated, get more sleep, walk more and stretch appropriately.
    Have a disciplined approach or a coach to carry through what you know you need to do.

22. BEST Success Practice to maximize the WHH continuum:
Be more connected to nature to avoid "nature deficit disorders" that leads to other maladaptive behaviors.
    Pray more and reflect on what is good. Be more positive, knowing that today is a good day to have a good day.

23. BEST Success Practice to maximize the WHH continuum:
Find reasons for joy and thankfulness. Smile "out loud" more each day.
Be positive.

24. BEST Success Practice to maximize the WHH continuum:
Find a wellness coach to practice diaphragmatic breathing and/or slow deep 478 breathing techniques. Check with your doctor beforehand.

25. BEST Success Practice to maximize the WHH continuum:
Test your water. Purchase and install the best water filtration system you can afford and change out the filter as required.

26. BEST Success Practice to maximize the WHH continuum:
Consume organic food from the USA. Clean fruits and veggies using the baking soda process of a teaspoon per 16 ounces of water before consumption.

27. BEST Success Practice to maximize the WHH continuum:
Follow a more restricted caloric intake, take a probiotic each day and practice a more vegetarian diet. Avoid red meats. Depression can be treated in part through diet.

28. BEST Success Practice to maximize the WHH continuum:
Formulate a list of your top twenty foods/drinks you consume in a week. Research them, and sort them using the template example. Those that fall into the lowest quartile on the left, should be avoided. Study the DASH, Mediterranean and MIND diets. Stay away from sucralose type artificials.

29. BEST Success Practice to maximize the WHH continuum are:
Whenever you visit a doctor, dentist, hospital, or clinic make sure you leave with a copy of the tests, diagnostics, and all images. Keep a List all medications, allergies, past surgeries. Gone are the days where we can trust the medical administrators to keep our records. Keep a file for each family member and be prepared to advocate and articulate details.

30. BEST Success Practice to maximize the WHH continuum:
Use paraben-free skin care, shampoo, shaving cream, and sunscreen products. Throw out any products with parabens, including some cereals, beer, frozen dairy products, and flavored syrups. Read the labels of the products you use or consume.

31. BEST Success Practice to maximize the WHH continuum:
People of faith live happier lives and experience less worry by practicing their faith in congregation with others.

32. BEST Success Practice to maximize the WHH continuum:
Pursue and vote for more policies and laws that promote economic freedoms , not social justice policies.

33. BEST Success Practice to maximize the WHH continuum:
If you are in the early stages of your work life (sixteen to forty years of age), find ways to do more at work, not less. Ask someone who is successful to be your mentor. If you are past forty, offer to be a mentor to a promising person.

34. BEST Success Practice to maximize the WHH continuum:
Create a special family code phrase to verify that you are speaking with family, loved ones and friends. Change the code periodically in person or by phone, not through text/email or social media.

35. BEST Success Practice to maximize the WHH continuum:
Minimize your "online" social media exposure and interactions.

36. BEST Success Practice to maximize the WHH continuum:
Proactively plan with your WAS/RIA/CPA, to develop what-if scenarios to deal with financial and emotional aspects of inevitable market down turns.

37. BEST Success Practice to maximize the WHH continuum:
For gut health, in a foreign country, never drink the local water and always peel any fruit skin before consumption.

38. BEST Success Practice to maximize the WHH continuum:
Pray, meditate and go to Church/Synagogue/Temple and congregate with others. Help others. Stay active. Detox from technology for a few days through a retreat.

39. BEST Success Practice to maximize the WHH continuum:
Constitutional republics and democracies with free market capitalism and low historic inflation produce more WHH than other countries. Limiting free credit or government-funded programs adds to the long-term stability of the economy. Limit your credit card debt.

40. BEST Success Practice to maximize the WHH continuum:

Exercise, Set goals, and act on goal identification achievement. Socialize in person, and share why you are unhappy (loneliness kills).

Understand that you cannot be happy or motivated all the time.

41. BEST Success Practice to maximize the WHH continuum:

When transitioning business or personal wealth, plan at least ten years prior and use WAS/RIA/CPA/attorney to customize your intention,s knowing they will change over time.

42. BEST Success Practice to maximize the WHH continuum:

Have more than one person aware of and educated on the legal, financial and health management aspects of your personal and business wealth and future intentions.

43. BEST Success Practice to maximize the WHH continuum:

Learn to take calculated risks

44. BEST Success Practice to maximize the WHH continuum:

Practice being more social in person.

45. BEST Success Practice to maximize the WHH continuum:

Create a solid routine, and be more conscientiousness.

46. BEST Success Practice to maximize the WHH continuum:

Make time management a priority.

47. BEST Success Practice to maximize the WHH continuum:

Adopt a growth mindset.

48. BEST Success Practice to maximize the WHH continuum:

Determine your personality type with one of the methods identified. You can adapt or change your personality.

49. BEST Success Practice to maximize the WHH continuum:

Adjust your ego drive and empathy as conditions warrant.

50. BEST Success Practice to maximize the WHH continuum:

Avoid time distractions, and find one hour a day to maximize your WHH.

51. BEST Success Practice to maximize the WHH continuum:
Sleep seven to eight hours per day.

52. BEST Success Practice to maximize the WHH continuum:
Set SMART goals.

Best Success Practice to maximize the WHH continuum:
Define what is a meaningful life for you. What is a meaningful life? It is specific to each person. For many, it's improving whatever it is we do each day. Be significant and be purposeful for yourself and others. Live a meaningful life to gain happiness for you and your loved ones.

If you are already accomplishing all the Best Practices above, congratulations. You can be a positive benchmark and role model for others on their journey to maximize Wealth, Health and Happiness.

Email me at **Peterjroman@protonmail.com** to share your approaches and stories. I would love to hear from you.

10

Customized Client Lifecycle Solutions© to Support Wealth Health Happiness Continuum

As clients demand more from advisors, I have provided you with a guideline of what to ask for or expect from your advisors.

I call it the Customized Client life cycle solutions© set. The first chart is a summary of nine (9) areas of focus to consider to help you support your efforts to maximize Wealth, Health and Happiness.

Each chart thereafter is a detailed inclusion for each of the nine aspects.

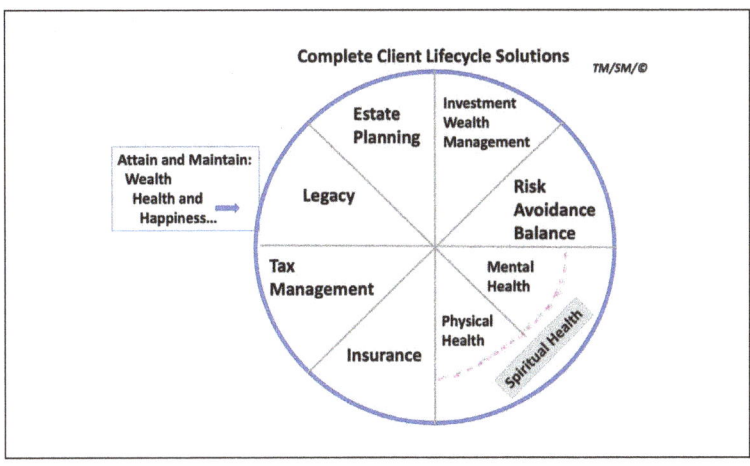

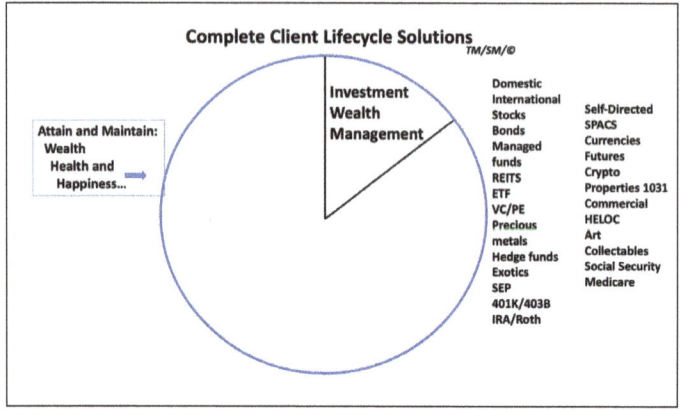

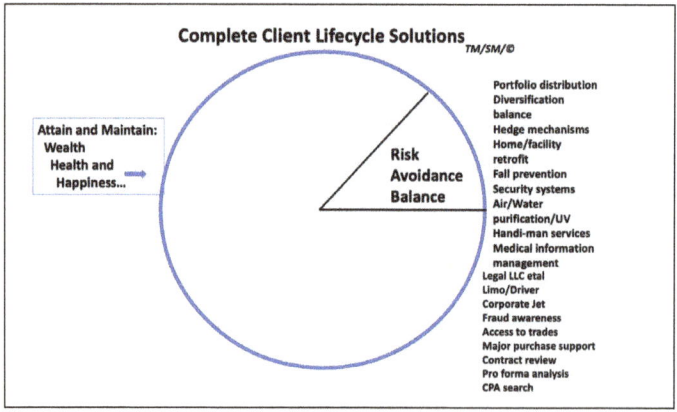

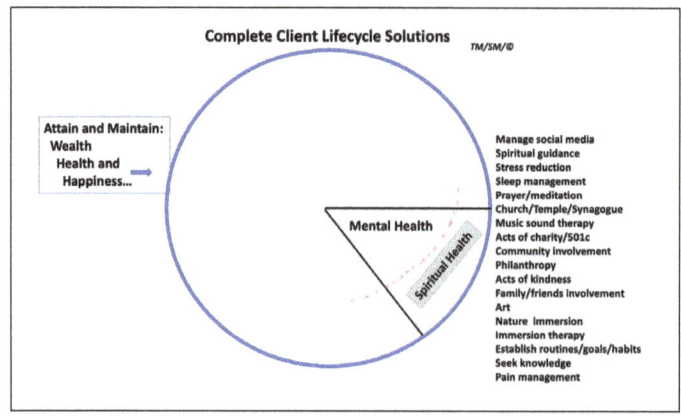

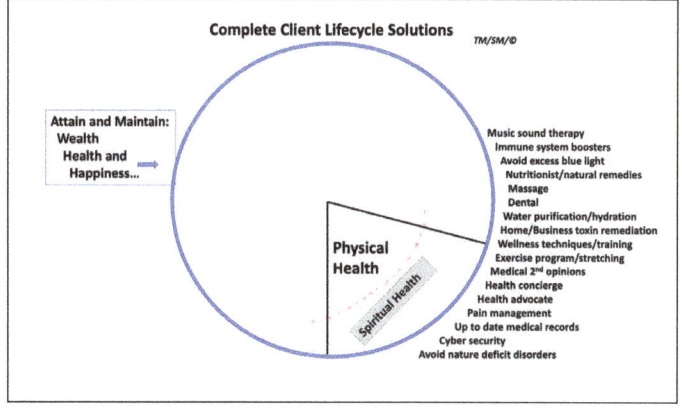

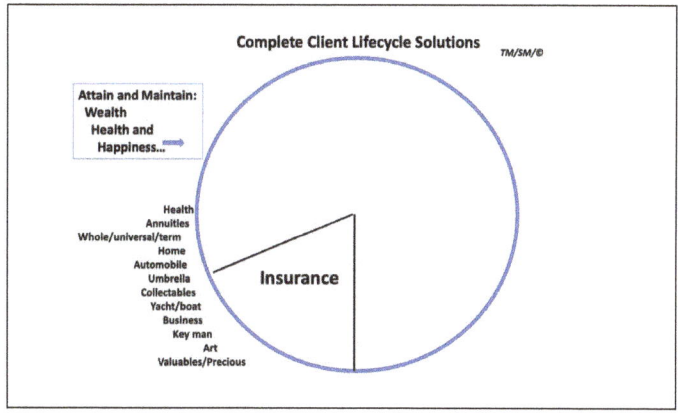

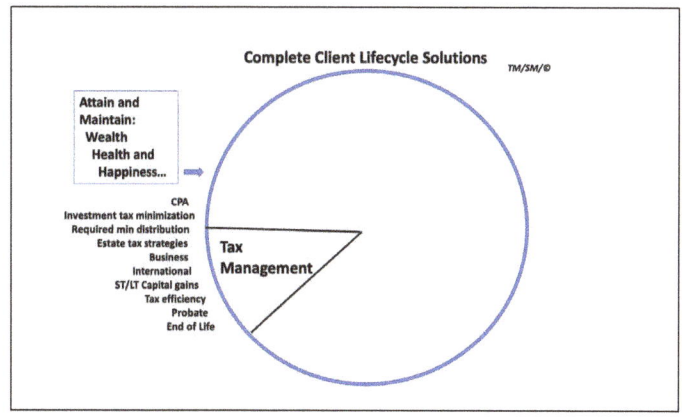

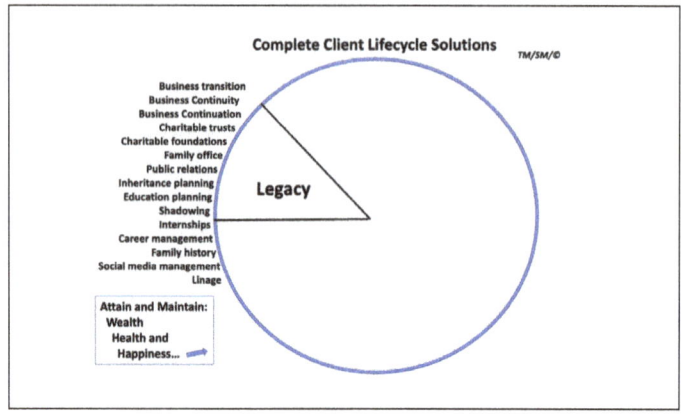

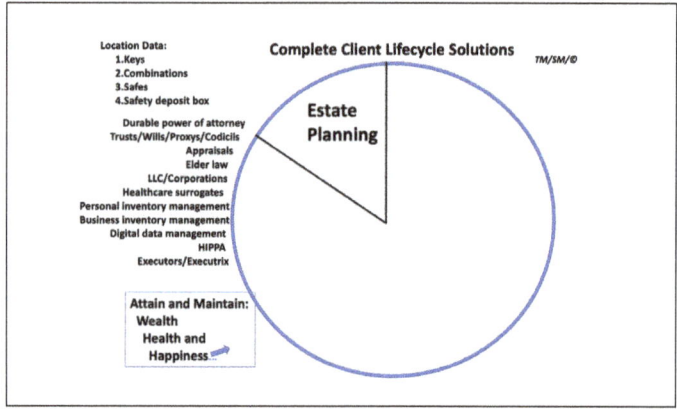

Go be Wealthy, Healthy and Happy, you deserve it!
Find your optimum equilibrium and continuum…

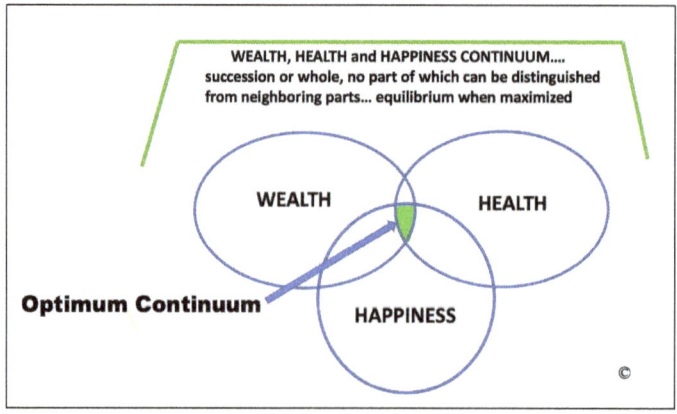

Notes and Sources

Ahuvia, Aaron, Wealth , Consumption and Happiness, *The Cambridge Handbook of Psychology and Economic Behaviour* (Cambridge University Press, 2008), 199-226.

Aubry, Jean-Pierre, and Laura D. Quinby "What Risks Do Near Retirees and Retirees Face from Inflation?" Center for Retirement Research at Boston College (May 15, 2024).

Benson, Alana, and Rachael Kim, "My Path to Generational Wealth: Start Early and Educate Yourself," *Nerd Wallet* (March 14, 2024).

Business World, "Metro Bacolod," interview with Frank Carbon, Philippines Chamber of Commerce and Industry President.

Cantley, Lewis, professor, Harvard Medical School Department of Cell Biology, email interview with *The Epoch Times*.

Cherry, Kendra, "How Your Personality Type Affects Your Health" (2022); medically reviewed Amy Morin, LCSW.

Diener, Ed, *Psychological Well-Being Scale (PWB)*© Copyright by Ed Diener and Robert Biswas-Diener, January 2009. Published in E. Diener, *Assessing Well-Being: The Collected Works of Ed Diener* (Dordrecht: Springer, 2009).

Dilorio, Cameron, "What Could A Dollar Buy You in the 1940s?" *Yahoo!Finance* (May 5, 2024).

DiSCprofile.com (2024).

Donghia, Mike, Remarks on Angela Duckworth's research in the Journal of Personality and Social Psychology (2007), Donghia Blog, *Epoch Times* (February 2024).

Donnelly, G. E., Zheng, T., Haisley, E., and Norton, M. I., "The amount and source of millionaires' wealth (moderately) predict their happiness," *Personality and Social Psychology Bulletin* (2018).

Esmaeilpour, Niloufar, Lotus Therapy & Counseling Centre.

Everly, G. "Psychological Aspects of Being Positive" Johns Hopkins School of Medicine (2024).

Franchell, Richard-Hamilton, MD, "6 Ways to Outsmart Bad Genes, *Psychology Today* (June 14, 2021).

Gilberto, Meghan K. Davenport, Margaret E. Beier, "Personality, health, wealth, and subjective well-being: Testing a integrative model with retired and working older adults," *Journal of Research in Personality* (April 2020).

Grainger, Charlotte, "The Five Personality Traits of Self-Made Millionaires," *Truity True You Journal* (July 23, 2024).

Green, Nigel James "The Deep Connection Between Your Health and Wealth," *Forbes* (July 3, 2020).

Hartog, J. and Oosterbeek, H., "Health, Wealth, and Happiness: Why Pursue a Higher Education?" *Economics of Education Review,* volume 17, Issue 3 (June 1998).

Hrynowski, Zach, Gallup senior education researcher, 2024.

Intuit Credit Karma, Forget doom scrolling, Americans now doom spend to cope with stress" (November 16, 2023).

Israelsen, Craig, American Association of Individual Investors (June 2024).

Jackson, Ashleigh, "Here's how much the average American has in their retirement savings by age," WKRN.com (May 5, 2024).

Johnson, Ben, "Attending Church Regularly Will Lengthen Your Life More Than Diet, Exercise, Longevity Expert Says," *The Daily Signal* (September 10, 2024).

Kaczor, Christopher, "How to Find Happiness 2010," *Columbia Magazine* (2010).

Kelly, Jack, "The Great Wealth Transfer from Baby Boomers to Millennials Will Impact the Job Market and Economy" (2024).

Keyishian, Amy, LearnVest, on Ray Linder's *What Will I Do With My Money?* (2020).

Kortmansky, Dr. Jeremy, associate professor of medical oncology at the Yale School of Medicine and clinical director of the Division of GI Medical Oncology at the Yale Cancer Center, 2024.

Kumari, Dr. Kumud, "The Concept of Happiness in India," *The International Journal of Indian Psychology* (December 31, 2022).

Lamberg, Erica, "Why the viral trend 'Chronoworking' is making waves among employees and employers," *Fox Business* (April 2024).

Lang, Kerry L., W. John Livesley, P. A. Vernon, "Heritability of the Big Five Personality Dimensions and their Facets: A Twin Study," *Journal of Personality* (September 1966).

Lawless, Lisa PhD and CEO. HolisticWisdom.com.

Lee, Jessica, J.D., Professional Vocalist, Advisor & Producer Creative & Coaching Divisions,

Lyubomirsky, Sonja, *The How of Happiness: A Scientific Approach to Getting the Life You Want* (New York: Penguin, 2007).

Malik, Brian, and Peter J Roman, "The Rule of 72 really can work," *Tribune Review* (April 9, 2015).

Map: Addy BinkSource Go Banking rates: Get the data Created with datawrapper.

McCain, Abby (January 2024).

Mineo, Liz, *The Harvard Gazette* (2017).

Murray, Iain, "Health, Wealth and Happiness," Competitive Enterprise Institute (October 14, 2004).

National Library of Medicine, *Frontiers in Psychology* (2012).

"New Study," *The Healthy* (August 22, 2024).

New World Wealth Report 2024, "Millionaire Growth."

Pinnell, Dr. Ron L., "An Investigation of the relationship among teachers' personality typologies and perception of organizational climate in secondary schools" (1989).

Raisbeck, Daniel, policy analyst at the CATO Institute, Fox News Digital.

Ramsey Research, "The Financial Literacy Crisis in America 2023," Ramsey (April 3, 2023).

Rissetto, Vanessa, MS,RD,CDN, "These Are the 10 'Perfect Proteins," *The Healthy* (October 11, 2023).

Roberts, Catherine, "Produce without Pesticides," *Consumer Reports* (April 18, 2024; updated May 17, 2024).

Routley, Nick, "Charting the Relationship Between Wealth and Happiness, by Country," *Visual Capitalist* (September 8, 2022.

Rudy, Melissa, "Olive Oil Consumption," Fox Digital (May 2024).

Russo, Roman, *Optimal Happiness* (2021).

Sandeman, Stuart. "Breathe In, Breathe Out," *Epoch Times Health* (May 2024).

Schwab's Modern Wealth Survey (2023).

Spitzer, Father Robert J. Spitzer, *Healing the Culture* (San Francisco: Ignatius Press, 2000).

Truity, "The Income Effect Personality Type," a research report by Truity (2019).

UPMC Health Beat (April 2024).

Varacallo, Patricia, DO, "This Artificial Sweetener Can Permanently Damage Your DNA,

ViveVenture, LLC, www.jessicaleejazz.com.

WebMD, "Is Retail Therapy Real?" (2021).

Wong, Belle, "Average Salary by State 2024," *Forbes Advisor* (March 6, 2024).

Some references to individuals and details in this book have been altered to protect their anonymity.

NO AI was used by the author and editor to write this book.

Acknowledgments

Thanks to Karen Lee Roman for being my critique and human spell check.

Thanks to Jill Shoemaker for her artistic inputs and guidance throughout.

Thanks to Laura Duffy for the creation of my Cover art and assembledge of content for publishing suitability.

I want to profusely thank my editor, Alan Axelrod for his patience. My previous experience was authoring, Newspaper, technical and academic papers. Alan's abilities enabled what you are about to read.

About the Author

Peter Joseph Roman was educated at Providence College and graduate studies at Syracuse University. He is Adjunct Professor of Marketing and Entrepreneurship, Carnegie Mellon University, MBA program (retired).

One of eight professionals recruited by Eaton Corporation, a Fortune 50 company, to start and profitably grow an electrical engineering services business globally, Roman and his colleagues brought the business to a $1 billion USD run rate in twelve years. Senior Director of the Eaton Electrical sector global accounts, he was founder and manager of Eaton's executive customer board of directors and now, the founder of "The Consultancy," which advises a wide range of companies, from small startups to large multi-nationals.

He has published many articles with newspapers and technical publications nationally on elder fraud prevention, information warfare, investing, technology, taxation, business development solutions, electrical engineering solutions and customer relationship management.

www.ingramcontent.com/pod-product-compliance
Lightning Source LLC
Chambersburg PA
CBHW051612120626
46551CB00014B/1762